History of
Orbis - 2 v.

Christian Histories, Christian Traditioning

Christian Histories, Christian Traditioning

Rendering Accounts

Dale T. Irvin

Maryknoll, New York 10545

The Catholic Foreign Mission Society of America (Maryknoll) recruits and trains people for overseas missionary service. Through Orbis Books, Maryknoll aims to foster the international dialogue that is essential to mission. The books published, however, reflect the opinions of their authors and are not meant to represent the official position of the society.

Copyright © 1998 by Dale T. Irvin
Published by Orbis Books, Maryknoll, New York, U.S.A.

All rights reserved. No part of this publication may be reproduced or transmitted in any form or by any means, electronic or mechanical, including photocopying, recording, or any information storage or retrieval system, without prior permission in writing from Orbis Books, P.O. Box 308, Maryknoll, NY 10545-0308, U.S.A.

Ishmael Reed's poem "Dualism," page 17, copyright © Ishmael Reed, is reprinted by permission of the author. Lucille Clifton's poem, "why some people be mad at me sometime," page 34, copyright © Lucille Clifton, is reprinted from *Next: New Poems* with the permission of BOA Editions, Ltd., 260 East Ave., Rochester, NY 14604.

Manufactured in the United States of America.

Library of Congress Cataloging in Publication Data

Irvin, Dale T., 1955-
    Christian histories, Christian traditioning : rendering accounts /
Dale T. Irvin.
      p. cm.
    Includes bibliographical references and index.
    ISBN 1-57075-207-9 (hardcover)
    1. History (Theology)   2. Tradition (Theology)   I. Title.
BR115.H5.I78   1988
270—dc21   98-28990
                                                                               CIP

In memory of
James Melvin Washington

Contents

Acknowledgments

Preface

1. **Faithful Histories**   1
   Contemporary Diversity Confronts the Singularity of a Christian Past   1
   Faithful Histories   3
   Critical Practices and the Meaning of Tradition   7
   Looking Ahead   14

2. **History and Tradition: From Crisis to Re-Creation**   17
   Rendering Accounts   17
   The Crisis of Modern History   21
   The Re-Creative Work of Traditioning   27

3. **The Accountability of Handing Over**   34
   A Double Accountability   34
   Tradition or Treason   39
   Solidarity with the Dead   43
   The Rhizomatic Structure of Tradition   46
   Accountable Retraditioning   50

4. **Theology of History**   53
   Tradition as the Theological Meaning of History   53
   History and Divine Revelation   57
   Toward a Theology of History of the Whole *Oikoumene*   72

5. **Narratives of Church History**   79
   History as "God-Bearing"   79
   Narratives of History and Hermeneutics of the Divine   82
   The Master Narrative of Church History: A Critique   86

6. **A Genealogy of Christian Histories and Traditioning**   100
   Genealogies and the Diversity of Historical Memory   100

Multiple Trajectories: A Genealogy of the Early Christian
  Movement   106
Genealogical Ruptures in the European Tradition(s)   116

7. **The Grace to Renew the Past**   123

Notes   145

Acknowledgments

I am honored to have had such a wonderful circle of friends and colleagues who have supported me over the years in the course of this project. While I cannot list all those to whom I am indebted, several persons deserve a special word of thanks for the contributions they have made to the book. The opening chapters owe much to Angela K. Askew, with whom so many fruitful hours of intense conversation were spent talking over ideas that eventually found their way into these pages. Akintunde E. Akinade read the entire manuscript and provided numerous and valuable insights that improved the work immensely. For his scholarship, but even more for his friendship, I am truly thankful. Harold Dean Trulear has likewise been a close friend and spiritual colleague, prodding me on in pursuit of faithful scholarship and calling me back time after time to the source of grace in life.

Kosuke Koyama, David D. Daniels, Joan S. Parrott, Michael Christensen, Rebecca Laird, Vicky Trulear, Bishop Ithiel Clemmons, Charles Amjad-Ali, Humberto Alfaro, Donald Dayton, Frank Macchia, C. Vernon Mason, Douglas A. Irvin, Mark V. C. Taylor, Peter Ochs, Mats Hansson, Melanie May, Barbara Austin-Lucas, Quinton H. Dixie, Patricia Wilson-Kastner, Keith A. Russell, Steven J. Land, Rickie Moore, John Chris Thomas, James A. Forbes, and Scott W. Sunquist have all been sources of inspiration, insight, and support. I wish them all to know how deeply they are appreciated. I wish to thank as well my fellow members of the Vatke Society (Sarah Winter, Ben C. Ollenburger, Kathleen O'Connor, Steven Kraftchick, Harold Washington, Pamela Gordon, Steven Cook, and John Sandys-Wunsch) who responded to earlier drafts of several chapters at our annual meeting.

Institutional support for this book came from New York Theological Seminary whose trustees provided a study leave that facilitated its completion, and Ellie Soler, our librarian, who so diligently helped me locate numerous journal articles and obscure references. I also wish to thank the librarians of Union Theological Seminary, New York, who so graciously provided me with assistance over the years.

William Burrows of Orbis Books has been both a wonderful friend and an enthusiastic supporter of this project. Without his editorial guidance, the book might not have seen the light of day. I owe a continuing debt of gratitude to Victoria L. Erickson, Douglas Irvin-Erickson, and Andrew Irvin-Erickson, the three people closest to me in my life whose love and patience are such a rich source of strength.

Finally, this book is dedicated to James Melvin Washington, who read it in manuscript form but did not live to see it in print. I consider it a tremendous privilege to have known James Washington as teacher and friend. The generosity of his heart was matched only by the brilliance of his mind. In countless ways he exemplified what it meant to be a Christian intellectual, renewing the culture, the grammar, and the memory of Christian faith.

Of course, all errors and infelicities are my own.

Preface

This book is the result of many years of struggling with fundamental questions of theology and history that have emerged for me from the study of world Christianity at the end of the modern age. The book is about Christian *traditioning*, the process of handing on the faith to a next generation. In the history of the Christian movement, the next generation of faith has not only been one that stands in temporal succession to a living community of faith. The "passing on" has often entailed a "passing over" as well, as the Christian movement has crossed religious and cultural boundaries in mission. The work of passing on has sometimes been dichotomized too sharply into categories of catechesis and mission, or evangelism and mission, by those who would separate the world into Christian and non-Christian regions. My argument is that situated as we are in a contemporary world that can be variously described as postmodern, postcolonial, or post-Christendom, these two processes need to be taken together to address questions that are fundamentally the same.

Over the course of its history, the Christian movement has engaged in practices of traditioning that have resulted in more and more diversity of expressions or incarnations of the Christian faith. In the contemporary world, such diversity has accelerated with the growth of Christianity outside the regions of the world culturally identified with European history, or "the West." Some would see such diversity to pose a problem, specifically to the notion of the unity of the Christian faith. I see diversity to be the strength of the Christian movement, and a part of the very fabric of Christian identity from the days of the apostles. But then this leads me to question what to do with the notion of there being such a thing as "the Christian tradition," or "Tradition" (with a capital "T"). The experience of diversity leads me to affirm in a positive manner the fact that Christian traditioning has taken place through multiple historical incarnations, or *traditions*, of Christian faith.

Most observers of world Christianity today would agree with Pius XII's assertion a generation ago that the church "does not identify herself with any civilization."[1] Nevertheless, the vast majority of Christian historical and theological writings continue to assume that the history of Christianity prior to the modern period was exclusively European. Thus the history of European Christendom continues to function as a master narrative of Christian tradition, legitimating European or Western theological domination in all its diverse forms and de-legitimating traditions that cannot be articulated through this narrative history. Church history is divorced from mission history (or theology from mission studies). Those churches that cannot trace their lineage directly back to a European ancestry are not considered to have a tradition "of their own."

The answer I offer in the pages that follow is a reappropriation of the positive meaning of the plurality and diversity of Christian traditions incarnated through the multiplicity of human historical experience. Human history itself is multiple, pluralized, and diverse. In place of history or History being the bearer of revelation through tradition, I argue for *histories* as the bearers of traditions of Christian faith. The Christian faith, I argue, embraces such internal pluralization, expressed through its historical multiplicity and diversity of concurrent articulations.

But how then do we intelligently narrate the story of the Christian movement, or the history of the Christian faith? In place of a master narrative of Christendom, I will argue for a more genealogical approach to Christian history which would allow us to narrate the diversity of its historical traditions. Such a genealogy of the contemporary Christian faith would be one that intentionally seeks to articulate its multiple origins, and uncover its significant ruptures, within a wider family of traditions. In the end I suggest that this conception of history and tradition best fits with the conception of catholicity as a community of churches in the world today. In the diversity of world Christianity I perceive the grace for re-traditioning the Christian faith, expressing the hope of a faith not yet finished.

1 | Faithful Histories

Contemporary Diversity Confronts the Singularity of a Christian Past

The ground has shifted beneath the edifices of world Christianity over the past half-century. Even a cursory glance at the centers of institutional life and energy reveals new configurations emerging around the world. Many of the institutional structures of Christendom that dominated world Christianity in the past are being challenged by communities and movements whose voices have emerged from the margins of a global economic system controlled for several centuries by the elite of Western European and North American societies. Often they are communities and movements that locate themselves within Roman Catholic, Protestant, Pentecostal, and Orthodox traditions of Christian faith, but their identities are not those of the dominant Western churches.

For more than a decade, I have sought to understand what this diversity means for Christian theological identity in America, specifically in my own case for Protestant identity after modernism. During this time I have been teaching in an urban seminary whose student body reflects the global diversity that is becoming more and more characteristic of the cities of the North.[1] On a regular basis I find myself negotiating through a terrain that is marked by differences of "race," culture, gender, orientation, language, confession, socioeconomic class, and age, often in mixtures and hybrids that defy any attempt to categorize them in a simple taxonomy of existing identities.

In this situation I repeatedly find myself asking the question of what and how to teach about Christian theology and tradition in a postcolonial or postmodern world. What sense do I make of the diversity of histories and historical memories found in the churches of the world? What understanding of Christian historical identity am I representing as I attempt to teach Christian history and theology? Given the rich diversity of contemporary Christian histories and identities, can anything be meaningfully taught as *the* Christian theological tradition, or *the* history of the Christian church? Isn't even the attempt to do so self-defeating, if not in some sense a part of the history of repression and outright oppression? At the same time, can we abandon all attempts to teach something that represents tradition as embodying the truth, without abandoning the incarnational claims of Christian faith and thus the integrity of Christian hope?

2 FAITHFUL HISTORIES

Here I want to be clear: the problem I confront is not with the diversity of languages, cultures, and historical identities represented in Christian churches across the world today. On the contrary, I have come to see such diversity as a gift and a resource for the future of the Christian movement. But the problem I confront is that much of the theological language, bequeathed to us through the various Christian cultural and theological traditions, reflects singular or totalizing conceptions of tradition and truth. The greater part of published theological material typically used to teach in a theology or Church history class continues to reflect a singularity of history and past Christian tradition that is alien to the contemporary situation of pluralism and cultural diversity we experience. The historical diversity I encounter in classroom, community, and church is not reflected in the inherited theological language and doctrine, nor in the textbooks I often try to use in transmitting tradition in a classroom.

In most of the history and theology textbooks I find, Christianity is represented as a predominantly or even exclusively European religion prior to the modern era. The history of Christianity prior to the modern period and the missionary expansion of the churches of Europe is therefore represented de facto through the history of Europe, often reduced more specifically to that of Western Europe. Church history and tradition are represented exclusively as the history and tradition of European peoples and the dominant European churches (Protestant, Orthodox, or Roman Catholic). Those churches and persons who do not bear European historical identities, or whose cultures are not derived from European experiences, are either depicted as not having a tradition, or as having a tradition that is not very old. They are "younger" churches, with "newer" religious traditions, situated in an eternally derivative position in relation to the "older" or "historic" churches of Christendom. If they are to claim a more enduring historical identity as Christian communities of faith, it would appear, then they must embrace an alien history and tradition—that of the West—as their own.

It is not unusual for me to hear someone from a Pentecostal church in conversation with a Roman Catholic say something to the effect of, "Well we don't have as long a tradition as you do." Or I might be asked by a Baptist student why she or he should be studying the history of the first Christian centuries, because this is not a part of her or his tradition. Students from Asian and African communities often know more about United States and European history (religious and secular) than they do Asian or African history, reflecting practices of natal exclusion that masquerade under the banner of conversion. At a deep level there is often found in these comments and experiences a rupture within historical identity which is superficially celebrated under the rubrics of Christian conversion, or the success of its missions. The result is often the inability to claim a longer religious history as one's own, and the imposition of an alien cultural tradition under the guise of a more authentically "Christian" one. These practices in turn serve to confine Christian tradition and identity to their various European historical expressions. But if the history of Christianity is exclusively European, then to be a Christian even in the postmodern and postcolonial world, one must abandon historical religious identities that cannot be traced to European ancestry, or so it would seem.

It is the disjunction between the singularity of the historical identity of the Christian past as represented in most of our theological discourses on the one hand, and the contemporary cultural diversity of Christian churches and persons on the other, that is the problem I am addressing in this book. The arguments I will be developing in the pages that follow entail a reconsideration of our conception of Christian tradition which would enable us to embrace the diversity of history and historical identity for Christian faith. Behind this is a more fundamental belief in the openness of God to human history, and in the opening of human history to God. The memory and expectation of the openness of God, and of our openness to God, I have found to be both the task and the content of Christian tradition. As these chapters will demonstrate, tradition joins together the disciplines of theology and history in a manner that mediates both the memory of God's openness in the past and our expectations of God's openness today.

Faithful Histories

Critical theological discussions of the concept of Christian tradition have certainly not been in short supply over the last half-century. Many of them have entailed issues of unity and diversity among the churches not unlike those being raised above. My own proposal is being added to the mix here not because I necessarily disagree with all that has already been said and written concerning the meaning of tradition. Mainly I have found that the discussions have not adequately moved beyond maintaining a dominant European historical identity for Christian theology. This cultural imprisonment in turn I have found serves to block a fuller realization of the embodiment of tradition in and through the diversity of our religious, political, social, and gender identities. For better or for worse, the diversity of the Christian churches in the world today requires consideration of both theological and historical representations in this direction. It is in line with the very thesis that this book will eventually lay out to argue for the multiplicity of Christian traditions through the perspective of global historical-cultural identities.

At this point I do not want to be accused prematurely of minimizing the importance of European forms of Christianity within the overall global experience, nor do I wish to be accused of disregarding the European theological heritage. What I am concerned to address in the pages that follow is the *dominance* of the European and European-American expressions of Christian theology, and the accompanying *exclusive identification* of Christianity with its European heritage prior to the modern period.

4 FAITHFUL HISTORIES

In recent years attempts to articulate theological beliefs which are reflective of diverse local historical-cultural contexts have gained a considerable hearing in the form of what are now generally called contextual or liberation theologies. These various theologies embrace the diversity of historical situations in the world today as starting points for their various projects of theological reflection. Even within the confines of what is often referred to as "the West" or "the North," the cultural community of the North Atlantic basin, contextual theologies representing diverse social and cultural identities have grown considerably. Working from the perspective of these contextual Christian theologies, I have sought to understand what it means to contextualize Christian history and tradition as well.

To contextualize is to argue for boundaries, limitations, and the particular. It is to seek after the localized form, or the particular incarnation in which and through which the enduring truth of life might flow. Without some commitment to that which transgresses and transcends the particular, the local becomes an idolatry. A major thesis of this book is that this is precisely what has happened to European historical identity, that what is essentially a tribal theological tradition (variously described as "the West," "Western Christianity," or "Christendom") has been universalized and thus has become an idol.[2] On the other hand, there is no life, no truth, no transcendence accessible to us that is not embodied in some form, or that exists apart from its embodiment in history.[3] To borrow an image from Ernst Troeltsch, the common spirit of life flows as a historical stream through banks of historical religious and cultural values, and in this case through a pluralism of historical churches.[4]

Nearly a century ago one of the founding figures of the academic study of church history in North America, Philip Schaff, sought in his own way to address the relationship between transcendence and history in terms of tradition. Discussing the formal (historical) principle of Protestantism, he argued that the dogmatic tradition "has not for its contents something different from what is contained in the Bible, but forms the channel by which these contexts are conducted forward in history."[5] Tradition for Schaff was the indispensable means by which the (transcendent) contents of the Bible were mediated through history to the church of the present. As a historian of *Protestantism* he implicitly acknowledged the several confessional channels of history along which these contents were being mediated: Lutheran, Reformed, and Anglican, for instance. As a *historian* of Protestantism, he acknowledged the changing forms of such traditions, arguing for such as indications of progress over against those who would hold fast to absolute, unchanging forms of Protestant or Roman Catholic tradition.[6]

The task of the historian was to maintain the witness of the past over against those who would dispose of it, without claiming the past to be superior to the present. Reflecting the dominant German historiography of his own day, he argued:

> The true church historian leaves to every age its own peculiar advantages, without concern. He presumes not with narrow prejudice to reduce all to one measure, but recognizes with joyful satisfaction, under the most different forms wherever found, the footsteps of the Lord, the presence of his Spirit, as secured to the church by his own promise through all ages.[7]

Schaff argued that the historian does not reduce the past to a common form, nor circumscribe the divine within the horizon of one point of view. The historian "does not *construct* history," neither does she or he "*correct*" it by contemporary standards. Rather, the historian "takes it up and *reproduces* it, as God has allowed it to occur in the progressive explication of his plan of redemption . . ."[8] History in this sense is the channel of mediation of a redemptive past insofar as it is the communication of the plan of redemption revealed in the past. According to Schaff, the historian's task was not *constructive*, but *instructive*, a point made even more pointedly by his contemporary, I. D. Stewart, in his text, *The History of the Freewill Baptists*, published in 1862.

Stewart's was an attempt to articulate an incipient historical consciousness for a community which had in many instances rejected much that could be associated with ecclesial precedents, forerunners, or a tradition. Against this perspective, Stewart argued for the value of the study of history. At the very start of his text, he wrote:

> History is replete with instruction, and suggestive of duty. It takes the experience of others and offers it to ourselves, admonishing us to shun their faults and copy their virtues. It may be said to extend our days, as well as our experience, by carrying us back into the past, where we seem to live with the men of other years, to participate in their labors, sympathize with their feelings, and share in their weal or woe. No person can read a faithful history without advantage, if he desire it.[9]

For Stewart the advantage of historical study was moral instruction, but it was also more. The reading (and writing, it would seem) of history achieved a mode of communication and even community with the past, what might be described as a covenant with the past. Writing and reading history brought one into a participatory relationship with others who lived before "our" days, thereby extending one's own identity to join with that of others in the past. The key term for me in this remarkable paragraph is *faithful history*, which no person could read without advantage.

"Faithful" in this context could mean what Schaff described as the historian's task to reproduce the past, in which case the term implies the accuracy of verbal representations or depictions, judged by the empirical traces and evidence left from the past itself and by the narrative logic of unfolding events. Alternatively "faithful" could be interpreted in the sense of belief-*ful*, a historical accounting so full of faith that one will encounter through it something akin to a divine (and unseen) presence operative in the events and in their accounting. I suspect that a little of both meanings resides in the author's preface. I would point out that while the former sense implies an accountability to the traces and evidences of the historical past itself, the latter suggests a willingness and commitment to encounter a presence beyond the material evidences of the past. The advantage of reading a faithful history comes very near to that of participating in a faithful community, and both suggest being a part of a faithful tradition.

But how much difference would Schaff be willing or able to embrace joyously today within his category of "different forms," I wonder. He suggests it is the church historian's task to search for divine presence wherever these forms are found; but can we find "the footsteps of the Lord, the presence of his Spirit" outside the channels of European history, or even outside the channels of Christianity? How encompassing is the "all," of "all ages"? Would a faithful history of India, for instance, be advantageous for a Christian seeking to find the footsteps of God in human history? And if so, then would not the history of India, or the history of Hinduism, be a channel through which the content of Christian faith could now flow?

So much was argued by the Indian Christian mystic, Sadhu Sundar Singh, early in the present century. Raised within the devotional life of the Sikh religion and the *bhakti* tradition of Hinduism, Sundar Singh was converted at age fifteen through a mystical vision of Christ and baptized as an Anglican. He went on to travel throughout the world, becoming an influential leader of the Indian Christian movement. And while he was not formally a theologian himself, nor did he join the ranks of the ordained clergy, his influence across the world was profound and would continue to shape Indian theology long after his death.

Reflecting a positive appreciation for Hinduism and the Indian religious tradition in relation to Christ, Sundar Singh suggested an image parallel to that of Schaff a half-century before him: "Christianity is the fulfillment of Hinduism. Hinduism has been digging channels. Christ is the water to flow through these channels."[10] One need not agree with the "fulfillment" conception of Christianity in relationship to Hinduism to appreciate the historical perspective Sundar Singh represents. He himself accepted the salvific value of Hindu devotional life, acknowledging the salvation of his own mother who was Hindu, for instance. Nevertheless, his own faith perspective was that of an Indian Christian, and as such he found Christ, the incarnation of God revealed to him through mystical experiences, flowing through historical channels cut by Hinduism. Boyd summarizes Sundar Singh's contribution to Indian theology:

> here we have one who is truly Indian in all his ways and thoughts and has yet entered fully, not into the Christian tradition of the West, but into the

heart of the Gospel. In his own oft-quoted words, "Indians greatly need the Water of Life, but they do not want it in European vessels."[11]

If the task of the faithful historian or theologian is to find the footsteps of God, or of God's Spirit, in history, then she or he must be able to find them in all human history. This means finding such footsteps in histories other than explicitly European, or even Christian, ones. In such a case we must be willing (to shift the metaphor here) to use new historical vessels for carrying the Water of Life. The historical and theological task before us in the churches is to make use of them by creating of them new vessels of Christian tradition, ones that will be more adequate for carrying the Water of Life than the dominant European vessels which have seen overuse in recent years. To do so will involve us in the project of reconstructing Christian tradition as channels and vessels through which the Water of Life will flow.

Critical Practices and the Meaning of Tradition

So we are brought back again to the fundamental question of Christian tradition as the historical forms through which transcendence differently flows. By now it should be clear that I do not subscribe to the "detraditionalization thesis" concerning modern life. This is the thesis that holds that the social processes of modernity (secularization, rationalism, and technology, for instance) have led to a decline of the significance of tradition in individuals' lives. Proponents of this thesis have argued in one form or another that social processes set in motion by the European Enlightenment, the Industrial Revolution, the rise of science, and the emergence of modern capitalism have all (with various degrees of causality) conspired to undermine the meaning and authority of traditions.[12]

Certainly the European Enlightenment, the intellectual fountainhead of modernity, opened up a sustained attack upon the authority of tradition. And there is little argument that these social processes unleashed across the globe have done much to undercut the authority and even legitimacy of historical religious traditions. Over the course of the last several centuries, however, the Enlightenment has succeeded in itself becoming a tradition, one resembling a religious faith more and more every day, and one still exercising considerable power within the contemporary world.

An alternative to the radical detraditionalization thesis which holds greater weight for me is that which has argued not for the demise of traditions in the modern and postmodern world, but their commodification and transformation into consumer products. Among the cultural theorists who have argued this point none has provided a more coherent or convincing description than Frederic Jameson.[13] Jameson believes that the totalizing effects of the market in late capitalist society have succeeded in commodifying history and memories completely. At both the level of mass culture and the level of highbrow culture, tradition has been transformed from being a source of authority into a means for the gratification of consumptive desires. History is successfully commodified, packaged, and sold back to a consumer population of tourists. In the process, the authority of tradition and the contextual identity of history are both subverted in subtle, yet pervasive ways.

It is difficult to dispute Jameson's thesis entirely. One need not look hard to see evidence of the commodification of traditions by postmodern cultural consumer practices. Nevertheless the commodification thesis does not satisfy me as being able to explain entirely the persistence of meaningful traditions in the contemporary world. Too much in the way of tradition and meaning continues to escape the effects of commodification and the marketplace. Jameson's thesis posits by its very logic the existence of some prior body of beliefs, practices, and habits, in other words a culture or tradition, which can then be commodified and sold back to a consuming community of identity. One might indeed purchase an identity in the form of clothing, artifacts, and customs which are learned. But the very process presupposes some prior or even inherent traditional identity which is being exploited by consumerism. The fact that African Americans are the targeted market for kente-cloth items, or that European Americans are targeted for classes in tracing European immigrant histories, suggests the prior existence and enduring authority of these deeper African and European cultural identities.

If all that could be said concerning the enduring presence of traditions amidst the postmodern world were exhausted by the detraditionalization and commodification theses, there would be little reason to go on with the writing of this book. Fortunately for the book, however (to say nothing of religion and faith), that is not all there is to say. For despite their disruption, and even their commodification, traditions remain enduring sources of meaning and identity for contemporary persons in community. On occasion, they may even themselves be sources for the disruption and subversion of modern and postmodern detraditionalizing forces.[14] What will hopefully become clearer as the arguments of this book unfold, is that the manner in which traditions coexist alongside one another in the postmodern world serves to qualify each one in a significant manner. Traditions today limit one another, illuminate one another, may challenge one another, and may even help to define one another to a degree that was not true for them in past periods of time. In doing so, traditions now enter into each other in fundamentally new or unanticipated ways, and they do so without being reduced to a common denominator or sublated into a higher synthesis.

I am not suggesting that the phenomenon of interaction is entirely new to traditions. On the contrary, traditions have always encountered one another and engaged one another across their boundaries in significant ways. What is unique for our contemporary world is the accelerated degree to which such encounters and coexistence are now taking place, often under social conditions that might appear to be less than optimal for the work of significant meaning-construction. Both those who hold to the detraditionalization thesis and those who support the notion of traditions being unchanging and unchangeably given, fail to recognize the dynamic process of rejuvenation and re-creation that has taken place across the centuries and continues today to give traditions ongoing life.[15]

Rejuvenation and re-creation have taken place in churches and other Christian communities of faith as well across the centuries. What is especially significant for these processes of renewal today is the increasingly diversified and pluralistic social reality of the churches. We are being challenged in a number of ways to recognize difference, heterogeneity, and alterity in our social contexts. Through them Christian ecclesial communities can discover the means by which their traditions, including even those that identify themselves as the One, Holy, Catholic, and Apostolic Tradition, are being made new.

I would go so far as to assert that the re-creation of Christian tradition is not an option, but an imperative of Christian faith. This is so not only because of the external demands for change and transformation foisted upon Christian communities today. One could certainly argue that the historical changes the world has witnessed over the last several centuries have been of such magnitude as to require of churches in the world new and more adequate responses of faith. But if this were the only reason for re-creating tradition, then one could rightly assess it as a purely reactive, and reactionary response. But I would assert that there are reasons internal to Christian traditions of faith that drive them toward rejuvenation and re-creation. The concept of the new, the inherent drive toward expecting the unexpected, the ability to embrace that which is unprecedented in history—in short, the ability to assent to change and transformation—are all concepts and practices which are welcomed and nurtured to varying degrees by the variant strands of historical Christian faith. One need not point out the failures and shortcomings of Christian churches over time from outside them. Acknowledgment of our manifold sins takes place from within, on a regular basis in fact, to call us afresh on the path to renewal.

Through the practices of repentance and conversion individual Christians experience being reclaimed and renewed. So it is with the wider community of faith as well, although on a different level of historical engagement. Baptism occurs once, and through it one passes into the community through the assent of faith, but confession and renewal happen again and again, to individuals and to entire Christian communities of faith. Both embody aspects of the more fundamental practice of *metanoia*, or the turning in a new direction called repentance and conversion. Conversion of course indicates a radical break with one's past, a fundamental change in direction. At the same time the overall narrative of *metanoia* incorporates the original direction in which one was heading, and the new direction toward which one is going. The practice of *metanoia* implies a process which can be narrated. As such it is a mode of discontinuity, but also a mode of continuity; a rupture in the course of one's own personal or corporate history, but also a means of overcoming the ruptures of history.

The practice of repentance is fundamentally eschatological in character. It calls into question or throws into crisis what has come before it in an act of judgment and decision. *Metanoia* compels us to narrate from a point of view on the other side of judgment and after the historical rupture, beginning from the discontinuity of the present with the past. One who has undergone conversion finds the meaning of history to be not an inheritance from the past irrepressibly bequeathed to the present, but in the present's outstripping the past. In the case of the narrative complex of a tradition, conversion is understood as an act of assent, rather than descent: one who undergoes conversion joins with a community of assent, in a break with one's community of descent.[16] The pages of the New Testament offer abundant evidence of such breaks in the experiences of the early Christian communities, cogently expressed in Galatians 3:28: "There is neither Jew nor Greek, there is neither slave nor free, there is neither male nor female; for you are all one in Christ Jesus."[17]

Being faithful to the history of a community of assent entails a more explicit act of commitment than is usually acknowledged by those within a community of descent. Intentionality and commitment become primary categories for understanding the past. Here I would agree with Juan Luis Segundo, that one's entry into a critical hermeneutical circle of historical understanding opens with an act of will or commitment.[18] In the case of liberation theologies, Segundo points out, this is a commitment to the oppressed.[19] Segundo goes on, however, to argue for a second precondition of his hermeneutical circle which is also in some sense an act of commitment, in this case the retraditioning of a new interpretation of the Bible (especially through the narratives of Jesus).[20] Segundo does not make as explicit his own Christian and biblical commitments in his description of the hermeneutical circle, but they are what in the end make his a *theology* of liberation. What Segundo and other liberation or contextual Christian theologians argue is that the coincidence of Christian commitment and commitment to the oppressed is inherent in the character of the divine (transcendent) identity that is revealed in Jesus Christ.

The Sri Lankan theologian Aloysius Pieris has also argued forcefully for this fundamental coincidence between the transcendent and the poor of history, making the case as well that it is not exclusively Christian:

> Christ, at once human victim and divine judge of *forced poverty*, lives in the oppressed in whom he announces himself to be unmistakably available as the recipient of our ministry (Matt. 25:31-46). *The struggle for the poor* is, therefore, the second constitutive dimension of Christian dis-

cipleship and is also the means by which Jesus is proclaimed the Lord of history. All christological speculations that flow from this liberational praxis do not compete with buddhological theories.[21]

Both christological and buddhological theories can properly flow from the praxis of struggle for the poor which he calls the second constitutive dimension of Christian discipleship. The first constitutive dimension, on the other hand, is according to Pieris the struggle to be poor, embodied in the practice of voluntary poverty which is likewise expressed through Buddhist and Christian monastic traditions.[22] Here we see the convergence of Segundo's two commitments, to the oppressed and to the Christ, in a community of assent which, in Pieris's terms, embodies a long tradition of voluntary poverty—in other words, monasticism. The narrative of tradition that emerges from Pieris's monastic community of assent is one in which christology and buddhology do not compete, but offer pathways of access into primordial experience. "Hence those who consult the collective memory (tradition) must be ready to transcend it at some moment or other if they wish to touch the core of the other religion," he writes.[23] It is a narrative which has as its starting point a form of conversion (the voluntary moment) and thus transformation. The outcome transcends even the tradition itself.

A community that emphasizes the dimension of assent, be it a monastic community in Sri Lanka or a struggling congregation of Pentecostal believers in the South Bronx, understands the rupture of tradition and experience, the crisis of life, as being overcome, inasmuch as the assent of conversion opens upon primordial or transcendent experience. In terms of our earlier metaphor it is a situation of the transcendent breaking through existing channels, overflowing the historical banks of identity in order to create them anew. History, tradition, and identity are not discarded, but transformed. In this case the meaning one finds in the channels of history does not lie in what the past was, but in what it has become.

History, for a community of assent, would appear to require something of an eschatological narrative direction. Contrary to the commonsense notion that time moves from the past to the future, for a community of assent the direction of meaning is from the present, or even the future, toward the past. The meaning of history, the purpose of history, lies not in the past but in the present in which we are reclaiming and rearticulating the past. Nietzsche said it well concerning the meaning of history for such a community of assent:

> there is for historiography of any kind no more important proposition than the one it took such effort to establish but which really *ought to be* established now: the cause of the origin of a thing and its eventual utility, its actual employment and place in a system of purposes, lie worlds apart; whatever exists, having somehow come into being, is again and again

reinterpreted to new ends, taken over, transformed, and redirected by some power superior to it . . .[24]

Such historical outstripping involves fresh interpretation of events through which previous meanings and purposes are adapted, reconfigured, and even transformed. It is in the present situation that we discover the imperatives that address us and send us searching for the meaning of the past, its purposes, and its inheritance.

But is a past that is so outstripped rendered completely ineffective, or emptied of any inherent meaning that might stand on its own? To say this would be to ignore the persistence, the lingering power and effects, of historical memory embedded in the very fabric of the languages, prejudices, customs, patterns, and intentions themselves out of which such new interpretations are fashioned. Despite Nietzsche's emphatic insistence on the will to knowledge overcoming or outstripping the historical inertia of events of the past themselves, in the end we cannot entirely disregard the manner in which the past continues to interpret us. For this reason the concept of a community of descent remains crucial for theology and tradition. Any faithful historiography must entail careful attention to the context from which one has descended, or a study of the past for the influences it has bequeathed to the present.

In the discipline of church history this has often been the point at which historical investigation begins. Here again Philip Schaff's words are worth quoting, for they articulate the commitment of one of the foundational figures of American church historiography over the past century:

> History, on the other hand, is the bearer of the Church; by whose means this last is made to possess a real existence, whereas, under any other form it could be nothing better than a baseless, fantastic abstraction, which for us who are ourselves the product of history, and draw from it all the vigor of our lives, would have no meaning or value whatever.[25]

The "us" who are the "product" of history are what I have been terming a community of descent. Schaff's assertion that history is the bearer of the church, or that all meaning and vigor in life are drawn from history, might well strike one as naive in light of the terrors of history that have erupted over the past century. Furthermore, from the perspective of the thesis that is being explored in this book, I am compelled today to inquire as to who the "us" is who Schaff intends, or whether the histories of which "we" are today in Christian churches a product are all the same. I will be arguing in this text that the vast majority of church histories and historiography over the course of the past century have envisioned the sole community of descent for Christianity to be a collective European historical community.

The narrative of descent is familiar to anyone who has studied in the discipline: from the Semitic community of first-century Judaism and the Greco-Roman world that gave rise to European civilization and the twin imperial orders of Rome and Constantinople; through Europe's Middle Ages and Reformation; into the modern era in which European colonial power dominated the globe. In recent years it has begun to be challenged by historians, missiologists, grassroots activists, and others whose work will animate the chapters that follow. For the time being, I would point out that even from within the circle of the historiographical defenders of the grand narrative of descent there has been a critical historical perspective raised against the hegemony that would confine the church's inheritance to a particular historical past.

Herbert Butterfield, himself a recent architect and defender of the narrative of Christendom's descent, nevertheless provides us with an illustration of its criticism from within. Butterfield argues as a historian for Christianity (and by extension he acknowledges any religion) living on two levels, or having two dimensions. Christianity is a primary force that has contributed to shaping a major civilization and society he says, but it also has a universal message which is not confined to that civilization and society. The former is its "mundane" level on which Christianity operates formally as any social religion does, providing the social cement for tribal bonding. The latter is its more "profound" level which summons, according to Butterfield, individual souls to salvation.[26] This latter, more profound level, operates both on and apart from the mundane level:

> It is in the nature of Christianity to transform history for those who have faith—to transform the meaning of the story and the mode of experiencing it even though the course of the world's events remains the same as before.[27]

For some who experience the transformation of faith and for whom a new meaning to the story is possible, the course of the world's events will not remain the same. For some a course of events different from those that took place in European history might even be brought into the circle of transformative theological meaning. These who would enable the transformation of faith to affect the course of the world's events I would term a community of assent. In the mundane bonds of social solidarity that tie them to others, both contemporary and of historical memory, I would see the workings of the community of descent.

I think Butterfield is right: it is the nature of Christianity to transform history. Transformation is not elimination, however. The assent of Christian conversion, proclaimed and embraced in the ritual of baptism, does not signify the erasure of the language, culture, and identity derived from one's community of descent; it signifies their redemption. The process of renewal does not bring about their erasure, but their transformation. This is not to say that there is no moment of discontinuity, or break, in the historical process of *metanoia* for either individuals or communities of Christian faith. But to contend that historical disconnectedness exhausts the meaning of conversion would miss the deeper meaning of *metanoia* that is found in the narratives and processes of renewal. To heed the call of faithful living is to stand in solidarity with those who have gone before us (a basis for the continuity of our various histories, cultures, and identities) as much as it is to challenge and transform them (which requires the embrace of a certain discontinuity or break with them).

Discontinuity and continuity are tied together in the one act of *metanoia*. Christian communities of faith are simultaneously communities of assent and communities of descent. Historical continuity enables one to lay claim to memory and values, and thus identity, bequeathed from the past. Historical discontinuity allows one to transform them in the direction of a future more representative of what one perceives to be indicated by the coming Reign of God. The task of historical reproduction of faith, or of faithful reproduction of history, has a double form, which is what we will come to see tradition to be. Assent and descent, construction and instruction—both are incorporated in the project of re-creating Christian traditions of faith. This in turn calls us within the Christian churches today to support dialogue among historians and theologians concerned with rejuvenating our traditions of faith.

Looking Ahead

The following chapters do not pretend to fully embody such dialogue. That project entails many more voices, from a much wider circle of persons representing communities of faith. The project of re-creating Christian tradition truly belongs to the whole church universal, which is to say the many churches of the world today. The chapters that follow have instead a more modest purpose, that of focusing on particular aspects of the project of re-creating tradition. They invite us to participate in a living, dialogical relationship between present and past, or among the presents and pasts of the many Christian communities of faith. There is thus something of a "meta-traditional" bent to the discussion that I will be undertaking in these pages, something akin to a theology of history which invites us to take up the project of reconstructing Christian traditions of faith. Redefining and reworking the heritage of the past actually creates the past, creates a new past, by creating the present which is to become the past that future generations will take over or reject on their own, and as their own. When we understand this, we can understand that the community being traditioned is the tradition itself, which is why rigid boundaries between the disciplines of history and contemporary theology do not make sense to me.

My metatraditional discussion in these pages is not intended to be the basis for a new universal theory of tradition, or Tradition. I am not searching for an all-encompassing theory of history or faith. I am in fact quite suspicious of the totalizing conceptions of imperial faith which have passed for "the Christian Tradition" in the past. But at the same time, I am equally suspicious of the totalizing dismissal of Christian tradition and history advanced by some today. Instead of either of these options, I am attempting in these pages to illuminate the processes of traditioning in order to enable wider participation in the project of their re-creation. The openness I seek to embrace regarding the Christian future is one in which difference and solidarity are joined together in an open-ended understanding of the presence of God in our midst.

To these ends, the following chapter will interrogate more closely the relationship between tradition and history (both the past which has happened and the telling of the past), with a constant eye directed toward the process of retraditioning. Chapter 3 will then explore the complex of accountabilities to which a tradition responds, both those that are incarnated within a particular tradition itself, and those that confront it with imperatives from beyond itself. By the end of Chapter 3 I will have raised the problem of multiple accountabilities being simultaneously addressed, something which is akin to answering several persons (both living and dead) who are asking different questions, and doing so (both asking and answering) at once. The model of dialogical living will suggest itself for us at this point, suggesting that traditions are living dialogues of faith in which we are engaged.

Chapter 4 will seek to develop a more comprehensive theology of history which can undergird the wider arena of historical accountabilities suggested in this study. Chapter 5 will then examine the dominant narrative accounting of church history which has rendered an account of the Christian past by means of the master narrative of church history. Constructed through the work of a number of modern historians, the master narrative I am examining in this chapter is one that makes Christianity synonomous with European history, and the history of Europe's dominant churches normative for Christian traditioning. Chapter 6 will engage in an alternative, genealogical reading of Christian history and tradition, exploring the implications of the multiple, global, narrative trajectories of Christian tradition that emerged in the first centuries of the common era; and examining the genealogical significance of the rupture between the classical world and European civilization. The genealogy of tradition I sketch here remains admittedly underdeveloped, for a full written history of Christianity is beyond the range of this particular book. Nevertheless, what I have provided I believe offers an approach to the written histories of Christianity that will enable us to retradition the faith in our own age.

Chapter 7 will bring the results of this genealogical narrative reconstruction to bear on the project of Christian traditioning and theologizing. This chapter will be exploring what my proposal means for contemporary theological endeavors, paying particular attention to the ecclesiological implications of these multiple trajectories of church history. It will conclude with a theo-

16 FAITHFUL HISTORIES

logical examination of the connectedness I believe is possible among communities of Christian faith, a connectedness that enables communities from different historical identities to embrace in a new way the catholicity of faith through their differences. Throughout this text I am seeking to push the boundaries of universality and particularity of faith at the same time. Chapter 7 will draw from this effort specific conclusions for the relationships among differing communities of tradition confessing the one Christian faith.

2 | History and Tradition: From Crisis to Re-Creation

> I am outside of
> history. i wish
> i had some peanuts, it
> looks hungry there in
> its cage
> i am inside of
> history. its
> hungrier than i
> thot.
> —Ishmael Reed[1]

Rendering Accounts

In a short book entitled *The Meaning of Revelation*, first published in 1941, H. Richard Niebuhr took up one of the more perplexing questions of Christian theology: the relation of divine revelation to human history.[2] More than fifty years after its publication it remains an insightful text, due in part to the persistent nature of the question of the meaning of history in our age. In his opening pages Niebuhr argued that in the modern era historical consciousness and historical methodologies have come to dominate virtually every field of intellectual enquiry. Such historical thinking (often termed *historicism*) has convincingly demonstrated that all human thought, including thought about God, is conditioned by its social historical location, Niebuhr concluded. Thus all thought is relative to its historical background or situation. There are no absolutes or universals that can be apprehended apart from their mediation through the relativism of historical experience.

Embracing such historical consciousness or historicism, according to Niebuhr, was not tantamount to saying that God is limited by the boundaries of human history or even Christian history. It did, however, require acknowledgment of the limitations of perspective for interpretation and understanding. In revelation, the divine reality discloses itself in such a way as to be mediated in a meaningful manner through the particularity of historical experience. Those who would seek to communicate the meaning of revelation are thus compelled to speak of what they know by telling the story of the events that compose their history.

> The preachers and theologians of the modern church must do what New Testament evangelists did because their situation permits no other method. From the point of view of historical beings we can speak only about that which is also in our time and which is seen through the medium of our history. *We are in history as the fish is in water and what we mean by the revelation of God can be indicated only as we point through the medium in which we live.*[3]

To perceive history as the medium in which we presently live, the water in which we swim, means history is not simply that which is past. History is, of course, that which is past, but it is the past we are in, the past made present as the medium in which we live. We use the term history not only to name the world of the past that has happened; we also use the term to describe the *telling* of what has happened in the past. The confusion this double usage can create is no small matter.

There are many who would argue that the telling of the past coincides, or at least ought to coincide, precisely with the nature of the events of the past themselves. Arguments to this effect are made by historical realists who assert the possibility of there being a one-to-one correspondence between these two modes of history. Such arguments tend to ignore, however, the subtle yet significant manner in which all acts of recounting or representing events of the past are themselves new historical events, located in new historical contexts of their own and separated from the original events they seek to recount. However close the acts of retelling might be to the events being told, there is inevitably some measure of historical distance between them.

Paul Ricoeur has offered a more adequate description of the relationship between the past and present through his appropriation of Aristotle's concept of *mimesis*, the imitation or representation of activity through language.[4] Ricoeur argues that the form of *mimesis* that represents or reproduces human experience through time is narrative. By their very nature narratives bridge distances in time, representing as one event a series of activities taking place sequentially through time. Furthermore, the narrative activity of retelling a history that is past does not itself perfectly coincide with the past being recounted. In one sense it is continuous with it, but in another, it is discontinuous. The linkage, yet distance, between the past and its narration can be understood as continuous discontinuity, or discontinuous continuity. In either case it introduces the problems that have come to occupy those engaged in the study of hermeneutics.

Niebuhr's observation that we are in history as a fish is in water suggests there is no recounting that is itself free from the mediations of the perspective of the ones doing the recounting. Often the perspective is injected unwittingly and unwillingly, for as the fish does not always see the water, so one does not always see one's own historical standpoint. While there is no such thing as standpoint-less thinking, there are certainly moments when one's standpoint is too subtle or too common to be seen clearly. This is in fact how most of our existence within history goes on: quite commonly, without direct observation, and without much reflection. Likewise, the acts of historical narration we carry out are often unwitting and unseen. Their telling takes place in countless and often minute acts of mimetic representation and interpretation, both written and unwritten.[5]

These standpoints or perspectives do not come from nowhere, nor do they drop from the sky, but they are themselves historical creations and the products of a past. Often they are so subtle and unwitting in the telling of a history precisely because they share so much with the history being told, for they are in part its creation. One of the reasons offered by historians for why we study history is that history itself (as that which is past) has created the conditions for the present, so that any given present can be understood in a significant sense to be a consequence of its past. Such an argument places emphasis on the continuity between the past and the present, or on the past and its narration, precisely because it views the past as effecting the present. The structuring effect of forces and events "of a past which is not definitely over" can be located in these representations and interpretations.[6]

Nevertheless, with Ricoeur we must acknowledge, the protests of historical realists notwithstanding, that the representations and interpretations are not identical with the events of the past. They might be its signs and representations, but as Bahti puts it, they are allegories (tropes that are "saying otherwise"). They cannot encompass the totality of the past, whether it be the universal past of human historical existence or even a much more limited past of a particular human community. They are the work of a present seeking to understand its past, even though or at times because those of the present understand it to be a past that is not over. They are the work of persons located in one historical place, seeking to connect with another, and even to establish their continuity of identity with it, but showing their own situation to be, though different, in some sense identical. Such narratives of identity reverberate between historical subjects and a past full of meaning.

But then they are limited, for history is limited—both the history that is the past and the history that is the narration of the past. "*The* past," argued Johan Huizinga, "is limited always in accordance with the kind of subject which seeks to understand it. Every civilization has a past *of its own*."[7] There is no history in general, and no history that is given. History is always particular, and its comprehension a task to be achieved. Huizinga argues:

> In reality history gives no more than a particular representation of a particular past, an intelligible picture of a portion of the past. It is never

the reconstruction or reproduction of a given past. No past is ever given . . . History is always an imposition of form upon the past, and cannot claim to be more. It is always the comprehension and interpretation of a meaning which we look for in the past.[8]

Imposing a particular form on a portion of the past in order to create an intelligible picture, history is a process of "rendering account," Huizinga concludes. *"History is the intellectual form in which a civilization renders account to itself of its past."*[9]

Albert J. Raboteau argues that in this capacity history functions "as a form of self-definition . . . It tells us who we are, because it reveals where we come from and where we've been."[10] So while it is a form imposed on a portion of the past, it is revelatory in its power and effect. As the collective memory of the past of a particular "we" who have been somewhere (which is assumedly different), history provides a reservoir for the formation of identity (what Raboteau calls "self-definition"). It is precisely because the past is somewhere else for a particular we, that it is somewhere different than where (and who) the we now are, that it has to be remembered and represented in order for the we to be able to render account of who they are in the present. Reflecting on the manner in which such identity of a subject of history is constructed from the heterogeneous moments of a past, Michel de Certeau concludes, "The problem of history is inscribed in the place of this subject, which is in itself a play of difference, the historicity of a nonidentity with itself."[11]

In other words, history remembers that which is different, in order to overcome such difference. Through the capacity to remember (or through the facility of memory), history seeks to tie the present to the past in order that self-definition or identity can be sustained. It is along these lines that Pierre Bourdieu notes in particular the specific function of social monuments and family albums:

> The images of the past arranged in chronological order, "the natural order" of social memory, arouse and transmit the remembrance of events worthy of preservation because the group sees a unifying factor in the monuments of its past unity, or what amounts to the same thing, because it derives from its past the confirmation of its present unity.[12]

But if history remembers the past in order to overcome difference, at the same time it remembers in order to make different. As a reflective practice which goes beyond the simple reflex of memory, history is infused with intentionality. Indeed Huizinga is quite correct in arguing that the past of a particular history is never simply given, any more than memory as such can be said to be given. History is gained. Like memory, it is infused with intentionality (although not always fully consciously such). As a practice it seeks minimally to create comprehension and meaning where such are perceived to be lacking; in the words of LeGoff, "the goal of historical work is to make the historical process intelligible."[13]

There is moreover a critical dimension to the praxis of history which LeGoff discerns to lie in the close link between "historical science" and "the lived history of which it is a part." He formulates it as an imperative for change: "we can, indeed we must, beginning with each and every historian, work and struggle so that history, in both senses of the word, may become *different*."[14] This critical imperative impinges on various forms of social and collective memory as well, calling us in LeGoff's words again "to act in such a way that collective memory may serve the liberation and not the enslavement of human beings."[15]

According to LeGoff then, the practice of history not only entails rendering account of the past in a manner that is intelligible, so as to render intelligible self-definition and identity in the present; it also entails changing conditions in the present, liberating participants of the lived history of which they are a part from structures or conditions that oppress them. One could minimally argue that such forces are primarily idealistic, and that rendering intelligible the structures and conditions of history is in and of itself an act of liberation, in this case from the oppressions of ignorance. LeGoff would appear to have in view liberation from material forces of oppression as well. But on both levels it is the fundamental question of change that is raised by his call to the historian to make a difference, in his particular case in the quest for social change that is implied in the language of liberation. Whether the matter is viewed idealistically, materially, or in some combination of the two, the question of change raises once again the problem of history's "nonidentity" with itself, the otherness of the past as well as of the future.

The Crisis of Modern History

Questions concerning the relationship among past, present, and future are not unique to contemporary historians. The problematics of change that are inherent in the temporal structures of life (and death) are perennial in the experience of human communities.[16] In the modern era these appear to have been accelerated by the geometrically increasing rate of social change. Since the rise of the modern North Atlantic[17] civilization, in the wake of the intellectual currents of the modern European Enlightenment, a number of historical ruptures have occurred which have increasingly severed ties that would bind the various presents of the contemporary world to their multiple and diverse historical pasts. The effects of these events have been felt on a global scale. One need only note the results of North Atlantic colonial domination, capitalist economic expansion, rapid technological advances, scientific development, and global urbanization/industrialization to discover how severe have been the disruptions and dislocations of this era. To an unprecedented degree they have unsettled and even severed social, cultural, and religious bonds that united people in communities across generations for centuries, fracturing historical connections and historical consciousness (the latter being part of the paradox of modernity which increased critical consciousness of the historical past even while, or perhaps in order that, it undercut the authority of the historical past).[18] As the material forces of modernity have swept across the globe, disruption has been experienced in virtually every corner of the world, including, as we shall see below, in the Christian churches.[19]

In his short reflection on a Paul Klee painting, "Angelus Novus," Walter Benjamin captured well the apocalyptic sense of carnage that has been brought about through these ruptures of history in the modern era. The face of this angel of history, says Benjamin, is turned toward the past, while the angel itself is propelled toward the future by a storm we call progress.

> Where we perceive a chain of events, [the angel] sees one single catastrophe which keeps piling wreckage upon wreckage and hurls it in front of his feet . . . This storm irresistibly propels him into a future to which his back is turned, while the pile of debris before him grows skyward.[20]

Here at the end of the modern experience Benjamin's image of the past as wreckage upon wreckage confronts us with the problem of history in crisis. If, as Niebuhr argued, human beings are in history as the fish is in water, then we must ask at the end of the modern era how we are to live in them when the waters have become so polluted as to render life impossible. The disruptions of the modern era have severed much of the historical ties that would bind people together into community. The carnage that has been wrought tempts one to abandon any hope for realizing meaning in the midst of this history.

The effects of these twin factors in part account for much of the cynicism, nihilism, and even despair that have found their way into several currents of contemporary postmodernist theory. We noted above that according to LeGoff the task of the historian is to render the past intelligible, and that this is to be done in order to make a difference in the future. But when the former task (rendering the past intelligible) is called into question on account of the disruptions and carnage that have characterized this modern past, the latter task (making a difference) becomes an equally questionable pursuit. Historical fragmentation has given rise to postmodern critics who no longer can narrate the connections between the past and present; apocalyptic disorder has tempted some even to abandon the task of making a difference in the future. Yet this is not to say that postmodern historiography has not grappled with questions of the meaning of history. Confronting the very dilemma of the seemingly impossible task of discovering meaning on history is itself in some sense a meaningful practice. Opponents of postmodernism might protest its skepticism, but postmodernists warn against facile assumptions of meaning in history or the temptation to rush to conclusions concerning continuities across time. To these ends the strong sense of historical irony that characterizes the postmodern turn in historiography serves as a corrective to some of the more questionable aspects of modern historical consciousness to which even theologians such as Niebuhr fell prey.

Among the more pernicious attributes that have characterized this modern historical consciousness has been the assumption that the historical horizon of modern European civilization coincided with the horizon of universal human history. The concept of universal history is itself a product of modern Europe. It emerged only at the end of the eighteenth century from the intellectual milieu of the European Enlightenment, and had at its center a particular human subject, the modern European. Historian Reinhart Koselleck writes:

> Previously, histories had existed in the plural—all sorts of histories which had occurred and which might be used as exempla in teachings... Indeed, history (*die Geschichte*) as an expression was plural.[21]

Koselleck argues that the concept of a universal history, or history in general, was "an outcome of modernity (*Neuzeit*)," the "new time" of progress.[22] To the emerging bourgeois class in European society humanity seemed now to be capable of directing history toward a single and all-encompassing goal, described by Immanuel Kant as a universal *bourgeois society* which administers law.[23]

From the historically conscious perspective of the Enlightenment, the world of human experience was one which human beings themselves were actively creating. The actor was above all else the modern "man" of reason, who had come to exercise control over all others, be this the non-European historical other or the other of nature.[24] The coincidence of this historical vision with Europe's worldwide colonial domination occurs succinctly in Kant's 1784 treatise, "Idea for a Universal History from a Cosmopolitan Point of View." All human history appeared from his all-encompassing perspective to be tied to the universal historical agency of European civilization. At the same time, the possibility of discerning universal laws of history now seemed within reach, given the vantage point European civilization had as observer of the whole of humankind. These universal laws, Kant argued, pointed toward a regular movement and direction, the goal of which was "*the achievement of a universal civic society which administers law among men.*"[25] The effect of their operation brought others into contact with European civilization whose historical identity, stretching from the ancient Greeks to the modern Enlightenment, constituted universal history.[26]

In the decades following Kant, the nineteenth-century German school of historicism delineated more carefully the methodological principles that would come to characterize much of modern historiography. Historicism argued that a thing in history can be known only through its context.[27] The attention of the historian was turned to the concrete and particular of history as these are found in their contexts. Historicism thus championed the multiformity and diversity of historical factuality, or what came to be called "historical relativism."[28] Critics of historicism (then and now) have argued that notions of historical relativity undermine commitment to transcendent truths or values. But for the theologian Ernst Troeltsch, living at the end of the nineteenth century, such relativism was not necessarily antithetical to universal truth. In *The Absoluteness of Christianity and the History of Religions* he argued:

> Relativity simply means that all historical phenomenon are unique, individual configurations acted on by influences from *a universal context* that comes to bear on them in varying degrees of immediacy. It means, therefore, that every independent structure leads one to a perspective that embraces broader and still broader horizons till finally it opens out onto *the whole*.[29]

For Troeltsch, the unique, the individual, the particular, or the factual in history could only be known in relation to its horizon (relative to its context). But this did not preclude successive opening to wider and wider horizons until one reached what could finally be called the "universal context of the whole." Moreover, successive opening to wider and wider contexts could be achieved across the distances of both time and space, the horizon of understanding becoming more encompassing in both temporal and geographical dimensions. In his last major theoretical study, *Historismus und seine Probleme*, Troeltsch argued that in the modern era a truly universal historical horizon had in fact been achieved, providing for the European bourgeoisie class (the universal historical agent of the modern era) a universal historical consciousness.[30]

The cultural upheaval of the modern European epoch, brought about through the activity of the bourgeois class, required a break with the heritage of the Middle Ages and the church in order for a new cultural consciousness to emerge, he argued.[31] The active agent of this new cultural consciousness was neither God nor the church, but the human actor who had attained historical consciousness. Early in the modern era the bearer of this history had been the nation-state, Troeltsch argued, a collective individual or an individual totality. But by the end of the nineteenth century, the cultural unity of European bourgeois civilization was unifying the separate European states.[32] The active agent or subject of this new European cultural epoch was the bourgeoisie, Kant's "world citizen." It was the actor who had already assumed center stage in Kant's 1784 essay referred to above, on "What Is Enlightenment?" He was the one who had courageously come of age, achieving majority status.[33] He was explicitly gendered male (the "entire fair sex" holding the step to competence to be dangerous, said Kant), and stood alone in public as an autonomous individual who made use of his reason. Having freed himself from the matrix of determinations, he had become the subject of history.[34] The world of which he stood at the center was "universal history" or simply "History." It was specifically the history of Europe's modern age, for Europeans alone appeared to him to represent the active, self-reflective race. Like Kant, Troeltsch believed that outside European civilization, true historical consciousness did not exist.

> The domains outside Europe lack historical self-consciousness and the critical knowledge of the past for which only the European *Geist* has experienced a need.[35]

Aware that the lack of anything even remotely approximating a uniform world culture precluded the possibility of there being one universal context for history, Troeltsch nevertheless argued that the absence of viable historical consciousness outside the domains of modern European intellectual life allowed for its *de facto* claim to a universal historical consciousness. In effect, he collapsed universal history into the history of Europe, resulting in an ideology he himself called "Europeanism" (*Europäismus*). He claimed to be justified in doing so because of the sheer quantity of facts known (at least to him) regarding Europe's past; but also because it appeared to him that only the European *Geist* called for such self-knowing. Troeltsch admitted that all of this could be little more than naive European pride at work, reinforced by a history of European Christian dogmatics locating Europe at the center of the universe.[36] Given the assumption that a social or cultural context is necessary for historical understanding, he acknowledged that all a European could offer is a universal history from a European perspective. Nothing could prevent one from writing a universal history from an Islamic or a Chinese perspective, he noted, although he was not aware of such histories or historical consciousness.[37] Ultimately, Troeltsch asserted, only God has a universal perspective on history. Our knowledges must always remain partial, fragmentary, and local. By the closing pages of *Historismus* Troeltsch had as much as acknowledged what Robert Solomon calls the "transcendental pretense" of European historical self-consciousness.[38] But he had also recognized that the solution could only be found with more history, not less.

Troeltsch himself did not resolve the contradiction which he identified in the pages of *Historismus*, nor did he abandon the transcendental pretense of the ideology of Europeanism (*Europäismus*).[39] His was one of the more articulate statements of the universal horizon of the modern European historical consciousness, but it was by no means the only one. He was essentially correct in asserting that this had become the historical consciousness of the modern bourgeois class, which through its colonial domination had extended its reach to virtually every land on earth. What he did not foresee, however, was the manner in which the false universality of modern historical consciousness would be challenged by the "subjugated knowledges" of the postmodern world. From within the horizon of modern historical consciousness a historian such as Johan Huizinga could proclaim, "Our civilization is the first to have for its past the past of the world, our history is the first to be world-history."[40] From the context of postindustrial society, postmodern culture, on the other hand, Jean-François Lyotard asserts concerning universal history that the "grand narrative has lost its credibility," its place now taken by a multiplicity of local, heterogeneous narratives.[41]

The otherness of these multiple histories, and especially their otherness to the master narrative(s) of the dominant modern West, or Europe, gives them potentially a critical and liberative capacity. This is a quality of the religious narratives of Europe's others in particular, for religious narratives by their very nature invoke experiences of otherness that delineate boundaries or limits. Interrogating the religious experiences of Europe's others (including the others who have existed within the domains of European civilization) can, among other tasks, help recover a more critical historical consciousness that resists ideological reduction to one social class's history. Charles H. Long calls the mode of investigation that recovers a more critical historical consciousness through religious experience "a form of the archaic critique, or, if you will, a kind of crawling back through the history that evoked these experiences."[42] It begins with a hermeneutic of suspicion, but then goes on to a hermeneutic of recollection and memory.[43] A critical *recursus*[44] thus functions at the same time to open the future to that which lies beyond the false universalisms of the modern European era.

As historical endeavors these narratives represent not an abandonment of the past, but allegiances to pasts that are different from that of the universalizing order of the dominant North Atlantic society. Critical historians of Europe's others seek for new, alternative modes of intelligibility which might well appear marginal, peripheral, or even unintelligible to those whose horizon is limited to that of the dominant European experience. Even in historiographical circles that one might assume belong within the horizon of the dominant culture, resources for appreciating pluralism and the diversity of histories are growing.[45]

The historiographical turn from universal history to multiple histories raises questions for the Christian religious past as well, not only because of the manner in which Christian doctrine has often depicted the universal historical horizon of salvation, but also insofar as it has been traditionally identified as the dominant religion of European civilization. Christian churches identified with significant sectors of the dominant classes who precipitated much of the global historical crises of the last 400 years. Relatively few explicitly Christian voices were raised in the North Atlantic world against the global political expansion, capitalist domination, and colonial oppression of the period.

In many European countries, state or established churches in fact provided religious ideological legitimation for the national regimes. Protestant churches in particular were closely aligned with the newer bourgeois class which emerged in the eighteenth century and has maintained its political and economic hegemony through the nineteenth and twentieth centuries. Churches prayed for the success of imperialistic ventures beyond national borders. In worship they displayed prominently the symbols of national political life. They admitted into the ranks of their communion prominent owners of factories, or merchants who benefited from exploitive trade practices. In the United States many tolerated, and some even went so far as to endorse, the social systems of chattel slavery and racial oppression. In light of its dominant history, rendering accounts of the Christian past is, in a postmodern context, intrinsically bound to endeavors for making a difference in the Christian future.

The Re-Creative Work of Traditioning

By the same token we should also note that the Christian movement even in the modern era cannot be totally reduced to its dominant European forms. Not all Christian churches and communities in the world embody traditions that can be said to derive from Europe, or that are the historical product of modern European expansion. The ancient Christian churches of Asia and Africa in particular can claim traditions of faith that do not belong to European cultural history. Few, if any, of these ancient churches were significantly identified with the oppressions associated with European colonial rule in the modern era. They were instead quite often themselves the target of missionary polemics by churches of the North Atlantic world. The rise of indigenous Christian churches in the modern era represents another form of expression of non-Western Christian identities whose histories are other than Europe's. Many indigenous and Pentecostal churches in the so-called Third World (better called the "Two-Thirds World," or more recently, "the South") have multiple cultural and historical roots which go deep into local, indigenous histories. Some even in churches whose histories involve European colonial missionary origins have taken up the task of pursuing alternative identities, calling for a radical break with the European Christian past in the process.[46]

Within the domains of the North Atlantic world significant Christian communities of dissent continue as well to embody traditions of resistance against the social and cultural hegemony of the dominant classes of the West. Since the period of the European Enlightenment, counter-cultural movements for revival and awakening have sought (with varying degrees of success) to challenge Christian cultural accommodation to the dominant European bourgeois identity. A number of communities that were formed within the historical streams of revivalism and pietism have continued to nurture a vital prophetic faith. In recent decades we have witnessed an increasing number of dissatisfied persons among even the culturally dominant churches of the North Atlantic world who are finding themselves in a post-Christendom context for which the history of Western imperial Christianity offers few resources.[47] Many in churches that formed as Christian communities of resistance or dissent in the margins of the dominant Western societies have taken up with renewed enthusiasm the task of discovering histories of their own, confronting the silences of dominant historiography of the modern era with new voices from the margins. They join others from churches and Christian communities outside the synthesis of European Christendom in their critical *recursus* through pasts that are different.

The question that these various historical experiences, both within and beyond the circle of European Christendom, raise for us concerns the viability of Christian tradition and identity in the contexts of the modern and postmodern worlds. In the same essay in which he defined history as a practice rendering account of the past, Huizinga made the observation that it is not the past itself which is given, but something called tradition.[48] Tradition is not so much an object as it is a semiotic process by which enduring social, cultural, and theological identity are mediated and appropriated across generations of time.[49] What are handed over and received in this process (the word is derived directly from the Latin term, *traditio*, which means the act of handing over) are narrated complexes of beliefs, values, commitments, and rituals that enable ways of thinking, doing, and being in the world. A tradition is, Tillich pointed out, "a set of memories which are delivered from one generation to the other." They are, however, not any casual collection of memories, but "the recollection of those events which have gained significance for the bearers and receivers of the tradition."[50] Tradition is the structuring complex that mediates social and cultural forms across human generations of time. It is the means (to borrow the words of T. S. Eliot in his oft-quoted essay on "Tradition and Individual Talent") by which "the dead poets [and] . . . ancestors assert their immortality most vigorously."[51]

A tradition then constitutes the effective presence of the past. It is not merely the repetition of the past, for mere repetition often indicates a loss of vitality and a failure of transmission.[52] It is not necessarily alive when its form and content are reproduced in new situations. A living tradition is neither immutable nor unchanging. Quite the contrary, it contains the seeds of change and even fosters the emergence of what is new. A tradition encompasses continuities, as well as discontinuities. It encompasses endings as well as beginnings, and declines as well as arisings, semiotically representing the deaths and resurrections of collective historical identity. To these ends a tradition that would sustain a people's sense of history and identity through time must incorporate within itself practices (semiotic, hermeneutic, or otherwise) that enable the community to transcend its own boundaries of time and space, that enable the past to become an effective history within a particular horizon of the present.[53]

The intentionality and decision which are manifested in the practice of tradition are as much the work of the living as they are the works of those now dead. Again, in the words of T. S. Eliot speaking of tradition, "It cannot be inherited, and if you want it you must obtain it by great labour."[54]

In this sense, tradition is an ongoing, constructive activity (traditioning) found wherever people in community remember a past and claim it as their own. It is a practice that makes present the historical past as memory and identity. Where there is a living sense of the historical past or a historical consciousness, there is an effective tradition and a moment of traditioning.[55]

In a fundamental way, the ruptures of history in the modern era have brought about a crisis in the meaning and practice of tradition insofar as they have made inaccessible "a suitable historic past."[56] Most Christians of the world have until recently assumed that both tradition and identity were given in an unambiguous manner. For the most part, they assumed the continuity of living generations with those who had gone before in their particular church community. Those who had gone before, be they ancestors, saints, or apostles, were considered to constitute a suitable and accessible past. Few Christian thinkers explored in any significant depth the importance of multiple historical experiences and contexts within the Christian movement. On the contrary, until recently the diversity among Christian churches and communities of the world has generally been seen by those in authority as a problem to be addressed and not a resource to be explored.

As we have already noted, however, the disruptions of the modern era have called into question simplistic assumptions of historical continuity with the postmodern world, including the continuity of tradition for it too can no longer be assumed to be unambiguously given. Modern capitalism has succeeded in dissolving bonds that had tied people together in community for millennia. Science has eroded the religious and cultural authority of the past as well, while the forces of technological change operative through urbanization and industrialization in a short period of time have transformed patterns of life that had endured for centuries. The resulting ruptures have affected the continuity of Christian tradition even within the churches themselves. Many of these same churches were identified with forces that precipitated these historical changes, leading to the anomalous situation of Christians defending and participating in movements which were contributing to the erosion of their own basis of authority.

During the period of the European Enlightenment in the seventeenth and eighteenth centuries, tradition in Western societies came to be associated with ignorance, subjected to the intense criticisms of scientific thinking and rationality, and identified with the *ancien regime*. In the North Atlantic world, "Tradition acquired the bad name which had become attached to dogma."[57] In many cases, these negative attitudes toward tradition and the past were carried by European colonial regimes with them, or were communicated in the processes

30 HISTORY AND TRADITION: FROM CRISIS TO RE-CREATION

of modernization and development that took hold outside European civilization. Ironically however, it was the same intellectual movement of the Enlightenment that gave rise to the modern practices of critical historical thinking and writing. As Reinhart Koselleck has pointed out, the rise of the practice of modern historical criticism in Europe was itself a result of the rupture with the past brought about by the Enlightenment and especially the French Revolution, resulting in a loss of the past as tradition.[58] The rise of historical critical thought can be seen to signal the loss of history's authority for the present (authoritative tradition) and a crisis in the modern age's ability to locate itself historically (effective traditioning), a crisis which has spread far beyond the confines of the North Atlantic world in which it was born.

We can see something of the ambiguity surrounding the meaning of tradition in its usage in contemporary Christian theological discourse. For some, the words tradition and traditional describe conservative theological or ecclesiastical projects that are attempting to retrieve tired truths of the past and shore up crumbling ecclesial orders. For others, tradition embodies unchanging truths which communicate living faith. For still others, traditional represents an anti-European turn toward renewing the precolonial values of the past. Untraditional means new, innovative, or even progressive for some, and heretical if not oppressive for others. Sometimes the language of tradition appears in theological discourse to identify beliefs and practices that are premodern, and at other times those that are non-Western and even postmodern. For many, tradition represents beliefs and practices that were criticized by modern thinking, yet for others, it carries within it a powerful and effective critique of the dominance of modernity itself.

An example of a positive assessment of tradition is found in the work of the contemporary Roman Catholic theologian Yves Congar. According to Congar, tradition is the deposit of truth, or the living transmission of truth by which the saving mystery of faith is communicated.[59] Orthodox theologian Vladimir Lossky goes even further, suggesting that tradition (or rather, Tradition) entails not only the process of the transmission of the truth of the Gospel, but is the mode of receiving it.[60] Both Congar and Lossky distinguish between the many traditions and the one Tradition, and argue for the superiority of the latter. Both theologians consider the former to be ecclesiastical or dogmatic historical forms (Lossky calls them "horizontal") but the latter to be heavenly, divine, authentic, and Holy.[61] Both theologians consider Holy Tradition to be a mystery that remains unspoiled by its historical forms and thus untrammeled by the criticisms of modern historical thought. For both, Holy Tradition itself is insulated from the discontinuity and change effected by modernity.

Protestant theologians have likewise sought to distinguish the divine deposit from its historical form or transmission. They have usually done so by identifying the former with the Word of God (conceived as being either the person of Jesus Christ or the written texts of Scripture), and the latter with the tradition handed on within a particular ecclesial community. For example, in a work that was written in response to Congar, R. P. C. Hanson identifies what he considers to be five distinctive meanings of tradition. Four of these have to do with authoritative ecclesial doctrines (what the church has taught from its beginning, or the whole teaching of the church that has been handed down from its beginning). The first meaning, however, that of the extra-biblical survival in the church of trustworthy historical information about Jesus Christ, Hanson challenges.[62] Hanson's analysis recalls a Protestant distinction between Scripture and tradition on this point, which he employs to separate historical information about Jesus Christ from church doctrines that are handed on.

A somewhat similar analysis is provided by Letty M. Russell in her recent consideration of a feminist understanding of Christian tradition. Drawing on ecumenical theological discussions, Russell distinguishes between process and content, or traditioning as a verb and tradition as a noun. She identifies two forms of the process or traditioning: " 'the Tradition' as the action of God's Mission in sending or handing over Jesus Christ to the world," and "the process of handing over that is part of the human way of shaping history"; and two forms of the content: "the 'deposit of faith' in the witness of scripture and church doctrine," and "confessional patterns of church life."[63] From a feminist theological perspective it is the practice of traditioning as a human historical process that she finds to be most important because of the need to create a new future. Feminist traditioning entails "talking back": "we often talk back to biblical and church tradition by appealing to the action of God in traditioning Jesus Christ into our lives," she writes.[64] But here we note the distinction between divine and human activities that cuts through the categories of process and content. Divine forms of the Tradition (as process or Mission) and the deposit of faith (content) are distinguished from human forms of the process of traditioning and the confessional patterns that form their content. In Russell's theological perspective, the divine criticizes and calls into question the human, enabling new forms of tradition to emerge from history. These new forms continue to mediate the divine Mission and deposit of faith in new situations. Throughout her text she criticizes older forms that she repeatedly calls traditional, without explaining how they could once have served to mediate the divine but fail to do so any longer. In the end, she too joins the critics of the traditions of the Christian churches who find in them more evidence of human failure than of divine grace.

In their own ways, both Hanson and Russell draw on the older Protestant critique of tradition that emerged from the sixteenth-century European context. The Reformation launched its polemic against the traditions of the late medieval Roman Catholic Church precisely by declaring them to be historical creations of the church, and thus without divine authorization. From the critical vantage point of the doctrine of *sola scriptura*, the Reformers rejected the authority of such historical traditions. Integral to their challenge to the Roman

Church was their belief that Roman ecclesiastical tradition was a fallible, historical creation without enduring significance. Yet the Protestant Reformation did not abandon the concept of tradition entirely.[65] Instead it located it within the written pages of the Christian Scriptures themselves (along the lines we saw above in Hanson's analysis), thereby drawing more definitive historical boundaries around tradition and linking its authority directly to that of the prophets, the apostles, and Jesus himself. The Reformers sought to purify tradition of what they perceived to be historical corruptions (a concern evident in Russell's work as well). To this end, they found in the doctrine of *sola scriptura* the principle that would enable them "to recognize and excavate . . . the renewing and saving Gospel from the mass of accretions, distortions, and actual contradictions that had been piled upon it through centuries of expansion and of stagnation."[66] Perhaps there is more than a touch of irony then in Jaroslav Pelikan's observation that in the years since the sixteenth century the Reformation itself has become a significant historical tradition.[67]

If the Protestant Reformation brought about a critique of tradition in the church under the banner of *sola scriptura*, the ascendancy of historical criticism in the nineteenth century brought about a critique of Scripture by demonstrating the manner in which it is infused with historical traditions. Conservative Protestant theologians such as B. B. Warfield of Princeton Theological Seminary sought to refute both the methods and conclusions of historical criticism, believing its corrosive effects to pose grave dangers to the source of authority for evangelical Protestant faith.[68] But by the beginning of the twentieth century, historical criticism had successfully broached the sacred walls of biblical authority, submitting the pages of Scripture to critical interrogations such as those which had earlier been turned against tradition. Historical criticism broke down the wall that divided Scripture from early Christian tradition.[69] In the end it left Protestant theology with the problem of how to rescue a divine Word of Scripture from the historical vagaries of the words of its scriptures. It is essentially the problem of how to retrieve a meaningful tradition from amidst the vagaries of modern history.[70]

Yet the imperative to retrieve them is a compelling one. Without them we fall victim to a collective historical amnesia that collapses all experience into the immediacy of the present. Without them we lose our sense of perspective and orientation. Most important from a theological point of view, we lose the benefit of experiences from the past that can reveal to us once again modes in which the divine is present in the midst of human history, amidst the multiplicity of human histories. If through tradition we find the bonds that join us together in community, and to that which is divine or holy, then crawling back through them is an act of love and devotion. We crawl back in order to crawl forward into a future that is once again meaningfully joined to a past. At the end of his massive study on the problem of historicism, Ernst Troeltsch concluded that the answer to the crises of modern history and historical consciousness lies only through history.[71] In a similar manner Letty Russell might argue that the solution to the problem of Christian tradition lies only through re-creating Christian tradition. From a vantage point at the end of modernity this can only mean an opening up to the multiplicity of Christian traditions and memories that await us in a postmodern world.

3 | The Accountability of Handing Over

To articulate the past historically does not mean to recognize it "the way it really was" (Ranke). It means to seize hold of a memory as it flashes up at a moment of danger . . . In every era the attempt must be made anew to wrest tradition away from a conformism that is about to overpower it. The Messiah comes not only as the redeemer, he comes as the subduer of Antichrist.
—Walter Benjamin[1]

> they ask me to remember
> but they want me to remember
> their memories
> and i keep on remembering mine
> —Lucille Clifton[2]

A Double Accountability

No community, no group, no society exists without a past. We did not plant ourselves here, nor are we free from the constraints and conditions imposed on us by past generations of human communities. All of us live with an inheritance which is passed on to us in the languages, cultures, artifacts, structures, and identities that precede us. Out of these we ourselves are constructed, prior to our reconstructing them. Reconstruct them we eventually do, of course. All of us who participate in the reception of an inheritance at some point come to make it our own, however blind we might be to the degree of ownership and intentionality involved. Quite often the acts of reception pass unnoticed by us while we are actively engaged in them, because they are too subtle, or because they appear to take place without significant disruption. Quite often it is as difficult to identify a break between the present and the past, or a break between an inheritance and its reception, as it is to identify a break between an event and its memory, or between an event and the signs and symbols that represent it.

The presence of a past that is simultaneously embedded in, and grasped by, those living in the present I have identified as tradition. Through signs and symbols, traditions represent mimetically the presence of a past that is not over. They effectively structure the present through the configuration of enduring practices they hand on. Through them enduring collective identities are seized and mediated across time. But here we encounter a passage of sorts from the material world of the past to its representations through traditions. It is not so much the past as such that is the object of traditioning as it is the social memory that claims to represent the past. This explains why we can find instances where specific claims concerning the past represented by a tradition have been called into question by critical historical investigation, without the meaning for the tradition being diminished. Traditions do not so much seek to render an account of the past that is bound to its evidence and traces as they seek to render a meaningful account of the relationship of the past to the present.

At the same time, traditions remain bound to the conditions of the past they seek to render an account of, for they are its product and share the very inheritance they are mediating. It might be considered a truism, but it is one worth pointing out, that the material world of the past has left us not only its symbolic representations but its material traces, and the former are always somewhat bound to the latter. Historians may argue over which of these takes priority for our contemporary interpretations of the past, but one can hardly dispute that there is some relationship between the two. Perhaps we need to be reminded from time to time that it was real people, women and men of flesh and blood, who inhabited the material world of the past. Their intentions, and their resulting representations, cannot be entirely dismissed, even as they become overwritten and sublimated within the historical process.

I consider it important to make this point at length in order for us to see the twin directions of intentionality in human history. In their work in meaning-construction, traditions embody this double intentionality, of past generations bequeathing a heritage to the future, and present generations claiming an identity from the past. When they are effective, traditions create dialogues across generations separated by distances of time. Present interpreters of texts and traditions bring to them new questions that are shaped by new insights, and draw from them new responses which are not necessarily ones the original authors had foreseen. At the same time, the texts of the past pose questions to those of the present who engage them, or pose options for living which we might not ourselves have foreseen. Authoritative traditions can even be binding on one's conscience, as is often the case for religious communities of faith. The direction of one's life in the present is partially constrained through this engagement, but the meaning of the past itself, embedded as it is in its texts and traditions, is likewise transformed. The resulting dialogical relationship between interpreters of the present and works of the past is one which is re-creative of both.[3]

The dialogical practice of traditioning in the Christian churches today does not proceed without difficulty, however, for those who are in the churches are not of one mind on the matter. For some, tradition is the life-blood of their religion, the means by which the community of faith is connected to the source of truth, whether it be a divine Revelation given in the past or the presence of the Spirit of God that continues to accompany the community in its present. For these, tradition is a treasure that is borne in earthen ecclesial vessels.

On the other hand, there are some for whom tradition is considered a dead weight that does little more than prevent the churches from taking on a vital and effective ministry. For them, it is tradition that prevents the church from instituting changes and a more creative response to the world around it. It is tradition that keeps the church from embracing new, more relevant expressions of worship and faith. For these others, the matter can be summarized in what have humorously been called the seven last words of the church: "we have always done things this way."

It is not uncommon to find these two opposite attitudes side by side in a single church or denomination, creating tensions in matters of doctrine, ministry, and practice. Often members of a congregation do not even recognize that their differences have anything to do with the meaning and role of tradition. This is because they are usually not consciously reflecting on the process by which complexes of beliefs and practices from the past are or are not being symbolically mediated to the present generation. Instead one party speaks of holding on to what is familiar, or of doing things the "right way" (that is to say, the way they have always recalled them being done). They intuitively sense the importance of maintaining continuity with the past, perhaps without even recognizing that what is at stake is the fundamental collective identity of the community of faith across time. Too many changes, or changes affecting the central core of identity, mean that one could not recognize one's church holding a faith that can be called "Christian."

Over against this party, on the other hand, are those who charge that the older ways of belief, worship, or ministry are increasingly irrelevant to the contemporary world. Times have changed, or conditions have changed, and so must the church if it wishes to speak to people today. Those of this other party are just as convinced that what is at stake is the viability of the Christian faith, for without necessary changes people will just stop coming to church and the Gospel message will falter. Quite often those who take this side of the argument are no more aware than their opponents are that what is involved in their conflict is a question of tradition.

Both sides of the argument seem to be struggling implicitly, if not at times explicitly, with the manner or degree to which a community of Christian faith today is, or is not, continuous with communities of faith in the past. On the one side, continuity with the past would seem to guarantee that what is specifically Christian is passed on to future generations of persons in the church, assuring that the central tenets of Christian faith and identity are preserved. Doing things in life and worship the way Christians did them in the past, saying the same things that Christians said in the past, and believing the same things that they believed in the past, are all dimensions of the project of perpetuating the faith. Connectedness with the past for them is a matter of continuity, which is why they refuse to "jump over" a recent past to get to a more distant past. They refuse to reject the faith perspective of the fuller tradition to retain only a narrower expression of it, such as the "pure Christianity" of the biblical period, the early church, or the Protestant Reformation. The fullness of tradition is understood to envelope the contemporary community of faith in a continuing history extending from the past into the present and future.

Yet one need not look hard to realize that expressions of Christian faith in the world today can by no means be so easily made to comport with the past as some traditionalists would have us believe. There is much in the thought and practice of the Christian past that is alien even to the most conservative Christians of today. How much of Calvin's life in Geneva should we emulate today? Are the spiritual practices of the community of Isaac of Ninevah as compelling as they once were for those who seek a higher spiritual life? Much that is a part of what many call Christian tradition can be considered as little more than a repository for theological fossils, even by the most adamant defenders of the unchanging thesis of tradition. The study of such fossils might shed considerable light on forms of belief and practice found in the churches of the past, but one could hardly argue that such forms from the past have remained unchangeably the same. As a historical reality, the Christian religion has changed over time, responding to conditions and situations of the social and cultural worlds in which it lives. From this perspective, it would appear to be the more faithful practice to liberate a religion from its bondage to the past.

Nevertheless even from such an emancipatory perspective, it is impossible not to see in the changing forms of Christian faith some continuous thread (or threads), which warrants consideration of the whole of the past. The imperatives that compel tradition to change seem to originate out of the present, challenging the past. To the degree that Christians would speak meaningfully to their surrounding world they must do so in symbols, languages, and categories that are appropriate to their contemporary world. To the degree that Christians would act in these situations in ways appropriate to their context, their activities must be judged adequate by the categories of the context. And to the degree that the structures and categories of these contexts do not conform to those of a meaningful Christian historical past, the tradition can be expected to change. At some point, no doubt someone will charge that such change has resulted in the abandonment of what is essential to the Christian tradition. To that person the matter of contextual change will appear to involve the loss of identity. But others will argue that the risk of such loss must be suffered if Christian faith and practice are to be relevant to the contemporary world.

At this point we can hear echoes of the *identity-involvement dilemma* that Jürgen Moltmann analyzed in the opening pages of *The Crucified God*. Moltmann was referring to the dilemma which, according to his analysis, had resulted from the contradiction between two fundamental imperatives that confront Christian theology and the Christian churches in the modern era. The contradiction had led to a twin crisis facing the churches which he summarized succinctly:

> The more theology and the church attempt to become relevant to the problems of the present day, the more deeply they are drawn into the crisis of their own Christian identity. The more they attempt to assert their identity in traditional dogmas, rights, and moral notions, the more irrelevant and unbelievable they become.[4]

The result of this twin crisis, Moltmann believed, was the secularism and unbelief of modern societies on the one hand, and increasing isolationism and sectarianism among the churches on the other. Those seeking theological relevance at the cost of identity were led to the former, while those seeking to preserve identity at the cost of relevance led to the latter. The analysis pointed toward the need to address both the imperative of relevance and that of identity for contemporary churches, for the failure to respond to either eventually led to the loss of both.

I find problems with the manner in which Moltmann formulated the twin crisis so sharply. For one thing, he seems to me to have postulated too clear a distinction between the European Christian past and the non-Christian, modern, secular European world of today.[5] For another, Moltmann's analysis tends to make the Christian past appear more monolithic than it was, and more coherent as a source for identity. Nevertheless his twin imperatives for contemporary theology can be usefully formulated as twin accountabilities for tradition. Those who would assert that a church must become more relevant in its teaching, programs, and worship are making (even if implicitly so) the claim that at least some of the doctrines and practices inherited from the past are in some sense irrelevant to the needs and conditions of the present. By calling for change, they are calling for a mode of accountability to at least some portion of the world of the present. Yet those who would completely abandon the inheritance of the past would be hard pressed to account for what is particularly Christian about their faith, for it is only the inheritance of the past mediated by tradition that provides what is specifically Christian for the identity of a church (including the foundational texts of the Scriptures). To the degree that they assert relevance over identity, they open the door to the loss of the historical content of belief and practice that form the Christian faith. On the other hand, those who would assert the primacy of past at the cost of making any concession to contemporary idioms of thought or practice find themselves increasingly unable to pass on this identity to future generations. Seeking to preserve the life of the tradition, they often end up losing it.

In rendering accounts through tradition, a Christian community is then multiply accountable to the present and the past. Accountability to the present has an ethical concreteness which is constituted in its social dimensions. In recent Christian ethics this has been primarily formulated as accountability to marginalized communities of the oppressed.[6] But such a critical primary obligation reinforces a more general insistence that tradition be held ethically accountable to concrete community or social life. On the other hand, the accountability of tradition to the past is equally concrete. Insofar as they can be said to represent unique historical experiences, or to constitute the consequences of unique events, the representations and concepts of a tradition presuppose the answerability of historical acts.[7] Traditions are answerable to the unique acts or deeds which constitute the past in both ethical (insofar as the imperatives are grounded in the concreteness of existence) and aesthetic (insofar as they seek to represent the whole of an act or event) dimensions. As the residue of meaning content, tradition (as representation or memory) holds together what would otherwise be unitary or unique deeds amidst the arenas of historical existence, and configures them in a meaningful pattern of life.

Tradition or Treason

The issues of continuity versus change, or identity versus relevance, raised in light of the ethical demands of accountability and the historical demands of answerability, lead us to consider what in Christian history has been one of the most difficult questions churches have faced over the centuries regarding their various traditions—that of orthodoxy vs. heresy. Although the language of heresy and apostasy continues to be utilized to undercut the legitimacy of particular beliefs or commitments, its application is far narrower than was characteristic for previous generations of Christians.[8] Christian communities of faith have generally become more tolerant of the pluralisms that characterize the modern world. Few today would regard the diversity of expressions of Christian faith in the world as evidence of heresy.

Nevertheless Christian communities continue to confront questions regarding the truthfulness or adequacy of their depictions of God and the world. On committees and boards; in house church gatherings and formal worship services; through the reflective work of individual church leaders and professional theologians, they struggle with fundamental questions of theological formulation. Often we can hear in these efforts criticisms of the inheritance of the past. But we are just as likely to hear questions regarding whether or not belief and practice conform to the biblical and historical contours of the faith. In line with numerous movements for reform and renewal in the past they can couch their efforts in the language of a return *ad fontes* (back to origins), regarded as being the source and authority for faith. They continue to face the question of whether their belief and practice represent faithfulness to the tradition, or mark its betrayal. This latter question we find reflected in the pages of the source itself, that is, in the Bible.

In the pages of the New Testament we find the word tradition (*paradosis* in Greek) used to refer to two different modes of historical inheritance. On the one hand, there is in its pages a generally negative reference to what is called "the tradition of the elders" (*paradosis ton presbuteron*, Mark 7:3, 5 and Matt. 15:2; see also Gal. 1:14) or "human tradition" (*paradosis ton anthropon*, Mark 7:8; see also Col. 2:8). In both cases the Gospel writers and Paul appear to be referring to a body of interpretation of Torah, quite possibly the oral traditions of the Pharisees which are known to us today through Rabbinic tradition.[9] The Gospel writers polemically contrasted this body of tradition with the authentic commandments of God found in the Torah.[10] Tradition, on the other hand, also refers in the pages of the Second Testament to the life-giving words of and about Jesus Christ that were passed on by the Apostles. So in I Corinthians 11:2 Paul praises his readers for holding fast to the traditions (*paradoseis*) just as he passed them on. The content of what he passed on we find in various forms in his letters, articulated most concisely as the "Gospel" in I Corinthians 15:3-8. A similar positive reference to tradition(s) occurs in 2 Thessalonians 2:6 and 3:15, although the possibility that this letter is not from Paul's hand, yet appears in the New Testament under his name (as a number of biblical scholars now argue), raises in an even more complex manner the ambiguity involved in affirming the authenticity of any particular rendering of tradition.

The ambiguity of contending voices for tradition in the Bible can be found in the very meaning of the word itself. Tradition is used in English to translate the Greek noun *paradosis*, which names the content of something handed over. In its verbal form, *paradidomi*, the term literally means "handing over." The Greek verb names the act of betraying, of handing one over to one's enemies.[11] So in Matthew's gospel Judas is described as the one who hands over, that is, the betrayer (*[h]o paradidous*, 26:25; cf. Mark 14:21, Luke 22:21, and Acts 3:13).[12] Alongside Judas the Gospels refer to Pilate's action as handing over Jesus to be crucified. Disciples of Jesus are warned that they too should expect to be handed over. In the same sense, Paul in I Corinthians 5:5 instructs the readers of his letter to hand over to Satan one of the wayward members of their community, suggesting that even the early Christian community was not above the treachery of betrayal, albeit in this case of one who has soiled the fellowship with his sinful actions.

But this is not the only meaning of the word in the Christian scriptures. In its positive sense the same verb (or its cognates) names the process of passing on authentic memory of Jesus Christ, and hence of Christian identity, from one group of persons or one generation to another. In this case, the act of handing over or delivering refers to the process of maintaining and communicating the memory and authenticity of identity from the past to the present and even future generations. We see in Acts 6:14, for instance, a reference to Hellenistic Jews defending the customs of Moses handed over to them, which is similar to a reference in II Peter 2:21 to sacred commandments identified with Jesus Christ that are handed over in the apostolic message.

The ambiguity and danger of the moment of handing over/traditioning are found in I Corinthians 11:23 where the same root word is used in both senses in reference to the common practice of the eucharist: "For I received from the Lord what I also delivered (*paredoka*) to you, that the Lord Jesus on the night when he was betrayed (*paredideto*) took bread . . ." The primary night of traditioning in the apostolic faith is a night of betrayal and death. Handing over, traditioning, is not only an act of passing on the authentic memory and identity of the past in a new historical situation; it can also be an act of betrayal and treason.[13]

The act of traditioning is in fact always closely related to the act of treason, for there must be a moment of both in each instance of historical change. In every act of authentic traditioning there remains something of an act of treason, otherwise it would not be an authentic act of handing over, of change. Without a bit of treason performed in the act of handing over, the tradition remains inseparably bound to the world in which it was formed, hence not only irrelevant but incomprehensible. Acts of treason and betrayal, on the other hand, are not unambiguous signs of the rejection of a tradition, but moments of contending for its authenticity. Acts of treason presuppose a traitor's decision to contend for the authenticity, meaning, or purpose of the tradition, either to reform it and restore it, or to displace it with another which the traitor at least perceives to be better. Conversion and betrayal are always matters of perspective.

At stake in every act of handing over are not only the memory and identity of the community, but the relevant values and commitments these give rise to. We are always reinventing our traditions in order to make them relevant, for the changes that occur through the passage of time refuse us the opportunity to lay claim to the timeless relevance of an unchanging memory. We are always excluding some aspects of our collective memories, recalling others, and reinventing tradition as we contend with new questions that emerge to confront us in faith. At the same time nothing less is at stake in this process than the meaning and identity of faith itself, for a truly irrelevant faith will soon die of its own irrelevance, and the identity of the community will pass into the arena of being a historical relic or part of the archive. There always remains an element of uncertainty in our acts of handing over, uncertainty in ourselves or in others as to whether these are acts of traditioning or acts of treason. To hand them over requires a significant measure of risk, in the words of M. M. Thomas, at times even "risking Christ for Christ's sake."[14] At the same time, however, not to hand them over, or to seek to hand them over risk-free, amounts to killing them, their ultimate betrayal or handing over.

Walter Benjamin wrote in 1940 in his "Theses on the Philosophy of History," "In every era the attempt must be made anew to wrest tradition away from a conformism that is about to overpower it."[15] This conformism, which is also an illusion of a timeless and unchanging identity, results in tradition no longer belonging to us but being alien to us, set over against us, mediating a past which is not our own. It is a situation in which the tradition has become heteronomous (the situation according to Tillich when we confront a law that is other than us, outside us, opposed to us, and oppressive[16]), not an instance of traditioning but of the failure of traditioning. At these times we find ourselves more distanced, more alienated from the past. Then we face more critically the task of reinventing tradition, which is the struggle not only to redeem the present but to redeem the past itself.[17] These are moments when even the dead are not safe, says Benjamin.[18] They are the moments when we hear ourselves or others saying that the traditional language no longer speaks to us, that the tradition appears to be empty of meaning or vitality for us. In these situations the past becomes other for us, heteronomous in a manner that closes off our relationship to it, and the dead become just that—merely the dead, no longer our saints or ancestors or companions. Traditions become artifacts relegated to museums where their vitality is lost even if their remains continue to be studied. The practice of traditioning is itself in danger of being little more than pastiche.

At other times the act of traditioning is successful, however, and Tillich's moment of heteronomy gives way to one of theonomy. In these moments tradition becomes a divine imperative as a life-giving commandment, the law of God which characterizes theonomy. In Moltmann's terms, we can say that identity and relevance coincide in an experience that is revelatory. An effective tradition is revelatory insofar as it is transparent to a divine or transcending imperative. It enables those who are addressed to respond to their world in a meaningful and thus relevant way. At the same time, it provides the ground for identity, becoming the context for belief and action. Receiving and holding the imperatives of tradition, we experience a mode of transcendence which is not a flight from this world but the return to it. Bonds of community across time and space are forged, not only among those of the living present but with those of the past. The experience of commonality across human time opens to an experience of transcendence in which not only relevance and identity are secured, but for Christians at least something of divine presence is mediated through history in tradition.

The degree to which such a tradition is experienced by members of a community as alienating or authentic becomes then a critical factor in evaluating the relative experience of heteronomy or theonomy. Quite often we find a particular articulation of tradition both alien and authentic at the same time. We find the community saying "yes" and "no" as it continuously confronts the process of handing over. This is particularly true in contemporary situations where multiple and competing voices can be heard laying claim to a common historical past and identity. Here in particular we are hearing the sharp polemics of tradition and treason. Feminist, womanist, gay/lesbian, black, and Latin American liberation theologians are all accused of treason in some quarters while welcomed as re-creating the tradition in others. Conservative evangelical Protestants and liberal Roman Catholics alike find themselves engaged in defending their perspectives on tradition while making counter charges regarding the treason of others. Some would seek through strictly historical, logical, or philosophical means to determine which (if any) among competing voices could lay claim to being the more adequate bearers of authentic Christian tradition. But the grounds on which such a search could be conducted are themselves determined by what one holds to be essential to the tradition.

Ernst Troeltsch pointed out almost a century ago that it is from the historical arena of practice and change that the norms of identity and valuation for religious community, or traditions, emerge.[19] In recent years, recognition that the authenticity of a particular moment of traditioning is a historical judgment has led to an increased appreciation for the theological significance of historical praxis.[20] Praxis has become for a number of contemporary theologians "fundamental theology," the doorway through which one enters theological reflection.[21] At the same time a wide range of theological concepts and doctrines generally addressed by systematic or dogmatic theologies have been reconceptualized in light of their social and cultural contexts. One recalls again Juan Luis Segundo's contention that social and historical commitments operate as preconditions within an active hermeneutical practice.[22] For Segundo, as for most liberation and contextual theologians, the study and production of theological discourses are directed toward participation in and transformation of the social practices of ecclesial communities, which is also to say the retraditioning of ecclesial communities. They seek to change the world through changing the historical conditions of oppression that distort social life.

Solidarity with the Dead

The praxis of liberation theology centers around solidarity with the oppressed. In many cases this includes the oppressed who have died, the victims of historical injustices and terror. Solidarity with oppressed generations of the historical past is an extension of liberation theology's commitment to various communities of the oppressed in the present. What Helmut Peukert, quoting Christian Lenhardt, calls "anamnestic solidarity" is required of a liberating theology of history.[23] The argument is compelling: the generation that finally achieves liberation, that realizes justice and lives in perfect solidarity, will owe much to those who have come before them in the struggle for justice, but who were victims within the process of liberation. The memory of unresolved suffering of the past will of necessity keep that generation from the full realization of the happiness of liberation, unless they engage in historical amnesia and forget the past. This forgetting would, of course, neither address the debt nor resolve the suffering.

> How can one retain the memory of the conclusive, irretrievable loss of the victims of the historical process, to whom one owes one's entire happiness, and still be happy, still find one's identity? If for the sake of one's own happiness and one's own identity this memory is banished from consciousness, is this not tantamount to the betrayal of the very solidarity by which alone one is able to discover oneself?[24]

Peukert can only resolve the dilemma in eschatological terms. Anamnestic solidarity leads him to consider the doctrine of the resurrection of the dead, and to assert that the resurrection of Jesus can only have reality within the practiced solidarity experienced as the presence of what Jesus himself referred to as the Kingdom of God.[25] But the eschatological dimension of universal solidarity necessarily entails remembering the past, or "the uncovering of this eschatological now in the past." Drawing on Walter Benjamin's "Thesis on History," Peukert concludes: "Anamnestic solidarity that affirms the other in annihilation anticipates redemption and lights up the vision of the rubble of history, as a presentiment."[26]

Anamnestic solidarity commits one to the memory of those who have suffered. Its universal or eschatological dimension, which opens on the doctrine of resurrection, encompasses the redemption of those who have suffered. Suffering and redemption are connected in the lives of these martyrs and witnesses of faith in a manner that sheds light on historical reality, both past and present. Historical solidarity with those who have suffered constitutes the dimension of witness, or martyrdom, which infuses theological tradition. Anamnestic solidarity joins historical accountability and historical illumination together in one act.

Christian contextual and liberation theologians who would practice solidarity with the oppressed are accountable, or answerable, to the historical past. The eschatological dimension expressed in the resurrection of Jesus entails an accountability of solidarity both with those who suffer, and those who witness to redemption through the reality of the resurrection in their midst. Hence the accountability of the present community of faith not only to the downtrodden of history, but to memory preserved in Christian tradition, summarized most conclusively in the messianic memory of Jesus Christ, whom God raised up through the power of the Spirit. Admittedly the redemptive contours of Christian memory have often been obscured in history, most notably perhaps in the histories of Western imperial Christendom. Nevertheless those persons of Christian faith who would seek to realize justice in the future remain accountable to the memory preserved in revelation, and even in dogmatic traditions, of the past.[27]

Admittedly the temptation to abandon a Christian historical identity can be attractive, given the burdensome nature of the dominant North Atlantic churches' history of oppression and persecution. The threat is that in order to address the oppressions of the contemporary world theologians would take Jesus at his word, and let the dead bury the dead while attempting to live without tradition. But in such a case the gods of death would be said to win their claims over the past, and Benjamin would prove to be correct, that even the dead are not safe from the enemy.[28] On the other hand, if indeed we in the contemporary world are, as Benjamin said, at a moment of danger, then we are, as Judith Plaskow and others have sought to do, to live dangerously. We must choose to take responsibility for re-creating our traditions, while being held accountable to the pain and suffering of our world and its historical past, in order to live through to the joy on the other side.[29] If we are at a moment of danger in which history, tradition, and the dead themselves are exposed to the gods of commodification or silenced by the gods of oppression, then we must live dangerously, even subverting tradition in order to be accountable to it or to redeem it.

But how do we re-create when the past seems to belong to those who so ruthlessly practiced their oppressions? The answer in part, I have already suggested, is to identify an alternative memory of the past, the memory of suffering and the witnesses of liberation, and assert their redemptive value over against the dominant forces of oppression. But as soon as we do so we confront the problem of identifying which memories and which witnesses even from the alternative past are to be authoritative for us today. We come up against the problem of multiple memories, and alternatives even among the alternatives. How do we live dangerously in a postmodern world of fractured historical horizons and many pasts?

A fresh look at the internal diversity of a tradition, and at the historical complexity of identity, is called for here. To some it appears that the modern critique of the authority of tradition has given way to postmodern fragmentation and the triumph of diversity. Concerns about the fragmentation of identity and the tribalization of historical memory, which appear to some extent to be results of the postmodern, are becoming quite common. I share many of these concerns, even though they sometimes appear to be exaggerated. In the end, however, I think they are largely unwarranted. In many cases these attacks on the postmodern experiences of fragmentation, heterogeneity, and difference tend to presuppose uniformity, homogeneity, and sameness to be more desirable social conditions, and even the norm prior to the postmodern experience. But they are not necessarily more desirable, nor were they ever the social norm, absent the presence of structures of oppression and exclusion which silenced voices of differences and eliminated voices of dissent. Multiplicity is the historical norm; social experience becomes more diverse through time. Historical unity and uniformity are products of social oppression and exclusion, which unfortunately have been dominant forces in the history of Western Christendom as much as anywhere else.[30]

The Rhizomatic Structure of Tradition

I am suggesting that diversity and differences are not so much problems to be overcome as they are resources for making things new. The differences we experience among our traditions, and the diversity we uncover within them, are resources that suggest alternatives from the past itself, available to the present for the construction of a different future. Whether it be at the broader level of social life, or at the more intimate level of one's inner life, the diversity and multiplicity of being refuse the reductionisms of historical uniformity or psychological essentialism. The pluralism of human historical experience, in both its social and its psychological dimensions, is reflected in the constructions of meanings and identities we carry, as individuals and within our historical communities. As Sampson concludes:

> We are fundamentally many, never just one—not many in the sense of many thoroughly organized and coherent personalities; for that is the error of our current way of thinking about human nature. Rather, we are many because we are members of diverse conversational communities, with various perspectives on the world, ourselves and others with which to frame our experiences and render them, us and others meaningful.[31]

Obviously the conversation is not without its tensions and conflicts. Yet the conflicts within a particular tradition and the struggles among the various traditions are often the generating forces that open up new directions for change. Such conflicts are manifested within the historical process itself as paradoxes, contradictions, and aporias. They are moments in history beyond which passage appears impossible, or points in its analysis at which its interpretations cannot be reconciled. Yet even the most superficial glimpse through the historical record shows that people have gone on, living with the contradictions and aporias, and even incorporating them into their identity to be passed on to the next generation. The concrete, historical practice of a community of people sustaining itself over time entails the reproduction of identity and memory amidst changing historical situations, through dialogue and conflict.[32] It is only at the level of mythology that things always remain the same.

The process of historical change means that any particular tradition encompasses differences within itself over time. Often it is assumed that the notion of a tradition implies continuity, or that it has a fundamental *identity with itself* over time. But historical changes introduce differences into a tradition, giving rise to its *non-identity with itself*. Religious traditions in particular are not the static monoliths their defenders often claim them to be, but are heterogeneous and multivocal arenas of contention and change. Composed of multiple voices that are different, and often in considerable disagreement with one another, they are pluralized internally.

As concrete (from the Latin *concrescere*, "to grow together") realities, they are collective endeavors that carry along multiple voices and a plurality of origins, and are open to multiple options as their end.[33] Traditions are very much like what the French philosophers, Deleuze and Guattari, call rhizomes: plants with subterranean, horizontal root systems, growing below and above ground in multiple directions at once.[34] A tradition, many common portrayals to the contrary notwithstanding, is not like a tree, organized with a major trunk and smaller (minor) branches, and drawing primarily from a single, dominant taproot that likewise grows in one direction. A tradition is more like a rhizome, agglomerating and stabilizing at times around common experiences or locations, but then branching off and spreading rapidly at other times, in several directions at once. It is a decentered, or multicentered, system flowing across multiple material and subjective fields. Even those traditions that are most like a tree, organized hierarchically, in the end succumb to rhizomatic pressures. "Transversal communications between different lines scramble the genealogical trees."[35]

In its rhizomatic structure, a tradition incorporates multiple accountabilities, and these too are both subterranean and above the ground. In its subterranean dimension, a tradition embodies multiple historical accountabilities to generations past. Its above ground structures can be considered, on the other hand, in light of its accountabilities to generations present and future. Addressing the multiple accountabilities past, present, and future entails a complex, indeterminate, ongoing dialogue. It's the very essence of a tradition, in fact, to keep alive the question of meaning and the vitality of its past(s), through its refusal to reduce historical accountability to a single voice or end it completely. It is the nature of a religious tradition in particular to keep alive its ongoing engagement with present and future generations, leading it rhizomatically to seek out new areas of cultural life and expression.

Guattari calls a cultural rhizome a "regime of pure multiplicities."[36] Hassan calls it "a culture open to syntagma and parataxis instead of hierarchical or generative models of organization."[37] Both descriptions are suggestive of the possibilities that reside within traditions, which empower people to act precisely because they contain within themselves the options and ambiguities of the past. As rhizomes grow below as well as above ground, in the daylight of the present, so the historical pasts that traditions incarnate grow more diverse genealogically as they become more complex in the present. "A multiplicity has neither subject nor object, only determinations, magnitudes, and dimensions that cannot increase in number without the multiplicity changing in nature . . ."[38] As the dimensions expand, the nature of the multiplicity is changed. There is no fixed place from within or beyond it where the multiplicity as a whole can be grasped or articulated, no single essence of the tradition. A multiplicity cannot be adequately described as a singular reality, a unity, a solitary One. "The notion of unity (*unite*) appears only when there is a power takeover in the multiplicity by the signifier or a corresponding subjectification proceeding."[39]

In Christian theology, this is often expressed as the economy of the Trinity, which describes the works of God in human history through the Christ and the Spirit. There is wisdom in those traditions that have refused to reduce God to a monolithic One, but have instead sought to depict the coincidence of Christ and Spirit, especially in the person of Jesus. "Takeovers" of the description of trinitarian history have been attempted from time to time: Monarchialism, Subordinationism, Modalism, and perhaps even Unitarianism. The inadequacy of these descriptive theological positions lies in their reduction of the multiplicity of God's divine personhood to singular categories of personal power.[40]

More successful in the history of Christian churches have been the imperial takeovers of ecclesial life, resulting in the ideological reduction of Christian faith to a singular, imperial tradition. The history of world Christianity is replete with the stories of orthodox parties attempting to exterminate heresies, of hierarchies suppressing dissent, of various factions seeking to dominate the institutional mechanisms so as to control the faith and practice of the community. It is not uncommon to find the history of world Christianity even at the end of the modern era being told as the story across twenty centuries of a singular, historical Tradition, which alone is adequate for the passage of faith.

Historically, of course, we find it impossible to reduce Church history to the story of one, holy Tradition. Even in the moments of its most profound historical takeovers, Christianity has been embodied in alternative and competing imperial identities. The great divide between the Eastern Orthodox and Roman Catholic hierarchies of the church gave rise to two versions of imperial Tradition which continue to refuse reduction to a common formulation of faith, and yet continue to experience transversal communication. A brief glance through the pages of any textbook on Church history shows how difficult it is to argue historically for the existence of anything like a singular Holy Tradition.

And yet, ironically, it is precisely on account of its rhizomatic structure, that we can indeed speak meaningfully of *a Christian tradition* in singular terms, in the same manner that we can speak meaningfully of One God in Christian theology. The concept of a rhizome suggests that multiple historical experiences, and shifting historical identities, can link up together over time to form an enduring, coherent structure that we can call a tradition. The symbols and practices incorporated within it are different, and they occur in times and places that are different. But a meaningfully structured differential/referential network emerges rhizomatically nevertheless, so much so that we can indeed speak coherently of it as a singular historical tradition. Signs, symbols, and practices link up textually within the network of a tradition, a process that Julia Kristeva calls "intertexuality."[41] Within the textual networks, signs and events are not bound to their own time and location of production, but can be transposed from one time and place to another. Tradition is a mode of intertexuality that links things forward and backward in time, by referring to differing symbols and practices across the differing planes of time and place.

The most effective practice by which traditions relay and relate symbols and events across time is that of narrative.[42] Through the mode of representation of emplotment, narratives provide the intertextual cement that binds into coherent institutions and movements what would otherwise seem to be only random events. Narratives organize a tradition's direction and intensity across times, terrains, and texts, creating a sense of a whole out of often disparate parts. The continuities, changes, ruptures, and transitions of history are rendered meaningful in the narrative process. As Hayden White has observed concerning the relationship between narrative and (in his case, literary) tradition:

> a historical narrative is not only a *reproduction* of the events reported in it, but also a *complex of symbols* which gives us directions for finding an *icon* of the structure of those events in our literary [and I would add theological] tradition.[43]

Narratives organize symbols in order to provide an icon of a tradition; but even the most enduring and stable of traditions do not remain forever unchanged, and so their narratives must ultimately remain open-ended. At each moment traditions open up to multiple possibilities and directions, among which contemporary participants and adherents must choose. The ethical *accountability* and aesthetic *answerability* of tradition at this present point of open-endedness remain the same as those that open the past. Accountability and answerability come to expression through solidarity with experiences of suffering and redemption. Tradition opens us to the present *aporetic* conditions of suffering and redemption, characterized by the ambiguities that inhere in every narrated moment of change. The point where open-endedness becomes a critical praxis (and not merely a potentiality) is the point where we are engaged in transposing anew. And this is the point where we are re-creating tradition.

Perhaps an example of a contemporary theologian re-creating tradition can help shed light on the process that I have been describing. One such theologian is Judith Plaskow. In the pages of her book, *Standing Again at Sinai: Judaism from a Feminist Perspective*, Plaskow explores the internal connections among tradition, memory, and identity as they are reshaped by, and within, a Jewish feminist context. Critical questions emerge from her experiences and commitments as a feminist, as she contends with the patriarchy and oppression that characterize the dominant Jewish tradition. But for Plaskow the task is not merely to analyze the oppressions of the dominant tradition.

> The project of creating a feminist Judaism fits into a larger project of creating a world in which all women, and all people, have both the basic resources they need to survive, and the opportunity to name and shape the structures of meaning that give substance to their lives.[44]

The task is one of critical, transformative engagement, or praxis, in both the material and existential dimensions of community life. She goes on in the next sentence to link this critical praxis explicitly with the project of re-creating tradition: "In the Jewish context, this means *re-forming every aspect of tradition so that it incorporates women's experience.*"[45]

Plaskow seeks to rethink and re-create the various aspects of her Jewish tradition by exploring in a fresh way the fundamental beliefs and commitments of the Jewish faith; successive chapters in the book address Torah, Israel, God, sexuality, and political life. Concerning Judaism's concepts and images of God, she develops a critique of the dominant patriarchal representations of the masculinity of the divine by drawing on social science and political analysis. Yet her reconceptualization of God does not abandon the tradition she criticizes. "In seeking metaphors to use for God, Jewish feminists never start from zero, but draw on the Jewish concepts and symbols that have come down to us."[46] The female images and concepts she begins with in Jewish tradition "must be ferreted out as a tiny minority strand."[47] But it is from Jewish heritage that they are ferreted out. These images and strands are self-consciously appropriated from a contemporary perspective shaped by feminist experience and practice. The result is the emergence of a feminist Jewish tradition, being given liturgical and theological expression, and bringing about new options for the community's collective experience of faith in God.

Accountable Retraditioning

Examples of retraditioning among contemporary Christian theologies can also be found. Some I have already indicated under the rubrics of liberation and contextual theologies. Black, feminist, and Latin American theologies emerged in the 1960s and 1970s to challenge the hegemony of the dominant modern Western theological schools over the latter's complicity in historical practices of oppression (racism, patriarchy, and class conflict). Doing so required an alternative historical identity, which in turn implied a "tradition of one's own." For Black theology, this was the alternative historical memory and tradition of the African-American community in the United States; for feminist theology, the historical experience of women as a social class marginalized

THE ACCOUNTABILITY OF HANDING OVER   51

by gendered oppression and patriarchy; and for Latin American theology, the historical experiences of the poor of the South.[48]

Alternative historical trajectories of faith have emerged from the various contextual theological projects in Africa and Asia as well. Many Latin American, African, and Asian Christian theologians have vigorously rejected the reduction of their histories to the missiological extension of North Atlantic churches.[49] In Asia and Africa, theologians have paid particular attention to the significance of other religious histories and traditions for Christian church identity, calling in some cases for a new baptismal immersion of Christian identity within the histories of non-Christian religiosities.[50] More recently in Latin America, a new appreciation for pre-Columbian, indigenous spiritualities which have survived among the people has emerged.[51] The religious life of the people of Latin America has in many cases blended Catholic and indigenous traditions, despite past official attempts to suppress such popular syncretism. Theologians such as Virgilio Elizondo have now begun not only to explore the spiritual values of these multiple traditions, but have argued in favor of the *mestizo* theological identity that emerges from the borderlands of Latin American cultural existence.[52]

Even within the dominant North Atlantic schools of theological thought and tradition (Protestant and Roman Catholic, liberal and conservative) a new appreciation for the complexities of theological identity can be found. It has become apparent to many that the social and theological world of Europe and North America has been more complex than the older historical narratives of tradition presented it to be. National identities, class conflicts, and differences among the religions of Europe have not been unique to the last century. The history of Europe, and of the *Corpus Christianum* which has so often been depicted as a unified, institutional basis for the cultural religion of Europe up through the nineteenth century, are far more diverse than the mythologies of "European Civilization" tend to depict.

The following two chapters will explore the theology of history and historiographical practices more adequate for multiple, *mestizo* modes of Christian tradition across the world today. By the end of this investigation we should be better equipped to evaluate the underlying tensions that exist between those who opt for historical singularity, and those who embrace the diversity of human histories for the mediation of Christian faith. It should not surprise us to find the tension between the one and the many reappearing at the heart of many of the theologies being articulated today. It is a tension that accompanies a project whose future remains open-ended.

Different communities of Christian faith remember different memories of the past. Every act of remembering, every articulation of identity, expresses a moment of traditioning, in some small degree. Out of these acts of remembering a complex of tradition emerges. This chapter has sought to establish a basis for a more positive assessment of these multiple traditions of Christian faith, and the multiple accountabilities they continue to uphold. It's a noisy conversation going on inside traditions, to say nothing of the conversation among them. We are in the midst of dialogical activity when we are traditioning, a critical dialogue carried on with other voices, of the past and of today.

None of us who is a part of the present moment can predict with certainty the outcome of the project we've embarked on. Which of our contemporary options will the consensus of the future come to hold as orthodox? Whose voices will emerge as the icons of the tradition, and whose voices will be regarded as idolatrous by the future? Any attempt to answer these questions is an attempt to re-form a tradition, to pass on and perhaps even regenerate meaning and identity in community. There is risk involved, the risk of dangerous believing, if the tradition is to be passed on to another generation. We can count on conflict, and on competing voices articulating multiple options for representing most faithfully the meaning of the past. But if members of Christian communities are to overcome the dichotomies of relevance and identity while being accountable to generations past and present, then they must struggle against the inadequacies of inherited articulations without disparaging these inheritances from the past. We need to listen to the array of historical voices within and beyond our own historical past, and learn to speak in a language that both belongs to it and transforms it, in order to create the past anew.

4 | Theology of History

The universality of the Church, its true Catholicity, is never something uniform or abstract. It expresses itself through the multiplicity of peoples and languages, through all the multiplicity of human persons.
—A. M. Allchin[1]

For history functions as a form of self-definition. In its pages we read ourselves. It tells us who we are, because it reveals where we come from and where we've been. History, especially religious history, because it touches on the deepest myths, beliefs, and values of our society, is personally important to us all. To change our view of history changes our view of ourselves.
—Albert J. Raboteau[2]

Tradition as the Theological Meaning of History

By now it should be clear that to talk about tradition is to talk about history. If history is the medium in which we swim, then tradition is the way of swimming. Or, to shift metaphors, if history is a surrounding cloud of witnesses from social worlds now gone, tradition is the effective memory which makes these witnesses present as ancestors and saints. Through the processes of traditioning, communities of the living are held accountable to persons of the past who no longer breathe air upon this earth. The theological claim which is made within a tradition of faith is that this accountability is not just to human persons of the past, but that it is, in some manner, an accountability directed toward God as well. What makes history theologically significant is the claim or belief that God is somehow implicated in its workings, so that a meaningful accounting or recounting of history as tradition reveals something about God.

We ought also engage the discussion of the theological meaning of history and tradition in terms of ancestors and saints. Too often the study of the historical past, or the discussion of history as a discipline, becomes an abstraction which loses sight of the fact that it is real persons whom we are recalling, that our memories reach back to embrace others who were once embodied in human form. It reaches to embrace real flesh and blood persons who once walked the earth, doing so by establishing their past existence and engaging them through the traces that they left.

Whether or not the memories that a tradition maintains correspond to material events of the past, or to real historical persons who once lived, are questions that historians must always be seeking to answer. Tradition can invent memories of persons and events, elaborate on them to the point where they become legends, or attempt to erase them when they fail to conform to its dominant shapes. It can do so without substantially invalidating the accompanying theological claims which are made by the tradition, at least until historical research convincingly demonstrates the historical inaccuracy of the tradition. The meaning of a tradition is found first of all in its theological claims and configurations. Nevertheless, these remain hollow claims, absent the collaborating witness to their historicity provided by critical historical investigation.

The manner in which we often use the term tradition to refer to accounts of the past that *cannot* be historically proven to be true, or that have an obvious ring of legendary accruement to them, reinforces the point that in the final analysis their meaning lies beyond the domain of pure historical research. By calling these memories traditions, we often permit them to remain within the working framework of an identity even though we know them not to be historical fact. They might lack the collaboration of material evidence or independent documentation; they might even have strong historical evidence against them; but such stories are often so deeply woven into the fabric of identity that to remove them would prove to be detrimental, if not impossible. The historicity of the identity itself is such as to require the ongoing acknowledgment of the tradition on which it rests. We might question the claims that St. Peter was the first bishop of Rome or that St. Thomas brought the Christian gospel to India, but we cannot question the historical character of the ecclesial identities of Roman Catholic and Indian churches which incorporate these traditions.

The historicity of these traditions lies not only in the fact that historical identities rest upon them. We call these stories traditions because they are "history-like."[3] They do not offer themselves as pure fictions or fabricated tales, but neither are they usually lacking entirely the collaboration of what could be considered independent historical evidence. They may not be historical in the sense that they can be proven to correspond to actual events of the historical past, but they are historical insofar as they are narratives of the historical past, and that as such they provide a basis for enduring identity. Narratives of the past set free from the documents and traces of their original situation are certain to take on new shape over time, as they are critically reformulated and creatively elaborated upon in new situations. It is likewise the very nature of a narrative to reshape the past in light of its outcomes or developments. Narratives by definition span distances of time and link events together in meaningful wholes called plots. It is not surprising then that the telling of a narrative can continue the process of emplotment, or re-emplotment. The shape of a narrative is not necessarily fixed by its past forms, but is open to being reshaped by the connections it makes between present and past historical identities.

So before we would too quickly dismiss the traditions of ancestors, saints, and apostles as being something other than historical truths, we need to look again at what historical means. The inheritance of the past that we call history, we have already noted, has two senses: history is that which is past, and history is the narrative of that which is past. Despite the efforts of some recent theorists of history to dismiss the importance of narrative, these two dimensions are not easily separated.[4] There isn't much in the human historical past itself that happened without narrative interpretation, nor is there any such thing as a past in and of itself, free from or incapable of being burdened with the narrative interpretations given it by its future.[5] Our use of the term history usually entails both dimensions at once: the world of past events, and the interpretive representation of them through narrative accounts.

These two dimensions of history serve in an important sense as limits to each other. Any narrative that claims to be historical (as opposed to being purely fictitious) is held accountable to the documents and traces of the past itself, a past that is only accessible to us indirectly through its documents and traces.[6] These material sources are themselves not free of an interpretive, narrative framework, be it a narrative that attached to them from the time of their production or whatever particular narrative is operational within subsequent episodes of their interpretation. Outside narrative, one might say, documents and traces of the past have no meaning.[7]

It is most often the narrative framework that we are seeking when we look for meaning from events in the past. In this sense, the objects of historical analyses do not correspond to what a philosophical realist might call "the real past," argues historian Leon Goldstein. Rather, historians arrive at the objects of their analyses through cognitive-constructive procedures, narrative being the most common constructive procedure they employ.[8] The narrative of history shapes the investigation and analysis of the historical past, and the results of the investigation of the past shape the historian's narrative. There really is no clear-cut means of identifying which comes first; the relationship between the narrative and the object is in the truest sense dialectical. The goal of any historical investigation and narrative is finally their joining together in a single act of remembering: a critical remembering which accurately represents the past by organizing a comprehensible whole.[9]

It is necessary to make this point once again because the study of church history, or the history of Christianity, is often represented in objective historical terms as if its subject matter were purely given, or capable of being grasped apart from the constructive interpretation of those of who were (and are) participants and observers. From this point of view, narrative interpretation appears to amount to little more than following the course of events that have unfolded. Historical continuities can certainly be discerned from amidst the temporal fields of events in the past, due to what Robert Heilbroner calls "the inertia of history."[10] They can also be grasped by the historical imagination of the reader. But such continuities are not synonymous with the narrative meaning, or narrative interpretation, of events. Nor is the content of church history free from the prefigurative theological interests of the historians investigating it. Claims to detachment and objectivity can only help to obscure the degree to which prior theological commitments are at work, determining selection of what is important to investigate, for instance, or shaping judgments concerning the significance of patterns of events. The historian's prior location in a tradition is often as important to the final outcome of her work as are the methods of analysis she employs to achieve historical understanding.

This is not to deny the need for critical social scientific methods within the discipline of church history. The methods of modern critical historiography are important, to the point that one cannot any longer easily defend their absence from the study of the Christian past.[11] If for no other reason, they are necessary for calling into question the illusions of objectivity that have for too long been fostered within the discipline of modern church history, and modern history in general. The memories which the historian labors to restore, analyze, and represent to a wider community of readers (or hearers) are not free of particular interests. They bear the marks of social location from the period of their original production, and from later periods of reproduction. They also bear the marks of the social interests of the recollecting historian, however much the historian may wish to avoid them. Every historian writes from a point of view, and every historian works with some commitments already in place. Church historians are no different, even those whose point of view is intended to discredit the claims of a particular history of the Christian movement, or to strip the religion of its illusions.[12]

Church historians work to tell a story. The implications of their story are theologically significant, for behind the critical investigations of the church historian lies the belief or claim (whether or nor the individual historian herself advances it) that God is somehow implicated in the story being told. The narrative of church history is, in the end, the material out of which the content of theological tradition is (re)constructed. It is *tradition* insofar as it is history effectively shaping contemporary identity; it is *theological* insofar as it has attached to it a belief in, or witness to, divine activity. Theological traditions lay claim to having some revelatory value, which forms the content of their meaning. Even when the claim being advanced concerns divine judgment, or when God appears to be hidden rather than revealed through a particular course of events, the theological character of the narrative invokes or implies some reference to divine activity (or its absence) in the course of events.

Meaning is hermeneutical, which is to say that the level of history at which meaning is found is that of interpretation. The meaning or purpose of the story is found in the narrative itself, not at the level of the material past. The divine is by definition unseen, and materially unseeable. God's "hand" in history is not found in the evidence and traces of the material past themselves, but in the interpretation and meaning of the past. It is the interpretive construct that is revelatory of God, mediating through material history the redemptive meaning or value of tradition. But then such a meaningful history is in some sense salvific, even if its significance is relegated to being an interpretation of salvation.

History and Divine Revelation

Theological understandings of Christian salvation necessarily refer us to the meaning of the person of Jesus Christ, and the events of his life, death, and resurrection. How this is so, or in what manner Jesus Christ is meaningful for salvation, remain questions that are hotly debated among Christian theologians. What is clear, however, is the point that Jesus Christ figures prominently in a Christian understanding of salvation. Indeed, it would not be stretching the point to say that what makes a particular theological set of beliefs *Christian* is that they in some manner relate to the person of Jesus Christ. Christians claim that in Jesus Christ God was acting in a unique and normative way, or that in the configuration of events of his life God's own self is revealed in ways that are determinative for future generations.

The memory of this person is public and collective. It is contained in the Gospel narratives which are recalled by a community of faith. Thus it is not just the historical person of Jesus Christ that is constitutive of Christian identity proper, but Jesus Christ as he is remembered in the community of faith, which has consciously constituted itself as his followers, as the community of his disciples. In this way, Christian claims regarding God acting in the history of Jesus Christ are extended to the history of Christian communities of faith which continue to experience the presence of Christ in their midst. It is along these lines of church history having continuing, derivative, or secondary revelatory value that theologians have usually moved when they have asserted tradition to be a source for theological reflection upon the nature and purposes of God.

At the same time, the ambiguities and terrors of church history make the claim that it has such revelatory meaning difficult to substantiate solely from the record of events themselves. Without some orientation of faith to provide an interpretative key, church history might appear to be little more than "one damn thing after another." The perception of meaning and purpose in history, despite the indications of history itself, is perhaps the greatest leap of faith the Christian believer must make. It is certainly a leap one must often make to discover God's hand in the details of church history. Making the leap, grasping meaning, finding purpose—all require something more than the historical record given to us. They require an ability to see beyond what is given in the record, to see with eyes that are more than simply historical. It is the capacity that the twentieth-century Protestant theologian Karl Barth called *analogia fidei*, the ability to see by means of an analogy of faith, that any church historian who would be a Christian believer must invoke.

For Barth, the *analogia fidei* was a mode of understanding which stood in contrast to the *analogia entis*, a mode of understanding derived from analysis of what is given in life.[13] The notion of an *analogia entis* suggested for Barth that meaning or truth discloses itself through being or history. Against this, he argued that the truth about God is not revealed directly in being or history itself, but only indirectly and in a hidden manner. Insofar as God reveals the divine self in human history, this revelation is never without ambiguity. The creative activity of God which gives history its character as history, Barth argued, is itself non-historical.[14] It cannot be located through historical investigative methods, although it is itself presupposed by history.[15]

In other words, the God who gives history its meaning, and who is the creative source of history itself, is never found immediately through history, but is only discerned through faith. Among Barth's contributions to twentieth century Christian theology, none has been more enduring than his insight into the dialectical veiling and unveiling of the divine in history.[16] Revelation for Barth entailed a mode of divine self-giving to humanity in history, an act of God which simultaneously revealed God and saved humankind. But God's person was just as much hidden by the events of history as revealed by them, Barth had to acknowledge. The hidden and revealed character of God, God's veiling and unveiling in history, required an *analogia fidei*, or eyes of faith, with which to see God revealed.

Early in his theological career Barth referred to revelation as the crisis of history, the moment of history's judgment which could only be understood as its negation. God, who is not human, calls into crisis every human effort to construct meaning or secure our own future. The place where such revelation occurred—the church which lived in human history—could only be a site of judgment. As his theological thinking unfolded, Barth grew in his appreciation for the positive content of revelation as well, as it has been received in the life of the church over the centuries and articulated as dogma. Eventually the church, and especially its history of doctrine, became for Barth a site of authority as much as judgment. He insisted, however, that the history of divine self-giving was eschatological, standing apart and over against all human history as the latter's judgment and end. In the final analysis the history of God remains inaccessible to human historical methods of investigation. It can only be appropriated insofar as God has given (revealed) Godself to human history. So the divine remains hidden, yet present to human history, to be grasped only through faith.[17] It is only through faith that we can perceive divine revelation, for we cannot reduce it to the categories of human historical experience.

Barth believed that the capacity of faith, the *analogia fidei*, allowed one to properly speak of revelation without reducing its apprehension to the course of history, whether it be biblical history or church history. He understood revelation to be God's self-manifestation through divine activities in history that revealed God's identity. It could be found not in a separate, sacred history, but in the proclamation of God's salvation, the "Word of God" which for him was preeminently identified as the person of Jesus Christ.[18] The history of the Christian church itself was not sacred history, nor was the church the historical center for meaning. The church was a de-centered reality, found near the center (*Nebenzentrum*), he argued.[19] Nor did Barth draw as sharp a line between the church and the world as his critics sometimes complained. The mystery of God remained open-ended according to Barth, God's openness to the world a consistent theme running throughout his theological thought. At the same time, the human person, Jesus Christ, alone in all of human history was (and is) the sacrament of the divine, Barth argued; the narrative of his life and activity constitutes the only adequate measure of divine revelation and meaning.

This did not mean for Barth that the study of church history was without value, for it was the site where the proclamation of the sacred history of Christ's person had occurred. The revelation of God through Jesus Christ was not continued in the history of the Christian church, but insofar as the history of the Christian church was the history of the reception of the Word of God that is Jesus Christ, that history was predicated on divine revelation. Without always saying as much explicitly, Barth found the content of divine revelation refracted only through the dogmatic history of the Christian church, and especially through those churches of the Reformed confessional tradition for whom the proclamation of the Word was central to worship. He resisted elevating the ecclesial tradition itself to the level of the Word, maintaining its critical distance as witness to the Word. Yet in the end his conception of revelation in history remained refracted through a narrow Western confessional ecclesial identity.

The Roman Catholic theologian Karl Rahner shared Barth's emphasis on Jesus Christ being the Word of God in history. Jesus Christ is God's perfect self-communication, Rahner often asserted. Likewise for Rahner, history was the realm of the provisional and dialectical, unfinished and ambiguous in its interpretations, yet the arena in which the Word was heard.[20] Unlike Barth, however, Rahner was not ready to concede that sacred history takes place only in the person of Jesus Christ and that the wider arena of human experience can be nothing more than the history of the reception of faith. It is true, Rahner argued, that the salvation dimension will be fully revealed in history "only in the Last Judgment, which itself is not a moment of history but rather the final unveiling of history." He continued:

> But all this does not mean that this profane history does not become transparent here and there and does not within its own sphere draw man's

attention here and there by signs and references to the question of faith and salvation and orientate the answer to this question in a particular direction. Salvation-history, which of its nature is a hidden history, works itself out in the dimension of profane history in which it takes place.[21]

It is by the Word of God that a particular part of profane history has been distinguished as salvation history, or consecrated as it were. It is only when the Word expresses them and interprets them, argues Rahner, that the saving acts become present in the dimension of profane history. And while the word provides rules for interpreting all history, it "does not occur always and everywhere but has its special place in time and space within history."[22] The absolute Incarnation of the Word in history is Jesus Christ, who is to be distinguished from what comes after him, including the church, its scriptures, and its sacraments, says Rahner. Yet the latter participate in salvation history because they follow from the Christ event, and thereby participate in being distinguished from profane history.[23] From here it is but a short step for Rahner to take from a sacramental ecclesiology to reaffirming the sacralization of the empirical history of the church, in his case specifically of the Roman Catholic Church. The wider salvation God is effecting in history is revealed sacramentally in the historical existence of the church, a theological perspective that was foundational for the understanding of the church articulated by Vatican II.

While not all Protestants agree with Barth, of course, nor all Roman Catholics with Rahner, these two thinkers articulate theological perspectives that are reflective of a more widely held, if unarticulated, conception of history that is, in the final analysis, captive to an ecclesiocentric perspective. The theologies of both Barth and Rahner were profoundly christological, but both tended toward articulating christology through ecclesial expressions, be they Word or Sacrament, in the church. The result is an ecclesial reduction of christology, and of theology in general. Translated into historical terms, both theologians articulate dogmatic systems in which the Western (Latin) genealogical heritage provides the content for Christian faith, be it Reformed or Catholic.[24]

A somewhat different historical memory informs Orthodox churches who lay claim to the inheritance of the Greek-speaking East, embodying as well a different understanding of tradition.[25] Tradition, according to Orthodox theology, is the living transmission in history of the faith and spirituality of the whole church. The one, unbroken, and continuing Tradition of the church is a holy Mystery which is not subject to the corrosive effects of human history.[26] While not synonymous with the history of the churches, it is the dynamic ground of their history, and the gathering of their history into God.[27] Theologically, it is expressed through the consensus achieved in the early Christian (Patristic) era that is summarized, according to Eastern Orthodox churches, in the Seven Ecumenical Councils.[28] However much this inheritance might demonstrate the ambiguity that characterizes all human history, for Orthodox theology, Tradition is not subject to the ambiguities of history, so much as it is the light that shines through them. In this way Orthodox theology continues to affirm the articulation of Tradition in the Patristic era despite the blatant effects of imperial political power that are evident in the theological expressions of the period. However much the history of Orthodox churches might reflect the ambiguities of history, Tradition, as a Mystery, remains untouched by them.[29]

Orthodox theology emphasizes love and obedience, the inner works of the Holy Spirit, as the bonds that join the church together in unity. It is these more than the external bonds of hierarchy or history that give rise to the catholicity of the church. They are expressed through the unity of Creed and Tradition, which is why dogma and liturgy are not regarded in the same historical manner as they generally are within Protestant churches, nor are they open to revision in the same way they were for the Roman Catholic church in Vatican II. For Orthodox theology Creed and Tradition are truly universal. Constantin G. Patelos claims with confidence: "[There is] One Undivided Unbroken Tradition of the Church. And according to our teaching, the Eastern Tradition . . . is the Holy Tradition of the Church of Christ itself."[30] On the other hand, Protestant and Roman Catholic theologies have both tended to place greater emphasis on the historical, institutional forms of the church as the location for salvation in history. Orthodox theology emphasizes the dimension of Mystery which is experienced in the whole church, both the hierarchy and the laity, in worship and in work. The institutional life of the church is not added on to the Mystery, but is the means through which it is made manifest. The church, with its history, has an iconic quality, so that Tradition cannot be reduced to the history of the church.

Nevertheless there remains a critical historical dependency of Tradition on the concrete history of the church or churches, even for Orthodox theology. That which is revelatory, iconic, and salvific is identified with the history of a particular church (or the churches). For most Protestant, Roman Catholic, and Orthodox theologians alike, salvation—defined in Christian terms as the reconciliation or redemption accomplished by God, through Jesus Christ and the Holy Spirit, in the world—continues to be identified with the church, or as being in the church. The life of the church, manifested in its holiness, unity, catholicity, and apostolicity, is salvific (historically effective) across time. The history of salvation in the world is thus closely related to, if not identical with, the history of the church, whether it be understood as the history of the reception of the Word, the history of the sacramental community, or the history that manifests Holy Tradition.

The last century has witnessed among many Christians a growing uneasiness with these ecclesiocentric formulations of the doctrine of salvation. Increasingly, the experiences of those involved in programs of interreligious dialogue and cooperation have called into question the notion that there is no salvation outside the church, or outside the Christian faith. The various political, liberation, and contextual theologies that have emerged over the last half-century have shifted the axis of theological reflection from answering questions of unbelief to addressing issues of social praxis. Understanding the relation of God's activity to human history has even been a central concern of the ecumenical movement which has undertaken renewal of the churches for unity and mission in the world.[31] Ecumenical efforts to renew the social witness of the churches in particular have struggled with conditions of modern society that lie beyond the ecclesial walls, calling the churches to a more relevant position. In a number of theological circles it is not uncommon to hear that salvation is not found in the church, but in the world. The church is seen to be not so much *the place* of salvation, but the agent of salvation. Certainly the church remains *a* place, or at least *ought* to be a place, of salvation. But it only does so by going outside of itself, giving itself to the world in mission and praxis. From this point of view, the history of the church does not, in and of itself, appear adequately to reveal divine activity in history or to be the location of salvation.

The search for a more adequate understanding of salvation and revelation in history has occupied a number of theologians across the span of the past century, among them notably Paul Tillich. From his early days as a leader of the movement for religious socialism in Germany after the First World War, through his years of teaching in the United States which culminated in the publication of his three-volume *Systematic Theology*, Tillich occupied himself with questions of the theological meaning of history. He recognized the challenge posed by the autonomy of modern secular culture, and grappled with the theological questions that it posed for his own time of historical crisis. He appropriated the biblical concept of *kairos*, a qualitative time or the fullness of time, to describe his experience of history in which the separation between the secular and the sacred was suspended and events in the world became transparent to theological significance of an eternal nature.

Experiences of *kairos* for Tillich were moments beyond autonomy (law of the self) and heteronomy (law of the other, or oppression). They were moments of theonomy, when the law of God becomes synonymous with the deepest law of the self, or when the depths of being become transparent to the eternal which is manifest through them. The preeminent moment of *Kairos* for Christian faith was the New Being of Jesus Christ, he argued. Yet the Christ event did not exhaust the meaning of *kairos*; such moments have continued since then in human history to derive their meaning and significance from the central *Kairos* of Jesus, the Christ. Tillich employed a theological method of correlation to give answers from the Christian faith to questions being raised by the present historical situation, demonstrating Christianity's philosophical relevance and existential vitality. The sources he drew on for theological revelation were the historical events of *Kairos* and *kairos*, witnessed to in Christian scripture and tradition, under the symbols of God, the New Being of Jesus Christ, and life in the Spirit.

The concept of a *kairos* suggests that every moment of history, every period of history, is open to dimensions of eternity whether or not it realizes these. There is a depth to history, to every historical period and people, which is eternally significant. This in turn means that every nation and every age has a depth dimension the realization of which can be considered its historical vocation. Tillich conceived of the special historical vocation given by God to every people on earth as being potentially of service to the whole of Christianity. He did not conceive of the vocation that could be expressed as the depth of a people's identity as being confined to Christian history, or to the history of European nations. "Every human group may become a 'bearer' of history," he argued.[32]

What characterized a group as "history-bearing" was first of all a center that oriented common life, and the power to maintain it; and second, a sense of vocation or goal which was its purpose, a "vocational consciousness."[33] Tillich perceived both dimensions to be grasped in the biblical symbol of the Kingdom of God. But could one consider all humanity, rather than particular groups, as the bearer of history? In the third volume of *Systematic Theology* Tillich did not think so, "For the limited character of groups necessarily seems to disrupt the unity which is intended in the symbol, 'Kingdom of God.' "[34] The ultimate meaning of human history will be realized only in the Kingdom of God. Only then will all human history be revelatory of the divine. The ambiguities of history remain as long as there is history, and history itself will not overcome them. He continued:

> [T]he aim of history does not lie in history. There is no united mankind within history. It certainly did not exist in the past; nor can it exist in the future because a politically united mankind, though imaginable, would be a diagonal between convergent and divergent vectors. Its political unity would be the framework for a disunity that is the consequence of human freedom with its dynamic that surpasses everything given.[35]

The aim of history, the Kingdom of God, does not itself lie within history. Yet, he claimed, if the notion of salvation is to have any historical meaning, then the salvation of which the Kingdom of God is a symbol must be related to human history. Salvation history must be definable in terms of time and causation, without being reduced to them. It must be capable of being narrated historically, even though "it manifests something which is not from history."[36] Saving history thus is not world history, nor the history of a particular group in history. It is not the history of the churches, nor the history of religion in general, for all of these remain ambiguous. At the same time, there are "manifestations of the Kingdom of God in history."[37] The final manifestation Christian theology claims to be Jesus of Nazareth who is the Christ, or New Being.

What then of the church that follows Jesus as Christ? Tillich argued that the churches "represent" the Kingdom of God, but do so continuing to share in all the ambiguities of history. Churches both manifest the reality of redemption in the present, and look forward to it in the future.[38] The church (singular) is wherever churches (plural) confess Christ as the central manifestation of the Kingdom of God.

> If we look at church history in light of this two-way relationship between the church and the churches, we can say that church history is at no point identical with the Kingdom of God and at no point without manifestation of the Kingdom of God. With this in mind one should look at the many riddles of church history which express the paradoxical character of churches.[39]

The paradox is preserved, yet the centrality of the church affirmed, within this dialectical distancing. Several pages later Tillich wrote:

> In view of this [paradox or riddle] one must ask: What is the meaning of church history? One thing is obvious: one cannot call church history "sacred history" or a "history of salvation." Sacred history is in church history but is not limited to it, and sacred history is not only manifest in but also hidden by church history. Nevertheless, church history has one quality which no other history has: since it relates itself in all its periods and appearances to the central manifestation of the Kingdom of God in history, it has in itself the ultimate criterion against itself—the New Being in Jesus as the Christ. The presence of this criterion elevates the churches above any other religious group, not because they are "better" than others, but because they have a better criterion against themselves and implicitly, also against other groups.[40]

I have quoted the passage at length to demonstrate a deep contradiction left unaddressed in Tillich's thinking. It is a question that continues to haunt all ecclesiocentric theologies of history today. For Tillich, the history of Christian churches, or the church, both manifests and points beyond itself to the event of New Being and the Kingdom of God. Yet if the Kingdom of God is truly more than church history, if sacred history is not limited historically to the church, then it must be manifest in history other than in that of the Christian churches. If the presence of the "criterion" is a quality of church history that no other history has, then sacred history is historically limited to the history of the Christian churches, and there is no point of historical judgment of them beyond themselves. Other histories must have a presence of the criterion of the Kingdom of God which is their own, and which can be the historical criterion of judgment for the Christian church as well. Otherwise, the criterion and judgment become idealizations, and do not qualify as history.

Tillich himself conceptualized the presence of Christian faith outside the explicit boundaries of the church in terms of "latent Christians," a concept similar to Karl Rahner's famous notion of "anonymous Christians." Yet neither theologian assigned any real concrete, historical meaning to these moments of faith beyond the boundaries of the church, or of Christendom. Latent or anonymous Christians are persons who are said to be members of the church implicitly. Their membership is without historical content, meaning, or form. They do not add to the manifestation of the Kingdom of God in Tillich's terms, because they are unmanifest as members or participants. They live in the light of the ultimate meaning of redemption, either through expectation or implicit reception, thus without explicit knowledge of the historical way of salvation. They are "traditionless Christians" by virtue of their own redemptive history being latently or anonymously Christian.

Tillich acknowledged an eschatological manifestation of historical redemption among such persons, symbolized as the Kingdom of God which is not in history but is the end of history. A similar universal historical horizon of salvation, and thus of revelation, is a theme that Wolfhart Pannenberg pursued as well in *Revelation as History*. Pannenberg began by noting the general agreement in contemporary Christian theology that revelation is the self-revelation of God.[41] He criticized Barth's restriction of revelation to the Word of God manifested in Jesus Christ, however, moving instead in the direction of Tillich's theology by posing the thesis of God's indirect self-revelation through the medium of human historical events. Yet such revelation is only comprehended completely at the end of revealing history, not at its beginning. It is only at the end of history that one can locate the manifestation of God.

> It is not so much the course of history as it is the end of history that is at one with the essence of God. But insofar as the end presupposes the course of history, because it is the perfection of it, then also the course of history belongs in essence to the revelation of God, for history receives its unity from its end.[42]

How then is the revelation known before the end? Its universal character is open to anyone who has eyes to see it, asserted Pannenberg. At the same time it is experienced proleptically in the fate of Jesus Christ, that is, in his death and resurrection. "The Word relates itself to revelation as foretelling, forthtelling, and report," he argued. Trutz Rendtorff drew the conclusions from this thesis for the study of church history, in a concluding chapter entitled,

"The Problem of Revelation in the Concept of the Church." The relationship of Christ to the church is such that the existence of revelation in the world is seen in the study of the Christian church and its history.[43] Like the other theologians we have been considering, Rendtorff understood this history to be entirely European, in that the history of the Christian church was a European history. The configuring history that foretold the ultimate revelation of God was the history of European churches, and by extension, the history of European civilization otherwise known as Christendom.

Pannenberg's thesis that Jesus Christ is the proleptic realization of the end of history was formulated in such terms as to imply that the modern realization of a universal historical horizon was the result of the biblical hope for the unity of humankind.[44] It is only a small step from this belief to the assertion that the mission of the church in history is to unify world history under its own banner, or under the banner of a universal political order. So the 1968 Faith and Order Commission's study project on the "Finality of Jesus Christ" concluded:

> So long as in the West Christianity was identified with a special 'Christian culture,' limited to Europe, no more could the germs of universality in the Christian message bear fruit either. *The universalizing and unifying of history started in the ages of mission and colonialism, and is now in this generation penetrating human minds everywhere as never before.*[45]

In one respect the statement just quoted is quite correct, in that the search for universal history is inextricably linked to the age of European missions and colonialism. The search has preoccupied more than missionaries, colonial administrators, and church theologians, however. Over the course of the last two centuries it has preoccupied all the social sciences in the European-American academy as well. The roots of modern Western historical thinking are often traced to nineteenth-century German Romanticism and Hegelian philosophy. The genealogy is itself an important historical argument, for the rise of the critical discipline of historical study in nineteenth-century Germany had as much to do with the need for national identity and theoretical justification of the state as it did with the pursuit of pure knowledge for its own sake.[46] From these roots the doctrines of historicism and the development of critical historical consciousness spread across the intellectual landscape of later modernity to become a general part of its makeup. Modern, critical historical consciousness is often itself represented as a progressive development, superseding earlier forms of consciousness in the West itself, as well as displacing other forms of consciousness of the past in non-Western cultural contexts.[47]

History entered the German university as a legitimate scientific discipline during the first decade of the nineteenth century. Hegel provided its systematic philosophical articulation in his lectures on the philosophy of history during the third decade. Hegel's philosophy of history provided a powerful argument for universal history being the self-realization of Absolute Spirit, so that the universal horizon of history and God's own self-realization become identical. With the publication of J. K. Wilhelm Vatke's *Religion des Alten Testamentes* in 1835, the spirit of Hegelian historical thinking found a home in the theological disciplines, in the first instance in the discipline of biblical studies. With Vatke's text, which was infused with Hegelian philosophy and the first biblical theology "to have a thoroughly historical character," the search for theological meaning in the particular facts of biblical history was begun.[48] In 1841 Johann C. K. von Hofmann employed the term *Heilsgeschichte* (salvation history) to name the universal theological importance of those particular events in the life of Israel that are recounted in the Bible as incidents in which God is acting in history.

A century after Hofmann introduced the concept of *Heilsgeschichte*, and in the aftermath of the Second World War, the question of divine revelation amidst the vagaries of the events of history continued to occupy theologians and biblical scholars in the North Atlantic world. Influential among them was G. Ernest Wright, whose book, *God Who Acts: Biblical Theology as Recital*, explored the implications of holding events in a particular history to be the primary mode of God's self-revelation. As is suggested in the subtitle of the book, it was not so much the events of this history in and of themselves that were revelatory for Wright as it was the events joined to a manner of telling (or confession) that carried the burden of revelation, an insight that has been pursued more recently by those engaged in the movement of narrative theology. Wright's primary focus was in biblical studies, but his implications were confessional. In his proposal he saw the means by which study of the Bible could be

> kept nearer to history and to the recital of history by faith than is possible by the systematic methodology which actually tends to separate what is felt to be the *intellectual* content both from the faith and from its rootage in history.[49]

Accordingly God both acts in history and provides the means by which these divine acts can be interpreted, that is, the Word. In a christological move which by now should be quite familiar to us, Wright argued that it is the person of Jesus Christ who provides the climax of Israel's history and the subsequent inauguration of a new history. But Jesus stands within a larger history, or the totality of events of Israel's history. These events and their interpretation joined together are "[t]he objective work of God in history which points forward to history's fulfillment."[50] Historical biblical events provide the primary data of faith, according to Wright. In them, and then through their mediation, God acts. Thus biblical theology moves from reflection on historical events to explication or proclamation of their theological meaning.

It thus must point in the first instance to this confessional recital of traditional and historical events, and proceed to the inferences which accompanied those events, became an integral part of them, and served as the guides to the comprehension of both past and future. Biblical theology, then, is primarily a confessional recital in which history is seen as a problem of faith, and faith as a problem of history.[51]

An even stronger emphasis on the "retelling" aspect of biblical theology characterized the scholarship of Wright's contemporary, Gerhard von Rad. For von Rad, revelation and faith were more properly located in Israel's telling of history, that is, in its tradition. This he called the "rewriting" of history.[52] Von Rad would go so far as to credit Israel with the invention of history,[53] a thesis which has drawn significant criticism in recent years.[54] Whatever the merit (or lack thereof) of the thesis of original historiography, von Rad was able to draw attention to the manner in which salvation history takes shape as a tradition. It is not necessarily a succession of discrete events taking place amidst the otherwise profane occurrences of everyday human history which can be distinguished as divine or salvific in and of themselves. The divine in human history remains hidden, to be found only through hints and signs that are deciphered or interpreted by those who would narrate such a presence. If the divine is immediately present to every moment of human historical experience, such presence is not meaningfully discerned and comprehended apart from a narrative mediation that provides the telling of divine history, which is otherwise called revelation.

As we have already seen, the field of theological inquiry felt the impact of Hegel's philosophy of history and the rise of critical biblical historical thinking, transforming the dominant shape of the Western theological landscape across the course of two centuries.[55] Not a few theologians embraced the notion that historical thinking was the inner dynamic and eventual product of biblical faith itself. Gerhard Ebeling for instance, writing in the early 1960s, recognized that the secularizing and historicizing character of modern European thought had achieved total domination of society and religion on a global scale. Like the legendary King Midas, for modern (European) humanity "everything, the whole of reality, turns to history."[56] But, he argued, historicalness, while it had presented a challenge to traditional ways of conceptualizing Christian faith, did not contradict Christian faith. Ebeling stated what had by the 1960s become a commonplace for many European and North American theologians:

> For the Christian faith stands essentially in a close relation to history. It is well known that the significance of history in Western thought goes back to the Old Testament. For God is here understood as the God who acts and reveals himself in history.[57]

THEOLOGY OF HISTORY 69

In his recent study, *God in History*, Peter Hodgson argues that the presence of God in human history is found as an immanent figure, pattern, or *gestalt* in human history that unifies and empowers. He sketches briefly the history of Latin Christian conceptions of salvation history, surveying the span of biblical, imperial Roman, late medieval, Reformation, and modern theologies of history. In developing his own constructive proposal at the end of the modern era that draws on historical philosophical categories of Hegel and Troeltsch, Hodgson argues:

> God is efficaciously present in the world, not as an individual agent performing observable acts, nor as a uniform inspiration or lure, nor as an abstract ideal, nor in the metaphorical role of companion or friend. Rather, God is present in specific shapes or patterns of praxis that have a configuring, transformative power within historical process, moving the process in a determinate direction, that of the creative unification of multiplicities of elements into new wholes, into creative syntheses that build human solidarity, enhance freedom, break systematic oppression, heal the injured and broken, and care for the natural.[58]

The historical process thus can be viewed as a dialectic of human and divine factors, giving rise to a patterned fabric or tapestry. The text of such patternings, the gestalt of history, appears as the vehicle of divine presence which can in turn further empower the historical projects of freedom and empowerment.[59] Through the figurings of Jesus's ministry and preaching of the coming reign of God, as questioned and qualified by the suffering of the cross, liberation and solidarity emerge as constitutive of both divine and human historical praxis. An open-ended teleology is intended in this configuring. A single goal, the telos of history, is the end to which the history of freedom is directed. But this is a telos in God, beyond history, which can only be experienced in history in manifold shapes or forms. In categories which are heavily dependent on Hegel, he argues that the history of freedom within history is the goal of history; "but in history it appears only in a manifold of ambiguous and incomplete shapes."[60]

For Hodgson, Hegel (read through the lens offered by Troeltsch, with an affinity for Whitehead and process theology) opens up the profound possibility of achieving a new cultural synthesis, a teleology within history, which will empower a new emancipatory praxis of freedom that stands at the end of a history whose roots reach back through Augustine to the Bible. He writes:

> My proposed theology of history is at heart an adaptation of this brilliant Hegelian vision [of philosophy of world history] to a postmodernist context. Instead of speaking of a single, more or less unified and progressive history of freedom, I believe today we must speak of a

plurality of partial, fragmentary, always ambiguous histories of freedom, struggling to survive, and sometimes prevailing, against the forces of domination and oppression.[61]

In this construal, both the Hegelian sublation (*Aufhebung*) of the past, *and the particular past the Hegelian vision sought to sublate, or to take up into a new synthesis* are left intact. There are many shapes of freedom on the present cutting edge of time, but the history of freedom itself is a singular historical trajectory of thought running through the history of Western intellectual life.

There is much in Hodgson's thesis that I find to be sound. With him I could affirm that God is present in the world, not as an individual agent, nor as a lure, nor as an abstract ideal; but in the shaping or patterning of transformative (reconfiguring) praxis.[62] God's incarnation in Jesus Christ he understands not as being located in the individual person of Jesus so much as in the patterning of his life, which continued after his death in the communal identity of those who gathered in his name.[63] But then one wants to argue with Hodgson, that if it is to be truly the *Gestalt* of the God who created all things which was manifest in Jesus, renewed through the resurrection, and continued in communal dimensions, it must also be a *Gestalt* found in history outside the historical constructs of Greco-Roman-Germanic-Anglo intellectual historical memory, and indeed outside the boundaries of church history itself. The *fundamental pluralism* of this *Gestalt* cannot be confined to the most recent edge of present-historical time, nor attributed simply to the postmodern context, although it is certainly found in both of these. The pluralism of the *Gestalt* that manifests divine presence, its fundamental hybridity, is characteristic of all times and places of divine manifestation, past, present, and future. Postmodern genealogical readings of history and historical memory are more adequate in representing this pluralism than are the singularity of Hegelian dialectics and the universalism of Troeltsch's historical consciousness.

Unfortunately Hodgson's access to a more genealogical approach to history is obscured by his arguments with other postmodern theorists. He engages in a surprisingly sharp critique of what he sees to be the "radical relativism" of the postmodernist theologians who have followed a Nietzschean pathway at the end of (modern) history.[64] The fault line that divides Hodgson from these Nietzschean postmodernists is found not so much between their respective approaches to figuring and tropes, nor between their respective embrace of worldliness and the carn(iv)al. It is not in their expressed commitments against domination, their respective relativisms, nor their skepticism regarding ultimate claims to knowledge of the truth from within the horizon of history. The fault line lies elsewhere, nearer their respective valuation of the particular historical identity of the Western European (Greco-Roman-Germanic) philosophical (and secondarily, theological) heritage. In Hodgson's own words (in a footnote on his differences with Paul Ricoeur concerning their interpretation of the philosopher's conception of the totalization of history), "The basic question is indeed how one thinks about history 'after Hegel.' "[65]

For Mark C. Taylor, Hegel (read through Nietzsche and Derrida) marks the totalizing end, a closure that is signified by its plenitude. "By rationalizing Augustine's unsystematic theology, Hegel's speculative philosophy effectively inscribes the end of history."[66] Through the triune figuration of God of classical Christian theology and Hegelian philosophy, Hodgson is able to affirm that God acts redemptively in history as the inward dialectic of identity, difference, and mediation which is history and secures the meaning of history.[67] For Taylor, on the other hand, such a totalizing vision of history is a denial of death and an act of repression. Following the seams of repression, he moves to unravel the closure of this logocentrism which is the work of "the unhappy person [who] desperately longs for saving presence."[68]

> Suspended between a past that has been lost and a future not yet possessed, history is the domain of discontent and restlessness, of striving and strife. Within the bounds of history, dissatisfied and unhappy subjects struggle to save presence by seeking saving presence . . . The very *search* for presence, through which the historical actor attempts to deny absence and embrace plenitude, testifies to the absence of presence and the "presence" of absence.[69]

The new cultural synthesis that Hodgson seeks appears, in Taylor's markings, to be the vain attempt of a melancholy subject seeking to transcend itself.

For Taylor, the end of the Western project called history coincides with the death of God proclaimed by Nietzsche. Here his indebtedness to Thomas J. J. Altizer and the radical theology of the death of God is apparent: for Altizer the death of God is announced in the radical character of the incarnation and cross, an apocalyptic event in which were joined beginning and end. Taylor follows, and then goes beyond by arguing that "the death of God is realized in the radically incarnate word. The disappearance of the transcendental signified creates the possibility of writing."[70] The end of history and the death of God bring about the writing of the book, and then even the book itself is subverted. The book he refers to is not merely writing, not the multitudinous texts of the postmodern world. It is rather the book that seeks closure, the book that holds beginning and end within itself, the "ordered totality" that is, like history, logocentric.[71] It is not writing, not just books (plural), but *the* book which is ended; not textuality, not inscription, and not scriptures, but the book of Christianity, that is, of Western Christian history whose final book was written by Hegel,

> Hegel, who wrote "the death of God," registered the disappearance of the self, and inscribed the end of history, is the last philosopher of the book.[72]

It is the end of the history and Christianity of the West that Hegel wrote. And it is the God of this history that Nietzsche proclaimed to be dead. The fundamental movement and enduring effect of history in the modern West was nihilism, Nietzsche asserted in a variety of ways. But as Heidegger would point out, "nihilism in Nietzsche's sense in no way coincides with the situation conceived merely negatively, that the Christian god of biblical revelation can no longer be believed in." Nietzsche's attack was not necessarily against Christian life or Christian faith. It was against Christendom, "the historical, world-political phenomenon of the Church and its claim to power within the shaping of Western humanity and its modern culture."

> Christendom in this sense and the Christianity of New Testament faith are not the same . . . Therefore, a confrontation with Christendom is absolutely not in any way an attack against what is Christian, any more than a critique of theology is necessarily a critique of faith, whose interpretation theology is said to be.[73]

Over against the declared end of Christendom, Hodgson seeks a future constructed from the remains of Europe's theological heritage. To do so he is driven to offer a coherent synthesis of the European historical past. Both Hodgson and Taylor invoke in countless ways the master tradition of the European theo-philosophical intellectual construction of the past. Throughout both texts, the authority of Augustine, Aquinas, Hegel, Troeltsch, and Barth lingers. Inscribed in the pages of both books is a tradition Hodgson seeks to regenerate and Taylor seeks to 'X' out. In Taylor's case he must conjure up the very spirits of a tradition he seeks to exorcise, reminding us again of the very history he would have us forget. Hodgson's appropriation of Hegelian dialectics in the service of uncovering universal meaning in history is no less problematic, for it was Hegel who forged the master narrative that made of modern Europe the telos of universal history.[74] The historian or theologian who would follow such configuring finds herself trapped within the confines of a European tribal history masquerading as Universal, for outside Europe can only be "people without history."[75]

Toward a Theology of History of the Whole *Oikoumene*

Is there an alternative way of remembering God in history, God at the margins of history, or God at the end of history, for diverse Christian communities? Is there a way for Christian theology to embrace God's manifestations in history outside Europe, and outside Christendom? Is it only the history of the Christian church, and the churches of European civilization in particular, which is revelatory and thus a source of traditioning? What if the direction of history were not that of a unified line of development, but were more rhizomatic and convergent? What if the presence of God in history was not as straightforward as imagined in the movement of biblical theology, but were a more complex presence happening in multiple historical locations simultaneously, hidden and revealed as Barth had imagined? What if God were to be found in historical contexts where there are Christian communities of faith, but elsewhere as well? How then would Christian theology look to history for the construction of a tradition? These are questions that are occupying a number of contemporary theologians from the South, Third World, or the Two-Thirds World (the terms are often used interchangeably).

In Latin America, North America, and Western Europe, especially among marginalized communities, appreciation for cultural diversity and pluralism has led to a deeper search for Christian roots outside the official domains of Western Christendom. A similar project has been undertaken in Asia and Africa as communities professing a Christian identity seek to be rooted in histories that are not explicitly identified as Christian. The search for more ecumenical historical roots for Christian tradition has led a number of contemporary contextual theologians in Africa and Asia to embrace the broader religious heritages of their continental communities. There has also been an accompanying theological commitment to grounding reflection in the deeper cultural contexts of each local situation. For many, the dominant forms of Western European theology (and their accompanying histories) are inadequate for articulating a faith that bears the marks of an originating experience of faith that is not European. The history of colonialism, imperialism, and missions has proven to be too costly, too destructive, and too dehumanizing for those who have suffered the oppression of European domination to simply forget. Third World theologians have instead turned to the suffering and oppressions of the colonized, missionized, Christian, and non-Christian peoples of the world in order to locate the criterion of judgment against the European-American political history, accompanied as it has been by its churches.

Choan-Seng Song took up explicitly the question of the relation of non-Christian histories to the church in the 1970s, in light of the history of China.[76] Positive theological assessment of China's history, Song argued, required the assumption that God has been active in all human historical experiences throughout time, an assumption he felt was shared in the prophetic tradition of Israel's Scriptures. Song did not assert that the history of China could be understood in religious terms as a Christian history in the manner that the dominant Western theological traditions identified European religious history as Christian; he instead called into question the identification of the Western church with the biblical history of Israel and Jesus Christ. In the history of Israel and Jesus Christ the salvific work of God is "intensely exhibited," he claimed.[77] "The people of Israel were singled out, under a divine providence inexplicable to us and even to them," a saving mystery to which Song responded doxologically.[78] Israel and Jesus Christ were not so much mediators of salvation, however, as they were symbolic of how God acts among nations and in histories. They constituted a historical paradigm for Christian theology, a paradigm which was distanced from other particular cultural historical experiences even though it continued to take on new historical textures by being reformed in its various historical locations.

Song argued for a link between the theology of history and the doctrine of creation in order to broaden the vision of redemption. D. Preman Niles, in response to Song, pointed out that this perspective still privileged the history of Israel as the sole paradigm of redemption, and thus "savors of spiritual imperialism."[79] Niles argued that creation serves as the theological ground for history in the biblical texts, and that in the doctrine of creation was found the ground for multiple histories of redemption. Not only should Christians assess in a positive manner elements from other Asian religious traditions (or historical paradigms), but Asian Christians should distance themselves from the history and theology held in Western cultural bondage and move closer to the traditions among which they lived.

Asian Christians who told their religious history as one derived from European missions often found themselves inheritors of "two stories," Niles pointed out.[80] One response to the tension between the two stories was to suppress the Asian cultural and historical one, and to graft Asian converts onto the extension of the other which was Western. Another option was to read Asian history and religious traditions as speaking a Christian message, an option which still did not permit Asian stories to be heard in their own right. Niles opted for a third response, one taken by the theologian of Korean history, Suh Nam-dong, who proposed that Asian Christians must not hurry to theologize Asian stories before attending to them in their own historical and cultural setting as counter-story and a counter-theology to the Western theological traditions. Asians needed to bracket off the Western history of Christianity to explore the meaning of Asian history.[81]

Among these theologians and historians there has been agreement that the history of European Christianity, tied as it is in Asia to the history of colonialism and missions, is unable to provide an adequate historical identity for Asian Christian communities. New paradigms and references for a Christian past are being sought among the "social biography" of the people. It is especially in the social biography of the poor and the marginalized of history that the dynamic of change is found, asserted Kim Yong-bock. The power that creates history is not found among lords and kings, where the dominant historiography of both European and China has located it; the motivating factors and generative powers of history are discovered instead in the social biography of the poor or oppressed, the *minjung* in Korean, who are the subjects of history.[82] Kim's historical methodology assumes that the direction of God's activity (or mission) in the world is not from within institutions which identify themselves as Christian to those outside the churches. Instead, the movement or activity of

God is among the history of the social outcasts, the marginalized, and the poor, in the change (or mission) they bring about, in Christian communities as well as in their wider society. The historical consciousness which takes shape through this mission is more broadly experienced in the history of messianic movements and peasant movements for change in Asia, and it encompasses Buddhist, Taoist, and Shamanistic as well as Christian religious traditions.[83]

Minjung theology has taken shape through reflection on the historical struggles of the lower classes of Korea, as these struggles have been brought to consciousness in stories, songs, dances, and other popular cultural expressions. A similar process of historical contextualization has taken place in other Asian contexts as well. In India, for instance, where history and historical reflection have been shaped through many centuries in diverse social, religious, and cultural traditions, Christian theologians have drawn on these historical memories and experiences for articulating Christian faith. Until recently it was not uncommon to find many European, and even some Indian, scholars of the opinion that Indian religions and cultures are not "historically minded," an opinion the Indian Christian theologian Samuel Rayan has found faulty.[84] Rayan pointed to the extensive civilization India has sustained over centuries, with systems of medicine and law, and their documentation. The patterns of historical movement most characteristic of Indian civilization are ones that are cyclical rather than linear; ones in which the social and the cosmic are closely interwoven; and ones in which human decision and activity figure prominently. This sense of history, the manner in which human choice affects its outcomes, and the resulting concern for ethics, Rayan argued, are found within the sacred texts such as the *Bhagavadgita*, a "hand-book of revolution."[85] Indian Christianity shaped through an encounter with the texts and traditions of Hinduism and Buddhism embraces not only the history of Indian civilization, but also the sense of history found in Indian civilization. Theologians and historians of Indian Christianity have challenged churches that have previously been theologically and institutionally dependent on the West to take up the task of incarnating their faith in their Asian religious and historical contexts as they undergo their baptism into the spirituality of Asian soteriologies.[86]

A similar incarnational process has been a task of African Christian theology over the last several decades, and a similar recovery of African history for Christian churches has taken place.[87] As in India, the presence in Africa of Orthodox traditions in Egypt and Ethiopia, tracing their continuity back to the age of the Apostles, represents an important symbol for Christian historical identity. The history of Christianity in North Africa through the first seven centuries of the common era presents a critical task, because it has yet to be adequately investigated in light of the larger history of Africa.[88] But beyond these experiences in which the Christian faith has been historically institutionalized in Africa, the histories of the whole of Africa belong to African Christians as well.

Colonial historiography of Africa created the myth that Africa had no history, or that the reality of the African past was eliminated by the onset of European colonial incursions. A similar myth has distorted African Christian historiography which locates the origin of African Christianity in the dynamic of Western missionary expansion. Through the recovery of the African past, however, postcolonial African historiography has attempted to address this myth. Thus Ajayi writes:

> In relation to wars and conflicts of peoples, the rise and fall of empires, linguistic, cultural and religious change and the cultivation of new ideas and new ways of life, new economic orientations and so on, in relation to all of these, colonialism must be seen not as a complete departure from the African past, but as one episode in the continuous flow of African history.[89]

This same principle applied to African church history locates in the diverse and complex historical experiences of Africans the dynamic of conversions to Christianity which took place through encounters with missionaries. The history of Western missions is not the history of churches in Africa. Emmanuel Ayandele has made this point succinctly, arguing that ". . . rightly considered, an African Church must necessarily be the product of an organic growth on the African soil, an institution in which Christianity is incarnate within the African milieu."[90] Ayandele noted that the churches most often studied by historians of African Christianity were those which most resembled Western churches, while the history of the indigenous churches had been presented as aberrant and outside the boundaries of legitimate Christianity.[91]

Such historiography has perpetuated forms of ecclesial colonialism through missions, and cannot comprehend the actual growth of Christianity in Africa. It has also subtly and not so subtly reinforced the colonial and postcolonial situation of oppression and poverty in Africa today. The narrative focus of mission historiography on missionaries and mission churches has obscured the theological importance of issues of cultural destruction, material poverty, intertribal strife, human rights violations, postcolonial imperialism, and other social problems confronting African nations today. The institutional approach mission histories have generally taken in African church historiography, argues Ogbu U. Kalu, has obscured the fact that God was always and already within African history.[92]

The history of Christianity in Africa is comprehensible only within the context of the history of Africa, a history African Christians share with other religious communities. The history of the African past belongs to African Christians; and through their relationships with other Christian communities, the history of Africa is part of the whole history of Christianity. Its themes, its issues, its narratives all must be African, figuring the work of God through God's African historical identity. Continues Kalu:

> Within this perspective, church history is about the understanding of God's activity among the poor and their responses to the presence of the Kingdom in their midst. It is a people's history of their perception of God's saving grace in the midst of their struggles for survival ... The definition of the term poor ... must include the poor in spirit who may nonetheless be rich in material things or be powerful. The church is the whole people of God and church history is the past of the whole people, the powerful as well as the marginalised.[93]

Many African church historians, be they of African descent or not, have recognized the need for a new conception of church history that would embrace the fullness of Africa's historical past.[94] The growth of Christianity in contemporary Africa can only be understood historically in light of Africa's history, both ancient and recent. Furthermore, the history of Africa and of African Christianity is still being made, and thus cannot just be studied without commitment and engagement. "History," wrote Mudimbe, "is a legend, an invention of the present. It is both a memory and a reflection of our present."[95] In the process of reclaiming the historical past African theologians and historians are re-creating African Christianity, a process that A.A. Mazrui and M. Tidy describe as "retraditionalization."[96] Reinventing tradition and re-creating faith are tasks that Eboussi Boulaga has linked in his search for a Christianity without the fetishes of Western ecclesial ideologies.[97]

Common to the work of these Asian and African Christian voices is the assumption that they cannot be articulated by the narrative that defines Christian history as being European. The diversity of historical perspectives on tradition that has emerged in their theological projects suggests that a plurality of narratives is required of Christian historiography and theological reflection. In the ecumenical dialogue that ensues one finds Church histories perceived to be dynamic and interactive, and no single trajectory of Christian tradition an adequate bearer of the message of redemption. Much of the historical dynamics operative within these traditions are opaque to those who stand outside their immediate circle of bearers.[98] Their "Otherness" to one another, however, need not be a barrier to understanding so much as it is an invitation to dialogue. At the same time it is an invitation to embrace diversity, pluralism, and the open-endedness of their own Christian traditions.

What can we expect from such an open-ended theology of history and historical narration? The next chapter will take up the question of historical narration more carefully, exploring a more adequate church historiography reflective of these insights into the theology of history. From the perspective that is gained by these historiographical considerations we will return to address the theological question of configuring the divine presence. We will not be able to escape the judgment pronounced on the traditions of Christendom from those outside its gates, which has been a major critique developed by contemporary liberation and Third World theologians. Nor will we be able to disregard the positive contextual appropriation of historical and cultural identities today, many of which have been forged outside the explicit domains of ecclesial Christendom. From these perspectives we hope to be able to articulate a fresh ecumenical understanding of Christian tradition.

5 | Narratives of Church History

The Christian religion has been primarily, although by no means exclusively, a European religion, and the principal religion of European civilization has been Christianity. It is generally agreed that to study the history of Europe involves studying the history of Christianity and vice versa.
—William A. Clebsch[1]

But what would be a history stemming from the oppressed? Are they destined to imitate and repeat a destructive cycle of events? The appearance of theologies of the opaque might promise another alternative of a structural sort, but only if these theologies move beyond the structural power of theology as the normative mode of discourse and contemplate a narrative of meaning that is commensurate with the quality of beauty that was fired in the crucible of oppression.
—Charles H. Long[2]

History as "God-Bearing"

The last chapter examined some recent directions being pursued in ecumenical thinking regarding theological appropriation of histories beyond Christendom. For a number of contemporary theologians, the doctrine of creation has offered a wider theological basis for developing a more positive ecumenical understanding of revelation and history. Creation provides the ground, the arena, and the widest possible horizon for understanding God's activity in human history. Affirmation of God's universal presence in, to, and through all creation would thus seem to require the affirmation of God's presence in, to, and through all human histories, however hidden that presence might yet be. This, at least, is the implication of Ogbu Kalu's point that Western missionaries did not bring God to Africa, but found God already there.[3]

But what then of the specificity of the Christian movement and its ecclesial life? Christianity makes claims about a particular person through whom salvation is experienced. The New Testament tells a particular story about redemption that involves Jesus and his disciples, and a new community called "the church" which emerged from that movement. The gospels intimate no clear break between the days of the apostles and later generations that would follow in their way, indicating that the story of human salvation will continue to be the story of the community that follows Jesus down to the end of the age.

In his recent work, *Not Every Spirit: A Dogmatics of Christian Disbelief*, Christopher Morse has taken up the question of the particularity of the Christian understanding of salvation, in terms of the relationship of Jesus Christ and the church to the whole of human history. Morse takes as the starting point for his ecclesiology the Apostle Paul's statement in II Cor. 4:7 that the treasure of divine grace is held in earthen vessels of human ecclesial existence.[4] This has often served as the basis for asserting *ubi ecclesia, ibi Christus*, "where the church is, there is Christ." Yet the import of this assertion lies in the fact that what the church does in its ministry and mission is to point not to itself as the earthen vessel, but beyond itself to the divine grace it finds in Christ. Hence the better affirmation might be *ubi Christus, ibi ecclesia*, "where Christ is, there is the church."

The resurrection narratives in the New Testament proclaim that the risen Jesus whom the church follows goes before the apostles into all the world. That is where he sends the apostles in mission. Biblically, Morse argues, the church's mission beyond itself is carried out through signs, wonders and sacraments:

> First is the sign of going into all the world. The wonder is that the world into which the apostles are sent is confessed to be one where Jesus Christ has already gone and is expecting them. Christian faith in God's sending of Jesus Christ into the world refuses to believe that there is any "world" of time and space and social circumstance into which the church is commissioned to go that Jesus Christ has not already gone. In this sense there are no "foreign missions."[5]

Already in his life and ministry prior to his death and resurrection, Jesus had gone into the regions of Gentiles in the cities of the Decapolis, and among the Samaritans. The gospels tell of his openness to the outsiders and those who were considered sinners under the terms of the covenant. Continues Morse:

> It is striking to think in this connection how much the dramatic plot and subplots of the gospel accounts, and the Christian liturgies based upon them, are shaped by what Jesus is said to have received, and not simply in a one-sided fashion to have given, to those who are more or less presented as outsiders, even subjects of consternation, within the cultural setting of his ministry.[6]

In the gospels then, Jesus is both recipient and dispenser of grace. So too the resurrected Christ continues not only to give but to receive from the world, in order to realize the fullness of grace. Even before the women brought their message of the empty tomb, the risen Jesus was presenting himself in new situations. As the risen Lord, Jesus' presence continues to unfold in new bodies and identities, receiving them as his own.[7] This is why in Christ are found multiple genders, classes, and ethnicities. Along these lines Andrew Walls writes, "As fresh cultural entities are incorporated into the community of faith, the full stature of Christ's body is revealed."[8] The narrative of Christian redemption entails both the sending and the receiving of the good news of Jesus Christ.

Walls does not envision incorporation to entail the loss of historical identity, but its enrichment, redemption, or fulfillment. Conversion to Christianity does not require the assumption of a foreign historical identity, he argues; rather, conversion redirects an existing historical identity in a new way, toward Christ.[9] The translation of the gospel into new historical situations is accompanied by the reception of new histories in the world Christian movement. Only in this sense, insofar as it is open to new identities, can any church realize its mission to be a sign pointing toward the fullness of Christ. Again, Morse summarizes:

> The dogmatic point is that faith shaped by such testimony entails a refusal to believe that the sacramental body of Christ in its witness to all the world as a eucharistic community of the baptized does not in turn need and receive from all the world witness of God's grace already there and sent on before in the incarnate, risen, and coming life span of Jesus Christ.[10]

This, then, is why the divine activity or revelation of God cannot be limited to the history of the church, but it can be narrated through it. The divine is equally close to every moment in human history, and all human history is equally close to God through grace. The plenitude of human histories and experiences are, have been, and will continue to be "God-bearing" in this sense. Interpretation of the events is never unambiguous, for God always remains simultaneously hidden and revealed through the events of history, at least until the end of time. On the other hand, the affirmation that God *is* at work in and through the Christian churches (which, given much of their historical past, requires no small exercise of faith) gives to them a particular sacramental or signifying meaning, reflected in the narratives of their existence.

Such an affirmation does not require one to deny that sacramental meanings can be found in other enduring narratives of faith, religious as well as secular in nature. Affirming the importance of particular configurations of the divine presence, revelation, and salvation within the history of the Christian movement need not exclude the affirmation of divine presence, revelation, and salvation beyond them. Neither should a broader affirmation of God's grace preclude a narrower focus on the narrative configurations of divine activity in and through Christian churches. Because the histories of the churches are important sites for experiences of salvation, they can be both sacramental agents and signs of God's salvation beyond themselves, even for those for whom Christian faith is not a commitment.

The question before us concerns the interpretive value of these agents and signs, which is to say, the hermeneutics and semiotics of the divine found in the sacramental lives of the churches and narrated through church history. Even if the churches are taken to be privileged signs and agents of salvation, by the very nature of the self-emptying grace they intend to signify they must abandon such a privileged position in order that they may have in them "the mind of Christ" (Phil. 2:5). Christian churches and communities of faith that would follow Christ must also heed his saying that in order to find their lives, they must lose them. Yet by their very nature, as we have already seen, the processes of traditioning and historical remembering of church history both tend toward holding on to the past, maintaining and even restoring it to memory. What is important here to affirm is that the theological meaning of "losing one's life" is not found in forgetting, but in remembering the past. It is not a matter of eliminating historical memory, but increasing it among the churches and the world Christian movement. The answer to the question regarding God's presence in the world is discovered through remembering more history, not less.

Narratives of History and Hermeneutics of the Divine

If churches are signs and agents of salvation in the world, they must share in some sense in the fuller realization of divine salvation that they signify. In the configurations of church history we discern something of the universal character and identity of the divine (although never unambiguously). God's self can be said to be revealed (not exhaustively) through the narrative of events in which God has been active.[11]

For most Christian theologies, the primary location for these events is the canonical text of the Scriptures, which narrate the formative stories of Israel's life and Jesus Christ. Particular histories of the Christian churches after the close of the apostolic era have generally been accorded derivative, if nevertheless equal, revelatory value as hermeneutical tradition. The structures and traces of their history have offered resources for interpreting divine activity in the world, resources that become available through the narratives of church history. At times, the doctrine that *extra ecclesia nulla salus est* ("outside the church there is no salvation") has tended to close off perception of salvation beyond the institutional walls of particular Christian churches. At other times, however, the biblical narratives of the universal historical horizon of salvation have challenged Christians to look beyond their own institutional life and experiences in faith.

Within their own lives, churches have often found particular events or experiences to hold the hermeneutical key for their larger historical experience. Certain events within the history of a church which, at least in the eyes of the interpreters of that history, manifest more clearly the divine presence and activity are lifted up in their identities. So the Council of Nicaea, the organization of Franciscan missions, or the Protestant Reformation take on a certain privileged status in various historical accounts of the churches. Such identities are never simply given amidst the conflicts and changes of history, but are always being constructed and reconstructed in the ongoing narrative interpretations churches offer of their histories. It is not God's self which the theologian of history attempts to construct from the historical memory, but a coherent interpretation of God's identity as it is configured amidst historical conflicts, divergences, upheavals, and change.

Over the course of generations of time, ecclesial identities are constructed out of difference and change. The church historians' narratives in this regard do not exhaust the mystery of God's personhood, but will often provide an interpretive whole that seeks to manifest divine intentionality through events of time. Change and discontinuity are the very stuff of historical experience; one need only to pick up a church history text to read of changes and differences in the churches through time. But if history is by definition that which is different, historical narration seeks to render differences understandable, coherent, or meaningful.

Historical narratives link differences across temporal spans through the semantic devices of a plot, creating a coherent story which, when supplied with adequate explanation and description, enables readers to make sense of the story, or to get its meaning. Through their imaginative constructs and narrative coherences, historians provide a figuring of the whole, which gives the theologian (if not always the historian herself) a figure of the identity of God. Faith communities summarize and expand on these narratives through corporate and individual practices of liturgy, fellowship, and service. They do so with varying degrees of blending, reflective of the impure nature of historical identity, and with varying degrees of change, as their histories remain open-ended. The identities that churches construct are in turn offered and taken on (to a greater or lesser extent) by those within them. Such identities are the way in which the boundaries of particular communions or communities are negotiated, their differences (both ecclesial and nonecclesial) articulated, and thus their inner lives constituted. By taking on the identity of a community of faith, one becomes identified with its history, and by extension one becomes identified with God, a process often simply referred to as salvation. The transformation of one's self and community is necessarily a transformation of one's identity through that of the community, and such transformation is both reflected in and accomplished by narration. Hence the salvific value of ecclesial narratives of identity.

Identities are never singular and static, nor are we given closed ecclesial narratives in the construction of them. To speak coherently of church life and church history, we must speak of identities and histories: of pluralized, divergent, and even transgressive historical narratives of events; of churches that change (narrated as growth or decline) over time; and ultimately of the nonidentity of churches with one another (heresies) or with their own historical pasts (reform and renewal). Furthermore, identities require translation over time, a discursive process that is different from narration. Where narratives overcome historical discontinuities to create coherent or continuous wholes, translations continue to mark the differences and reinscribe the otherness of simultaneous identities, establishing rough coherences but never full commensurability between (or among) them.

In terms of historical identity, narratives can be translated from one location to another, but their meanings do not remain the same. In the end the practice of translation leaves identities external to one another, while at the same time the open-ended character of narratives and identities leaves open the question of a future in which such differences are overcome. For this reason both narration of ecclesial identity and translation among them in an ecumenical context are tasks which an ecumenical theologian must keep before her.

At this point, however, we must raise a concern about the reductionism that narratives accomplish, for in overcoming differences that which is considered different can easily be discarded or subsumed. For any historian to tell a narrative of the past requires a significant amount of reduction, condensation, and even suppression. In the selectivity of the historian, we have already noted, ideological commitments and prejudices are always at work, rendering accounts of the past from particular points of view or social locations. Moreover, the historical past is never completely visible or transparent to historical observers seeking to find its traces and recount them in narrative form. Crucial evidences concerning the historical past can be, and quite often have been, lost. This is the case with the history of the St. Thomas Christians in India, for example; despite a sizable body of oral and legendary material, documentation that would count as historical evidence has been lost or destroyed, obscuring the historical reconstruction of the tradition.[12]

Then there are situations where the history of a community has been intentionally obscured, or rendered opaque, at least to a significant number of those seeking historical understanding. These are often histories and historical identities which, to invoke the metaphor employed by W. E. B. Du Bois at the beginning of the twentieth century, exist behind "the veil."[13] African Americans, argued Du Bois in *The Souls of Black Folk*, live with a "double consciousness," one of which exists behind the veil of oppression otherwise known as "the color line." This other consciousness remains fundamentally opaque to the dominant community of oppressors. The opacity behind the veil extends, says Charles H. Long, to the language, culture, and historical memory of persons of African heritage in the United States.[14] The specific meaning of the history of the other remains invisible to the historiography of domination, or of the dominant class (which are in the end one and the same). It inhabits an alternative historical space and offers an alternative historical narrative of meaning and identity.[15]

Charles Long's analysis doesn't contradict the statement of William Clebsch, quoted at the head of this chapter. Clebsch implicitly acknowledges the presence of Christianity's other histories, although he appears unable or unwilling to assign them narrative significance. While not excluded from his historical vision, they remain nevertheless opaque to it. The suggestion that Christianity has not been exclusively a European religion at the beginning of a book that studies it exclusively as a European religion should be enough to alert us to a presence beyond the European narrative of Christianity, which Long asserts is intimately bound to the religion of the oppressed. In that case the narrative of world Christianity is not so much a story of the march of the church across countless borders as it is the transformation of the Christian movement in new social and cultural locations. This is also why the history of world Christianity can only be told through various narrations providing the identity of Christians in diverse social and cultural locations today.

The period we are currently living through has witnessed a radical transformation in this direction. In what some are calling a paradigm shift, Christianity has been transformed from a religion numerically and ideologically dominated by its North Atlantic forms, to being a truly global and multicultural religion whose numbers are predominantly in the southern hemisphere.[16] In this process the rise of contextual theologies has facilitated a new appreciation for the local and the particular in the historiography of the churches, along with a new awareness of the cultural diversity of churches and their theologies.[17] This is true not only among communities whose cultural roots lie outside the domains of a European cultural heritage (in Asia, Africa, or Latin America, for instance), but among those of the North Atlantic world as well. Churches and denominations long dominated by Western European cultural expressions have begun to experience diversification in both the form and content of their faith. While we might dispute the extent to which the shift has actually been realized within any one church, or within world Christianity as a whole, the fact that a shift of some sort is taking place is hard to deny.

Here the challenge to engage in historical reinterpretation is also an opportunity to participate in historical transformation. Appreciation for the cultural diversity of contemporary global Christianity can bring about an increasing interest in the historical diversity of the Christian movement through time. The degree to which the Christian churches have manifested diversity historically is not an easy question to answer. Before doing so we would need to consider what actually constitutes diversity, or whether mere succession in time constitutes continuity.[18] No doubt there is a great deal of diversity of expression in

Christian life in the world today. We need to ask, however, whether what is often represented historically as the greater unity and uniformity of church and theology in the past is itself a historical reality, or whether it is instead a product of imperial domination of Christian historiography practiced in the past; in which case it is not the diversity of the churches *per se* that has changed, but the domination of theology and historiography by churches maintaining imperial memories of Christendom.

One could safely assume that both suggestions are true, that the degree of diversity we find in the church today is a change from the more uniform experience of the past, and at the same time, that the Christian past was not as uniform or monolithic as the historiography of the religion made it seem to be. We need not determine the precise levels of either dominance or diversity in this case, nor could we without invoking some nonexistent historically objective point of view which, I have already argued above, does not exist. By the same token we can take note of the changes in power relationships which are taking place in our own era of church history, and allow them to inform our re-reading of both the historical past and the past's historiography. We could thus affirm that churches of the past were indeed more socially and culturally diverse in their structures and practices than the dominant historiography of Christianity represented them as being; in which case it is the power to narrate, closely associated with the insurrection of subjugated knowledges, that has made the difference in contemporary ecumenical historiography. Narrating the transformation of Christian faith can then be seen as a part of realizing the transformation of the Christian faith, and vice versa.

The Master Narrative of Church History: A Critique

At this point my task is not so much to assess the current state of church historiography as it is to re-read the long narrative of church history in light of the emergence of local and contextual theologies world-wide. The emergence of these new theologies through the insurrection of subjugated Christian knowledge across the past century has been accompanied by more local and genealogical approaches to church history. The project of Black theology, for instance, has been accompanied by a significant body of scholarship investigating African-American religious history. Feminist theology and women's history have likewise emerged hand in hand over the course of the past century. There is already an enormous, and growing, body of historiographical scholarship delving into the study of particular episodes or histories of the churches. Yet, for the most part the overarching narrative of Christian historical identity has remained fairly well fixed in the historical canon, and in the discipline of church history as a whole.

This longer story of the Christian church I call its master narrative. It is for all intents and purposes what passes for the overarching narrative of

Christendom, which is what is often better called Western (or European) Christendom. Its basic plot is familiar to anyone who has read a church history text, and it continues to shape the curriculum of church history not only in schools of religion in the North Atlantic, but virtually everywhere in the world where Christian history is taught. According to its configuring, Christianity emerged from first-century Judaism and spread almost exclusively through the Greco-Roman world, first among Jews of the diaspora but quickly among Gentiles or "pagans" as well. By the beginning of the fourth century Christianity had permeated every sector of the empire, and with the "conversion" of the emperor, Constantine the Great, became the official religion of the Roman Empire. Guided by the theological consensus that emerged from the teachings of the "Church Fathers," the orthodox faith of one, holy, Catholic church thus triumphed over adversaries outside and heresies within. The study of church history in the first act is the study of *Patristics*.[19]

In time the empire divided into two distinct branches which became the two branches of European civilization. The two churches that emerged (Eastern Orthodox and Western Catholic), embodying Christian tradition respectively in Greek and Latin forms, drifted apart after the fourth century and formally separated in 1054, the year in which they excommunicated each other as schismatic. For several centuries, the Latin church of the West witnessed barbarian invasions that brought about the decline of civilization (the Dark Ages); followed by the rise of a new Western imperial order under Charlemagne and the Franks who claimed the heritage of the Roman Empire and emphasized the ecclesial institutional authority of the Bishop of Rome. A new cultural formation had emerged in the East by the time of the eighth century, the so-called Byzantine empire, which continued the Roman imperial order located by Constantine in the city of Constantinople.[20] From the seventh century on the Byzantine empire faced the ascendancy of Islam which eventually converted or conquered (the difference is one of religious perspective) more than half of world Christendom to the way of the Prophet Muhammad. The city of Constantinople itself finally fell to the Muslims in 1453, and with it the Byzantine empire (although the significance of the Ecumenical Patriarch of Constantinople did not end for the Orthodox churches in communion with him).

The study of this *medieval* period of the church thus entails the history of two Christendoms, one brought to an end and the other reborn in a new beginning. In the West (the place of Christendom's new beginning), this period reached its pinnacle with the work of the scholastic theologians (the epitome of which was the grand synthesis of St. Thomas Aquinas) and the humanism of the Renaissance. The chief endeavors of Western Christendom outside its own boundaries were bound up with the Crusades against Islam which were military endeavors to re-Christianize the Holy Land. At the end of the Medieval period a new era of overseas exploration and expansion opened up as

European nations began to undergo rapid scientific and economic development, and as the Crusades against Islam gave way to a new era of exploration and discovery. The Protestant Reformation, centered in Northern Europe, is alternately considered as the last chapter of the medieval church or the first chapter of the emergence of a new civilization which is more often associated with the rise of the new bourgeois class in Western Europe.

This new period, which began after the Protestant Reformation, marked the birth of *modern* civilization. Church history during this period divided into Protestant and Catholic streams (Reformation and Counter-Reformation). The narrative also began to differentiate between social, political, and theological developments "at home" in Europe (or Christian lands) and "overseas" (in mission lands) as Christianity was carried by European colonial and ecclesial powers to non-European contexts. The North Atlantic remained the center of theological power and the only "approved" arena for the production of theological knowledge, while the mission churches that took root and grew in non-European situations were considered to be by-products of the extension of North Atlantic knowledge and power. At home in the North Atlantic world, the rise of the Enlightenment and modern secularism brought about new and vigorous intellectual challenges which were in turn the central concerns of modern theology in the nineteenth and twentieth centuries. Overseas churches (often referred to as "younger churches") fell within the narrative domain of mission studies through most of this period, with liberation and contextual theologies finally given birth in the last half of the twentieth century.

This narrative of Christendom is rather firmly entrenched in Christian theological thought. It reaches beyond the historical discipline proper in what Harvey J. Kaye calls a "grand-governing narrative,"[21] or François Lyotard calls a "meta-narrative,"[22] broadly influencing Christian theological studies and pastoral practice. Left unexamined, it functions as a working mythology (often behind the scenes) shaping methods and content of other theological disciplines such as systematics, preaching, ethics, pastoral care, or biblical studies. Left uncriticized, it functions as a working ideology, reasserting the dominance of the North Atlantic world and European-centered modes of knowledge/power. The message this master narrative conveys is not only that Christianity is historically the religion of European civilization, so that to tell the history of Christianity is to tell the religious history of Europe; the Christian tradition becomes incarnationally European, and the solidarity that tradition achieves with the historical past is a solidarity through narrative strands of Western cultural history.

In recent years the discipline of church history has witnessed a growing sensitivity to the ideological components of European domination that inform the narrative, without mounting a successful challenge to the basic contours of the narrative itself. Such criticism has in fact been going on for more than a century, in various forms taken up in either religious or political ideological terms. One can mark the reassessment of the "Europeanization of Christianity" thesis with the publication of Adolf von Harnack's massive, multi-volume *Lehrbuch der Dogmengeschichte* in 1886-1890 (translated into English as *History of Dogma*). Harnack's history argued that Christianity was essentially Hellenized during the Patristic era, a process which in his narrative was configured as a corruption of the original faith. For Harnack, this process reached a certain conclusion in the Protestant Reformation, which marked both a return to biblical Christianity and the end of unified Christendom.[23] While he did not advance directly the thesis that God was at work in these events of the Protestant Reformation, his narrative reflected a Protestant theological working assumption that events of the sixteenth century have authoritative status, as tradition. At the same time, the predicament created by the end of unified Christendom set an imperative before the reader for continuing historical activity, which by the end of the nineteenth century when Harnack wrote was part of the background for what would become the modern ecumenical movement.

Harnack's history was explicitly dogmatic, and intended to address questions of a more normative theological nature. A somewhat different perspective can be found in what is arguably among the most important textbooks of Church history in the North American context this century, Williston Walker's *A History of the Christian Church*.[24] First published in 1918 and reprinted twice more (in 1959 and 1970) before being totally revised for a third republication in 1985, *A History of the Christian Church* is by any standard of historiography a significant accomplishment. At what might be called the micro level of narration, its pages are full to the bursting point with historical facts and analysis, covering significant individuals and movements across two millennia of Christian history. Walker's history concerned itself with biographical details far more than the dogmatic themes of Harnack's history. Yet the overall narrative, at what might be called the macro level, was one of triumph, although tempered by a sense of the complexity of historical events.

Walker's long narrative of the struggle, controversy, and triumph of Christianity traced the religion's emergence from Judea and Galilee across the Mediterranean world of the first century of the common era under Roman imperial rule. Nurtured in the twin intellectual matrices of Judaism and Hellenism, Christianity spread west and north to the imperial cities of Rome and Constantinople, a spread that was only possible because of the triumph of the Pauline doctrine of freedom from the law. In contrast to Walker, Butterfield stated his theological evaluation of Rome's role in the spread of Christianity quite explicitly: "The Roman empire of the first century A.D. appears to have been providentially ordained for the purpose of facilitating the Christian mission to the Gentiles."[25] Walker's *A History of the Christian Church* was far more subtle in its evaluation, leaving instead to the selection of data the impression that the Roman imperial context provided the historical basis for the development of the Christian church and its doctrines.

According to Walker, in the Roman imperial context of its early years Christianity confronted a twin crisis: at the doctrinal level, in the form of Gnosticism, Montanism, and other heresies; and at the political level in the form of opposition from Roman imperial power itself. The triumph of the church over the former came in the form of the triumph of the *logos* doctrine in the West, the story of which occupied the greater portion of Period One of Walker's history, "From the Beginnings to the Gnostic Crisis." The triumph of the church over the latter was narrated in Period Two, "From the Gnostic Crisis to Constantine." Its conclusion came with the Emperor Constantine's embrace of the Christian religion in 312, an event that Walker called a "fateful union."[26] Under Constantine, who became the ruler of the entire Roman world in 323, Christianity was not only legalized as a religion, but was promoted by the imperial regime. This was a status that, except for a brief time under the emperor Julian who died in 363, Christianity would thereafter retain within the Roman world.

Already by the fourth century, however, tensions among the various geographical regions of the Roman empire were beginning to manifest themselves as tensions among churches. Many of the controversies around heresies reflected cultural and geographical divisions among peoples of the empire. Period Three of Walker's narrative was entitled "The Imperial State Church." In that section he divided his attention almost equally between developments in the Greek- and Latin-speaking regions of the empire. Such was not the case for Period Four of the narrative, however, which covered the early Middle Ages and which, for Walker, began after Pope Gregory the Great and the end of the sixth century. Now the historian's attention was not so balanced: the churches of the western, Latin-dominated regions of the empire were given more than thirty pages of attention by his text, while the Greek-speaking churches of the eastern regions received only two. Thereafter the eastern churches disappeared almost completely from Walker's narrative horizon, which was narrowed almost exclusively to the history of western European peoples and nations in his Period Five.

Period Six, "The Reformation," formed the climax of what had now become a narrative of Western church history, occupying more pages than any other single period of Walker's text. The history of the Reformation in turn branched into multiple narratives of national churches articulated historically as parallel developments and dominated by the story of German and Anglo-American Christianity. In the denouement of Period Seven, "Modern Christianity" remained dominated by German and Anglo-American Protestantism, even as it began to witness a new global spread of the Christian churches. The ideological development from imperial Rome to the modern age of European-American nations was secured in seven periods.

NARRATIVES OF CHURCH HISTORY   91

Despite the historical coherence of Walker's narrative, finding any common intellectual thread through this massive work that could be explicitly deemed as having revelatory value is virtually impossible. The absence of a perspective that could be considered theological or interior to the life of the church gave the work a scientific or objective flavor which lent a certain agnosticism to the question of permanent theological values. Walker indicated as much in the opening pages of the text where he wrote:

> Christianity entered no empty world. Its advent found men's minds filled with conceptions of the universe, of religion, of sin, and of rewards and punishments, with which it had to reckon and to which it had to adjust itself... Many of these ideas are no longer those of the modern world. The fact of this inevitable intermixture compels the student to distinguish the permanent from the transitory in Christian thought, though the process is one of exceeding difficulty, and the solutions given by various scholars are diverse.[27]

On the surface, then, it would appear that this historian of Christian thought was concerned only with the transitory in that thought, and the persons and movements who shaped it. The permanent, which we can assume to be that which has revelatory value or represents the enduring truth about God, appears to escape the historian's grasp. Or perhaps it is truer to say that for Walker, *consensus* among historians concerning what is permanent escapes them. Each, it appears, is left to become a student on her own, making for herself the distinction between what is transitory and what is permanent, cognizant of the manner in which the transitory is what the historians deal with, yet strangely assured that the permanent is intermixed with the transitory. The nature of this intermixture is hardly spelled out in the pages of the text that follow. The problem, it would appear, is that whatever such an intermixture might have been taken to mean in the past, the rise of modernity, with its particular rational and scientific world view, renders the ideas of the ancient Christian world (and perhaps those of the medieval and premodern Reformation worlds as well) strange and alienating. The rupture of modernity appears to have severed for Walker a simple intermixing of the divine and the human in church history.

Herbert Butterfield offered a slightly different point of view concerning what now prevents a simple intermixing of these two. Butterfield too believed there were two dimensions to the history of Christianity, the mundane and the profound. The mundane, however, he tended to consider not so much in terms of modern rationalism as in the political formations of Christendom—ancient, medieval, and modern. He was explicit concerning what he regarded as the relationship between this mundane dimension of social-political life and the profound level of faith or belief which could only be lived out on the individual level of commitment. For him, history was not merely the intermixture of the two, but the transformation of the mundane (what Walker calls the transitory) by the more profound (what Walker calls the permanent) dimension of the Christian religion. Faith is required, Butterfield argued, to see such transformations; otherwise one would only see a continuing course of worldly events.[28]

Butterfield's language of transformation implies a narrative unfolding of progress or development, of church history moving across successive ages or periods in a generally positive direction. Walker's *A History of the Christian Church* also suggests as much. The history of the church, in the pages of the text, unfolds through a series of triumphs and advances, stretching across seven periods of time, in a geographical movement which is generally to the north and west of its beginning point. In other words, the historical direction of the Christian church is from Palestine to northern Europe, then westward across the Atlantic to the United States, reaching a kind of double-*telos* or conclusion in the original text, in German and North American church histories. The early period of church history that witnessed the triumph of the Catholic church whose life, sacraments, and doctrines communicate the presence of the Risen Christ ended with the "fateful union" between Church and state under Constantine. The imperial arrangement under Constantine became a theocratic state after Gregory the Great in the West, a condition that would continue after the Reformation of the sixteenth century in the national Protestant churches. The narrative branches of modern Christianity then grow from the multiple national trajectories of Protestant churches and missions. Broadly seen, the entire story of the Christian church becomes situated within the horizon of the modern European–North American world, whose questions of national formation and modern philosophy shape the history of the churches.

All three of these historians—von Harnack, Butterfield, and Walker—would agree wholeheartedly with Clebsch that Christianity has been almost exclusively a European religion prior to this modern age. While in its contemporary expression it is culturally diverse, it appears to them to be bound entirely to a European past prior to the modern era, of dominant imperial formation. The history of Christianity is represented in these texts (and indeed in virtually every introductory survey or compendium of Christian history) as being a European cultural history for the far greater part of its first two millennia of history. This long European narrative expands only toward the end of its second millennium, in the modern era, to become more inclusive of the multiplicity of human experiences and cultures beyond the political and cultural borders of European civilization and the North Atlantic world. The cultural diversity of the Christian churches beyond various European forms appears to be confined to relatively short periods of time, at the dawn of the Christian movement and then again toward the end of the modern era.

The ideological effect of this grand narrative is to make the contemporary diversity of world Christianity a product of the modern expansion of European and European–American missions. The diversification of a singular, orthodox Christian tradition comes very late in the long narrative of Christendom, and then has no organic or theological connection with whatever diversity was experienced and expressed in early Christian history. In Protestant historiography the shift from being a European to a world church is often linked to the expansion of Protestant churches through foreign missions and colonialization.[29] Karl Rahner maintained a similar three-fold narrative of history for Roman Catholic identity, differing from the historians examined above only in the later date to which Rahner ascribed the shift. For Rahner, Vatican II was the theological watershed that marked the dogmatic end of the modern European church and the emergence of a world church.[30] The opening of Rahner's third period might be moved back by Protestant historians to an earlier date, but the effects remain the same: the emergence of truly "world Christianity" is confined to being a modern or postmodern event and to the creation of modern Europe.

Rahner's thesis is reflected in the pages of the ambitious Roman Catholic history that was first outlined in 1958 and began to appear in print during the period of Vatican II. Under the general editorship of Hubert Jedin, the *Handbuch der Kirchengeschichte* is a multi-authored history translated into ten volumes in English under the title, *History of the Church*. Its overall purpose is "to give a reliable account of the principal events and leading figures in Church history."[31] In a longer historiographical essay that opens the first volume in English, Jedin argued:

> Church history is not the Church's cabinet of antiquities; it is her understanding of herself and therefore an integral part of ecclesiology. He who studies the development and growth of the Church in the light of faith enters into her divine-human nature . . .[32]

Church history is thus not the history of Christianity. Where the latter examines external historical events and their meanings, the former seeks the transcendent, inner elements of the life of the Church. Like any other history, Church history is bound by its sources and seeks the causal connections among events. But beyond these, "Church history as a whole can be understood only as the history of salvation: its ultimate meaning can be apprehended only by the eye of faith."[33] Ultimately, profane history and salvation history will become one and the same, so that the history of the church and the history of the world will teleologically coincide. The inner theological character of salvation is found now in the grand narrative of church history, however, which thus passes from being a particular history to a universal one.

The universal character of church history itself then can be figured at the end of the narrated time. Jedin quotes Pius XII's 1955 address to the Tenth International Congress of Historians, where he stated, "the Catholic Church is not identified with any civilization."[34] Such nonidentification is recent, however; the narrative of *Church History* only reaches the ends of the earth in the later volumes of the work. The Church first expands and forms within the Greco-Roman world, then undergoes Germanization where it becomes the inner life and direction (entelechy) of the West. Only with the breakup of the West is the church then planted through missions world-wide. From there it engages the modern global world of industrialization, secularization, capitalism, and revolutionary change. The Preface to Volume 10, *The Church in the Modern Age*, summarizes again this narrative sweep in a concise way:

> the Catholic Church, which has ceaselessly claimed to be universal, has actually become a world-church in our century. Restricted in antiquity essentially to the lands around the Mediterranean, cast back in the Middle Ages to the West by the encircling Islamic wall and the Eastern Schism, and still Europe-oriented in modern times despite the world-mission that had got underway, it developed in the twentieth century into a world church.[35]

One of the central themes of the narrative in these volumes is explaining the delay in becoming a world-church, narrated as a deferral in missions. The first volume makes several scattered references to the church outside the Greco-Roman world. After that the history goes silent on churches and events outside the unfolding Greco-Roman-Germanic-Western European tradition, other than to narrate conflicts with Jews, the Orthodox churches of Byzantium, and Islam. Consolidating the inner life of the Church in the West occupies the vast majority of pages in the work. Volume 4, *From the High Middle Ages to the Eve of the Reformation*, finally realizes that goal. This period "for many appears to have been the high-water mark of Christian civilization."[36]

Jedin's own "Preface" to Volume 4 informs the reader that the editors decided to separate this volume from the following Volume 5, *Reformation and Counter Reformation*, giving Volumes 3 and 4 over to the theme of the making of the Western Church, and Volume 5 to the "shattering of Western Christendom in the Reformation and in the Age of Confessionalism, together with the opening up of new lands through voyages of discovery and the missions. . . ."[37] But then without explanation, Jedin notes that "The beginnings of missionary work in Asia, Africa and America, which belong chronologically to the present volume [4], are only treated in Volume 5."[38] In other words, while the beginnings of the church in Asia, Africa, and Latin America might appear to belong *chronologically* to the high period of European Christendom, *thematically* they are related to the shattering of Christendom.

When they finally are narrated, the origins of Asian, African, and Latin American missions are related as a "springtime" that is part of the Roman Catholic movement of Counter Reformation and Reform. Mission history progresses and then stalls in Volume 6, *The Church in the Age of Absolutism and Enlightenment*. Missions are only briefly mentioned in small chapters in Volumes 8 and 9. Churches in the world beyond Christendom only enter the story at the end of Volume 10, and there consciously on the periphery (coming after the main lines of theological development of the mid-century).

The short historical genealogy of the churches outside Western Christendom in all of these works renders the churches theologically dependent. They lack a longer, more authentic form of tradition of their own. Whatever their theological accomplishments might be, they can only be considered as historical additions to, modifications of, or deviations from what is essentially a grand European religious history. In its stronger form this master narrative makes Europe's religious history, or a portion of that history, revelatory and binding for Christian communities of faith whose historical-cultural identity is not derived from Europe. The "human" element in the divine-human character of the church is European; and since Western European history was in its high period essentially Christian, the history of Western civilization is essentially revelatory in a way the histories of other cultures are not. Without always saying so explicitly, this is the effect of much Christian historiography: one studies a predominantly European history in order to learn the meaning of Christian faith wherever one may be, or be from, on earth.

Such a meta-narrative of church history allows the diverse Christian cultural experiences, communities, and theologies of Asians, Africans, Native Americans, and Pacific Islanders at most two or three centuries of history of their own, before they are traced back to being grafted onto the more narrow narrative stem of European church history. Often in such construals church history is depicted as a tree (a tall pine, suggests Justo González) with a main trunk (the Western European–North American narrative) and smaller branches taking off occasionally along its growth which are marginal to its overall upward development.[39] In either case the main or exclusive trajectory of Christian history moves westward, from the Orient to Europe and North America.[40] To be a Christian appears to require one to claim European ancestry, whatever the actual genealogy of one's ecclesial identity might be.

Such an exclusive historical identification of Christianity with a dominant, imperial European past displaces the dynamics of other social and cultural realities, however long or short the history of the latter might be. It denies churches and peoples who do not recognize our/their story being told in the grand narrative of church history the possibility of a history of our/their own, confining us/them to the negative historical and theological space of the non-European. The archive of Christian historical identity is maintained in European cultural lands, and continues to be maintained by Western European communities of faith.

Non-European church history can only be configured as an absence, which in turn leads to the assertion of the absence of God from history which is outside Europe (and thus by definition outside the church). The story of churches that are not grounded in European history and culture can only be fitted into the framework of the master narrative as latecomers to church history, and then only through displacement, suppression, and alienation—all acts of violence that pass for theological conversion. Furthermore, the rupture this master narrative poses between the historical churches of European ancestry and the contemporary churches of the Two-Thirds world of the South renders the greater portion of "authentic" church history inaccessible or irrelevant to the contemporary theological inquiry of the latter. The province of church history from the ancient and medieval periods is assumed to belong exclusively to communities and individuals of European descent. The assent of persons of African, Asian, and Native American historical-cultural descent can only be registered through the displacement of these identities, taking on a history that is not one's own.[41]

Wittingly or unwittingly, the meta-narrative thus constructs two classes of Christians, and renders most of the churches of the world today global "children" in relation to their European "parent(s)."[42] Even though some of the non-European churches are now recognized as adult children by the parent church or churches, they are situated in narrative relationships that are generational and paternalistic. As global children of a Western parent, they are "offspring" through Western missionary expansion. Within the framework of the master narrative, those churches and communities which claim to be cultural and historical heirs of the Western European past—primarily churches of the nations of the North Atlantic, but including those of the European nations of Australia and New Zealand—are parents who sent out missionaries from the eighteenth through the twentieth centuries. The "younger" churches founded by European missionaries are regarded as if they have no direct historical claims to a Christian tradition on their own, for they cannot rightfully lay claim to having a European heritage, and without such a heritage they cannot claim to be institutional inheritors of the tradition. The meta-narrative that renders some churches younger makes them appear to have, instead of an immediate relationship to the sources of Christian faith, a mediated relationship. Their access to the Christ of faith is mediated historically by the missionary activity of modern Western European churches.

Lest it appear that I am drawing this historiographic conclusion too sharply, I cite as an illustration the essay by Ulrich Koepf published in the volume, *Towards a History of the Church in the Third World*.[43] This particular article is doubly significant because it appeared in a text seeking to assert the basis for developing a fuller historiography of Third World church history. Taking as its point of departure the discussion concerning periodization of non-European church history, Koepf's essay represents a broad, if usually unarticulated, consensus that churches in Asia, Africa, Latin America, and Black North America gain access to the Apostolic Christian tradition, and thus to Christ, only through the historical mediation of European churches. Koepf suggests that we should think of "universal history," that is, the history of the whole of humanity or, in this case the whole of Christianity, as a tapestry. The meaning of any part of the tapestry is only grasped by reference to the work as a whole. Likewise, all local histories of Christianity must refer to the Christian whole, which has "an upper time limit" or "a clearly definable beginning."[44] He draws the implication for church historiography:

> To present a church history of the "Third World" from a regional or even a national standpoint seems to me impossible. A church history of the "Third World" can only be presented if we keep in view the essential coherence of Christianity as a whole.[45]

The purpose of doing so, he argues, is to point toward the manner in which the Third World can be included within the study of church history as a whole. To this end the Third World, he argues, has not been ignored even by European church historiography. But the Third World rightly has no independent place of its own within church history. It enters the purview of church history, which is at the same time the purview of European history, only with the history of missionary and colonial expansion beginning in the sixteenth century.[46]

> There is *one* point common to the church history of all regions and countries of the "Third World": none of them was the result of a direct revelation, an appearance of the Risen Lord. Apart from those churches whose tradition reaches back to the period of the primitive Church and belong essentially, therefore, to the ancient world, all of them owe their existence to the labours of European and North American missionaries.[47]

What constitutes the universal reference for European churches—their direct cultural and institutional continuity with the ancient churches, and through them with resurrection appearances—negatively constitutes the universal reference for the history of the Third World, and for churches of the Third World. The presence of churches of the Third World in universal church history is for Koepf marked by their absence. European history shares the same horizon as Christian history; European churches have an unmediated relationship to the resurrection by virtue of tradition, constructed culturally and historically as a European heritage. The relationship of churches of the Third World to the resurrection, on the other hand, is mediated through missions. European history and the Christian religion appear to be identical from this perspective, which is held by many Christian theologians and church historians. So absolute is this identification that a respected historian of Christianity such as Owen Chadwick can call attempts to de-Europeanize Christian history ridiculous.[48]

The question we must ask at this point is whether the history of the Christian churches is adequately or accurately configured as an *exclusively* European narrative. Even the most Eurocentric forms of the master narrative of Christendom have recognized the continuing existence of churches beyond Christendom, but these have been regarded as marginal to the mainstream of Christian history. This same marginal status, outside the mainstream of the dominant Christian tradition, lends itself to their retrieval in an age that has begun to appreciate history from the margins of society and culture. The manner in which many of these traditions have been rendered "heretical" by the dominant ecclesial memory of the tradition should not dissuade us from considering the manner in which they provide alternative means of traditioning Christian faith, especially as many of these movements represent episodes of dissent or continuing modes of resistance against the dominant political form of the tradition. The fact that these alternative traditions might have figured little in the dominant accounts of Christian tradition in the past does not preclude them from becoming significant for rendering accounts of the global Christian future in the present.

Excluded they have been from much of the configuration of Christian history written in the West. David Barrett points out in the introductory chronology of Christian history in his *World Christian Encyclopedia* that until the middle of the fourteenth century of the common era, less than half of the world's Christians resided in what is known today as Europe. The rise of Islam in the seventh century of the common era set in motion a historical process of conversion which eventually witnessed many of the world's Christian communities in Africa and Asia becoming Muslim. With the fall of Constantinople in 1453, even the ecumenical patriarch of the Eastern Orthodox (or Chalcedonian) churches was no longer located within imperial Christendom. Nevertheless, significant communities of Christians continued to exist in Asia and in Africa, many of them under Islamic rule. The assertion that Christianity has been exclusively a European religion for most of its 1,900 years, which undergirds the conclusion that Christianity has an exclusively European heritage, is not historically accurate. However dominant in numbers and power the Western European church became after the fifteenth century, it is not the sole historical trajectory of Christian tradition. Even Kenneth Scott Latourette, one of the primary architects of the grand narrative linking world Christianity to a European identity through the modern missionary movement and Western colonial expansion, qualified the thesis as a relative one:

> Until almost our own day, Christianity has been confined chiefly to one cultural stream, that of the Occident. *To be sure, Christian minorities have from time to time been widely spread among peoples of other cultures.*[49]

Like Koepf's acknowledgment of non-European churches whose traditions reach back to the ancient church, Latourette's qualification suggests that the

European experience of Christianity can not be regarded as exclusive, even if it has been dominant. The historical dominance of Christianity in a European form can not remove the historical origins and development of churches outside Europe, even if it seeks to suppress them. However much the horizon of the modern European colonial metropolis might have seemed to extend a singular narrative identity across the world, post-colonial and post-modern churches remember something different. The diversity which seemed to present a problem to many within the churches in the modern ecumenical era now is being embraced as the solution to the problem of imperial domination in the period after modernism.

Yet this does not necessarily mean that Christians and churches can, or must, abandon historical identity nor the long memories which the master narrative of Christendom was able to hand over as tradition. To this end the following chapter will seek to go back over the ground of early Christian history, and to construct an alternative paradigm to the master narrative, one that will be tentatively described as an interlocking field of ecumenical (or world) Christian traditions. In the diversity of historical traditions found even in the earliest period of the Christian past, we find resources for the diversity of the Christian churches of the future.

6 | A Genealogy of Christian Histories and Traditioning

Finding the real identity beneath the apparent contradiction and differentiation, and finding the substantial diversity beneath the apparent identity, is the most delicate, misunderstood and yet essential endowment of the critic of ideas and the historian of historical developments.
—Antonio Gramsci[1]

... we can embrace multiple perspectives out of the New Testament without collapsing the diversity and without dissolving the tension, because we know that truth is more complex and mysterious than one formulation.
—David Rhoads[2]

Genealogies and the Diversity of Historical Memory

Different communities of Christian faith hold differing memories of the past. They have different histories and different identities. This is the simple truth of our ecumenical era. There is no single set of experiences, no single collection of historical memories, that is common among all Christian communities of the world today. Christians of the world do not agree on the boundaries of their canons, the significance of common events in their pasts, or the essential dogmas of their faith today. They did not do so at the time of the beginnings of the movement in the days of the apostles, and have not done so over the course of their 2,000 years of history. Vatican II's "Decree on Ecumenism" says it well:

> However, the heritage handed down by the apostles was received differently and in different forms, so that from the very beginnings of the Church its development varied from region to region and also because of differing mentalities and ways of life.[3]

Whatever our theological evaluation of the situation might be, the Christian churches of the world are diversified, and often divided. The divisions are often painful, and without doubt often contradict aspects of the message of the gospel itself which calls on its hearers to love their neighbors. The "Decree on

Ecumenism" continues by noting that "the lack of charity and mutual understanding" are also causes for divisions among the churches.[4] But if we suspend judgment for a moment concerning whether particular theological positions are orthodox or heterodox, and whether a particular community is schismatic or a member of the One, Holy, Catholic and Apostolic Church, we can only be amazed by the great diversity of historical manifestations of collective Christian identity.

On the other hand, Christian communities of faith have much more in common than might at first appear to one who is surveying the theological landscape. Despite the controversies and tensions that have separated them, individual Christians and churches have been influenced by one another, and have mutually defined one another in subtle, and often not so subtle, ways. All major Christian communions or faith traditions now have formal and informal organs of dialogue, and all are involved at some level in various ecumenical endeavors. A great deal of historical and theological dialogue has taken place over the years even in situations of overt controversy or disputation, as opposing sides have engaged in mutual polemics and discord. Furthermore, historical and cultural influences tend not to respect the dogmatic ecclesial boundaries churches have so often labored to erect. Ideas have a way of seeping out of one community and into another. People cross over the ecclesial frontiers of denominations and communions, bringing with them much from their former traditions and identities, contributing to the reshaping of the ethos of their new church locations.

Christians who are different often find when they have had the chance to spend time together in worship and praxis that they share much in common with one another in their faith and understanding. Christians of the same communion, on the other hand, often find themselves in worship and praxis with different identities and commitments which can, over time, effectively divide them from one another. No model of history is adequate that does not account for both the convergence and the divergence of collective human experience. No understanding of tradition is accurate that does not account for both the centripetal and the centrifugal forces at work in time.[5] Finding identity beneath the contradictions and diversity within identity (as Gramsci said in the passage quoted at the head of this chapter) are the concerns of both the historian and the theologian of Christian tradition.

Among the factors that keep Christian churches and communions of the world divided are the different memories that they maintain. But such historical memories are not found evenly dispersed across the field of ecumenical life. The history of Christianity, as any religious history, has witnessed the distorting effects of the exercise of domination and coercion, obscuring some memories and enforcing the canonization of others. Hence the search for commonalities among the differences and differences among the commonalities is hampered by the unevenness in historical memories within and among Christian histories and traditions. Some of these histories are well known and easily accessible in the archives of ecclesial memory. Others are more obscured, intentionally hidden, or only fragmentarily available in the archives of traditions. The ecumenical project of dialogue requires a more intentional exploration of the latter in order for it to go forward.

The methods by which one uncovers and interrogates historical traditions that have been subjugated or hidden for significant periods of time (often for many generations) are necessarily different than the methods that have been commonly employed for writing the history of the dominant ecclesial communities of the West. Different ways of reading different records in the archives of traditions are needed if we are to begin to uncover lost or hidden histories.[6]

Charles Long has referred to the historiography that the oppressed practice to recover these histories and historical identities as " 'crawling back' through one's history."[7] When the practice is explicitly linked to relationships of power, it constitutes a historiographical practice that Michel Foucault referred to as a *genealogy*. Foucault, in turn, traced this historiographical method to the philosophical work of Friedrich Nietzsche (a genealogy of the genealogy, if you will). Contrary to the common sense notion that since history moves "forward" in time (from the past to the present), historiography must move in the same direction, Nietzsche argued that historiography begins with the location of the one who is telling the history, and moves backwards into time to interpret and transform the past. Thus he argued:

> the cause of the origin of a thing and its eventual utility, its actual employment and place in a system of purposes, lie worlds apart; whatever exists, having somehow come into being, is again and again reinterpreted to new ends, taken over, transformed, and redirected by some power superior to it . . .[8]

History, in other words, is a process of the present outstripping the past, and of every present being eventually outstripped by futures which cannot yet be imagined. Historiography involves fresh interpretation of events through which previous meanings and purposes are adapted, reconfigured, and even transformed. The meaning and purpose of the past are not given so much by it to the present as they are given to it by the present generation of interpreters. It is a conclusion none of us can escape, that however much we might hold ourselves accountable to the contours of the past, we who inhabit the present cannot finally dictate what others in the future will ultimately deem to be the meaning of our actions, or the worth of our endeavors. No matter how much we attempt to shape the heritage we will hand on to them, in the end the task of narration outstrips the lives and events that supply the content for the narrative.

Nietzsche's historiographical investigations raise explicitly the issue of power, and specifically the question of who has the power to narrate. His genealogical method seeks to expose the specific and detailed workings of power. A genealogy may operate on the same field of historical experiences and evidence traversed by the historiography of domination, but it does so seeking to subvert the "tyranny of globalising discourses," said Foucault.[9] It is "the union of erudite knowledge and local memories which allows us to establish a historical knowledge of struggles and to make use of this knowledge tactically today."[10] Thus a genealogy entertains the claims of local, discontinuous, and illegitimate historical knowledges—knowledges which have in many cases been separated from their material social locations, or knowledges which have been partially (if not totally) erased by the effects of domination. Nietzsche's own genealogy of morals pursued the origins of bourgeois Christianity in order to disclose a subversive identity behind its mask of timeless truthfulness.

Following him, Foucault argued for a genealogical conception of history which engaged in analysis of the details and accidents of every beginning, and of the descent of "numberless beginnings whose faint traces and hints of color are readily seen by a historical eye."[11] Through such genealogies he sought not only to uncover the power exercised by claims of timeless origin, but to uncover hidden knowledges, and to trace their dispersion through the domain of social practices, thus bringing into play their full subversive power.[12] A genealogy thus does not seek to render the opaque histories transparent to the dominant historiography, but seeks through the mechanisms of an alternative historiography to empower the opaque in the quest for freedom. The method uncovers dangerous memories, memories that hold subversive power.

J. B. Metz has argued that even the dominant churches of European civilization contain such dangerous memories in their liturgies and theologies.[13] More prominent has been the presence and the effects of dangerous memories among the oppressed, as James H. Cone has demonstrated concerning the African-American historical-cultural ground out of which Black Theology emerged.[14] The invisibility of the African-American religious community in the antebellum south and the cultural synthesis achieved by the union of Christianity and African religions invite genealogical methods of historical investigation to uncover their effects and transmission.[15]

Genealogies also suggest blended and hybrid memories, bringing about historical connections not previously anticipated or engaged. The multiple trajectories of one's family tree do not necessarily interact in their own time and context, but are joined by later events in which families and trajectories merge. Family genealogies often join previously separated histories in unique configurations that were unexpected and even unwelcomed by their various progenitors. So it is with intellectual and cultural genealogies which narrate the merger of previously separated trajectories of history. The resulting historical configurations are blends, and understanding them entails narrating multiple historical trajectories through time. As Homi K. Bhabha argues, we can be in the same temporality with different historicities.[16]

All historical occurrences are hybrid to some extent; the genealogy merely uncovers the dimensions of their hybridity. In doing so, it subverts the pretensions of historical singularity at work in the narratives of a singular historical community or truth moving through time. If, however, they narrate the historical disjuncture and originally discontinuous episodes of time, genealogies also narrate the coming together of unlikely, yet actual, historical junctures in which blending and mixing have occurred. They not only narrate the ruptures and fractures of historical experience, but the connections which overcome these and make of the past a genealogy and even a tradition. It is this third aspect of the genealogical method, which is not emphasized by Foucault, but which finally makes for a narrative "of our own," that we must finally examine in searching for a narrative of Christian history and tradition.

This is the dimension of "connection" which is often associated with Dilthey's conception of historical consciousness. Through it, historical research and writing reflect a deeper connectedness of living, historical relationships. A genealogy need not reduce the ruptures and disconnections of history in order to establish the connection of the present to its multiple pasts. Quite the contrary, it is precisely the ruptures and crises of history that the genealogy seeks to narrate, opposing any overarching transcendent teleological claim which might reduce the significance of the events of crises and change. Not the unified history of Spirit, but the manifold diversities of historical incarnations of Spirit in different times and locations on earth provide the content for the genealogies of Christian tradition.

The task of church history is thus not to be constructing a singular identity, but uncovering the diversity of identities that characterize Christian communities. An adequate historiography of the Christian church must seek to convey something of the pluralism of the past, in order to account for the diversity of contemporary Christian life. The global diversity of world Christianity today requires a more diversified understanding of Christian tradition than that which is given in the dominant master narrative of Western Christendom and its tribal historical consciousness. Postcolonial, postmodern narratives of church history must be more global than the master narrative of modernism if we are not to remain captive to the political imperialism of Western Christendom. The struggle against cultural and political imperialism within the Christian churches today requires a reconsideration of the master narrative of world Christian tradition.

Fortunately for this struggle, the Christian faith has indeed demonstrated an extraordinary pluralism of expressions and incarnations in history, beginning with its earliest texts and experiences. These differences have themselves been seen by Christians of the past as indicators and effects of God's universal grace. The unifying tendency, the drive to reduce the options and expressions of faith, has not gone unchallenged through the long history of the Christian movement. One need only to read the history of those considered by the dominant churches to be heretics and dissenters (or to read the history of Christianity *as* the history of heretics and dissenters) to see the diversity of Christian traditioning at work. It is from the perspective of cultural diversity that the idolatries of ethnic, imperial, or national history can be criticized.

The linkage between political/cultural diversity and the critique of the idolatry of political/cultural identity is seen in a letter from an anonymous Christian author in the second or third century who wrote concerning Christians:

> They reside in their respective countries, but only as aliens. They take part in everything as citizens and put up with everything as foreigners. Every foreign land is their home, and every home a foreign land.[17]

It is only when every foreign land becomes recognized as a homeland that the idolatries of homelands can be effectively criticized or made a foreign land.

But the faith and identities of homelands do not remain permanently separated or distinct from one another. As we have already noted, cultural identities have a tendency to seep across historical political boundaries of power that separate peoples from one another. Cultural ideas and influences migrate, as do the peoples to whom they initially belonged. New hybrid identities result, which by their very nature bear within themselves a critique both of the initial power arrangements that sought to keep cultures separated, and of any ongoing analysis that would conceal their mutual interaction. The theme of cultural hybrid identities opposing imperial history and imperialism is reflected in the work of the contemporary literary critic Edward Said, who himself represents the hyphenated identity of Palestinian-American. Of the "hybrid counter-energies" at work in history Said writes:

> The authoritative, compelling image of the empire, which crept into and overtook so many procedures of intellectual mastery that are central in modern culture, finds its opposite in the renewable, almost sporty discontinuities of intellectual and secular impurities—mixed genres, unexpected combinations of tradition and novelty, political experiences based on communities of effort and interpretation . . . [18]

To make his point, Said then quotes the twelfth-century Christian writer, Hugo of St. Victor:

> The person who finds his homeland sweet is still a tender beginner; he to whom every soil is as his native one is already strong; but he is perfect to whom the entire world is as a foreign place.[19]

The progression suggested in Hugo St. Victor's words, from a tribalist to a multiculturalist and then beyond, is suggestive for ecumenical historiography today. The place where one can feel at home within several existent traditions or identities is not itself the stopping point. Discovering one's history and tradition to be blended and mixed is not, in and of itself, enough. For we are always moved beyond these, by history itself ironically, to what the twelfth-century Anglo-Saxon monk called "a foreign place," which I take to be the beginning point for the re-creation of tradition. In the end the indicator of re-created tradition is not to be found in rendering every foreign land native, but in rendering every native land foreign. The mission of the Christian movement (to draw on a language that has more often in the past been used to describe the process of churches crossing boundaries of identity) is not to coerce others into taking on a particular Christian identity, so much as it is to convert Christian identity to new, and indigenous, modes of religion and spirituality.

Multiple Trajectories: A Genealogy of the Early Christian Movement

It is in search of a more politically and culturally diverse tradition that the genealogy of the Christian movement (re)turns to the historical narrative of Christian tradition. What we find at the beginning of Christian history is already genealogical diversity. The movement that was born in the West Asian Jewish context under Roman political rule was, from its inception, multiple and pluralized.[20] The Judaism in which Jesus of Nazareth was nurtured gave evidence of being affected by complex cultural influences from Persia and the Hellenistic world. The land of Israel lay at the crossroads of empires whose armies have swept across its borders for centuries, leaving behind a well-scarred landscape and opening its borders to new cultural waves of influence.

By Jesus' time, various parties or schools of practice had emerged within Judaism, which Josephus, the Jewish historian of antiquity, referred to in Greek as *hairesis*, (the etymological basis for "heresy"). Judaism in both Israel and the diaspora was divided over ways of reading and understanding the heritage of Temple and Torah. The earliest Christian movement, called the "Nazarene party" (*Nazoraion haireseos* in Acts 24:5), emerged from this context as a new party or movement, following the messianic way of Jesus of Nazareth but situated among the other parties in Judaism. The Nazarenes themselves were not of one mind regarding the message and meaning of their faith. Careful readings of the four Gospels and the various Epistles from different geographical and theological perspectives that compose the canonical books of the New Testament show not only diversities, but conflicts emerging among the family and followers of Jesus. Thus conflict and controversy were already found within the early Christian movement as well as between the movement and other Jewish groups in the first years following Jesus' death and resurrection.

It was conflict with the religious authorities in Jerusalem, according to the book of Acts, that first scattered the followers of Jesus to other cities outside the land of Israel. There they began to take their message beyond the members of the Jewish synagogues in the diaspora to persons of other religious and cultural identities. Wherever the Christian message spread in other cities of the ancient world, it quickly began to engage the cultural and religious forces in those places. By the end of the first century (and well before the canonization of the Christian New Testament) Christianity had taken root in new cultural locations and had undergone translation into new languages.[21] In some cases it appears that Christians seemed to forget, conceal, or repress crucial aspects of their inheritance from Judaism. In others, new meanings or insights emerged from the process of translation, which is always also a process of transformation in meaning.[22]

The greater part of the Christian movement continued to maintain its essential continuity with the faith traditions of Israel, however discontinuous this might have appeared to be to those who were opposed to them. Adherents read the Hebrew scriptures, although by then usually in the version translated into Greek. They continued to look to the city of Jerusalem as the symbolic and eschatological center of their messianic movement because their movement had emerged, according to the book of Acts,[23] from Jerusalem following the events remembered as Easter and Pentecost, spreading in multiple geographical directions before heading west toward the city of Rome.

These multiple narrative and linguistic trajectories of faith are symbolized in the diverse linguistic communities represented before the Apostles on the day of Pentecost in Acts 2:8-13. It is theologically significant for Luke that the events on that day included Parthians and others who resided outside the boundaries of Roman imperial rule. The episodes in Acts 8:26-39, of the Apostle Philip and the conversion of the Ethiopian royal treasurer, and in Acts 10, of the Apostle Peter and the conversion of the Roman centurion, Cornelius, suggest the Christian message spread in multiple directions, which finally leads in the book of Acts to the Apostle Paul preaching in Rome (28:16-30).

The dominant narrative trajectory of the book of Acts itself is theologically that of the Apostle Paul, or Luke's traditioning of Paul. The book culminates with his journeying from Jerusalem to Rome, the imperial city of Caesar, but in chains. Yet Paul's is not the exclusive trajectory of Acts, nor was it for much of the early Christian movement through its first centuries of existence. A genealogical reading of the book of Acts invites the reader to consider these several narrative trajectories initiated from the Day of Pentecost in Christian history. The city of Rome represented the symbolic end of the ecumenical endeavors of the Apostolic age for Acts, and the conversion of the emperor represented the end of the ecumenical endeavors of the church through the patristic era according to many (if not most) of the Christians of the Mediterranean basin and the Greco-Roman world on whose eastern shores Christianity had been born. Yet even from within this world an important sign of Christianity's truth and meaning was discerned in its ecumenical appeal beyond the boundaries of the Roman Empire and Greco-Roman civilization. Many early Christian teachers, writing from within the boundaries of Greco-Roman culture, referred to the spread of Christianity among peoples outside the Roman Empire as a validating sign of their faith.

The cluster of peoples from the Jewish diaspora who are reported by the writer of Acts to have heard the Gospel in Jerusalem at Pentecost are Parthians, Medes, Elamites, and other residents of Mesopotamia. Early Christian traditions follow the story of Christianity moving eastward to Edessa, a city just east of the Euphrates river and thus beyond the border of the Roman Empire. The name of the Apostle Thomas, one of the original disciples of Jesus, is closely associated with the founding of the church there in the middle of the first century of the common era.[24] Thomas is also recalled as the apostle who journeyed to India in or around the year 52, to establish Christian communities in both the southern and northern regions of the subcontinent.[25] The story of Thomas evangelizing in India in the first century of the common era, while historically unproven, still grounds the tradition of the Mar Thoma churches in that land today.[26] Questions concerning the historical accuracy of the traditions of Thomas in Edessa, India, and other regions east of the Roman Empire do not invalidate the direct theological linkage that they provide to the apostolic memory.[27]

By the third century of the common era these traditions can be documented historically as distinctive national-cultural communities of faith in the East, in Syria, Persia, Armenia, and India. Their rich spiritual traditions, including the forms of monasticism practiced among women and men, and their liturgical contributions are important resources for all Christian traditions.[28] During the fourth and fifth centuries, as Christianity in the Roman world adjusted to its imperial embrace, the tradition of Persia in particular developed a distinctive identity other than that of being Roman and imperial. After the fifth century, the major expressions of Christian tradition east of Antioch were considered to be heretical by the imperial churches of the Roman world. The Armenian and Syrian traditions were condemned as Monophysite, and the Persian or Assyrian church as Nestorian.[29] While the Syrian churches remained within the imperial orbit of Roman political control until the advent of Islam in the seventh century, the Armenian and the Persian or East Syrian churches (usually referred to as Nestorians by the Chalcedonian churches of the West) were beyond the Roman imperial domain.

The Armenian church was closely related to the ruling regime of the kingdom of Armenia. The Persian church, on the other hand, existed as a minority religious community, from time to time tolerated by the Sasanid dynasty which came to power in Persia in 226 of the common era, but always opposed by Zoroastrianism, the official Persian imperial religion. From the Persian capital of Seleucia-Ctesiphon, the patriarch of this church looked first to the school of Antioch, and then later to Nisibis, for theological direction. Theodore of

Mopsuestia (350-428), first accepted as orthodox but then later condemned in the West, was considered the standard of orthodox teaching in the Persian East where he was called "the Interpreter." His status and influence in the Persian church were roughly comparable to that of Augustine in the Latin church of the West. Theodore gave the Persian church its exegetical methods and its emphasis on the humanity of Jesus, the reason it was called Nestorian in the West.[30]

The comparison of the role of Theodore in the Persian East to Augustine in the Latin West suggests further parallels as well. In the late eighth to early ninth centuries under Islamic rule, the Persian patriarch, Timothy I, claimed the Persian church to be the inheritor of the See of Peter, similar to the claim more often made by the Bishop of Rome.[31] Indeed, an observer who was privileged to survey the entire situation of world Christianity at the turn of the first millennium would have readily recognized the Persian Christian tradition alongside the Latin and Greek traditions as one of three equally rich historical trajectories of Christian faith.[32] Possessing vigorous missionary tradition,[33] at its height the Persian church reached from the Euphrates to the border of Korea, spanning a distance of some 5,000 miles across Asia.[34] At the peak of its historical growth under Islam, the church numbered some 250 dioceses with fifteen metropolitan provinces among Persians and Mongolians and five missionary provinces in China and India.[35] David B. Barrett estimates that the total number of Christians within the Persian church reached twelve million by the year 1000.[36] The fact that this church was eventually decimated and brought close to the verge of annihilation by the end of the fourteenth century, after the conversion of Mongolian and Turkish conquerors to Islam, and especially during the reign of terror under Tamerlane at the end of the fourteenth century, does not diminish its significance for churches of the world today.[37]

The Persian tradition of Christianity was theologically articulated through a series of six synods held from 410 to 544. (Moffett cites an initial synod of Seleucia in 315 as well, but no records from it have survived.[38]) These six synods not only unified the Persian tradition, but coincided with the separation from the Chalcedonian traditions of the West. Stephen Gero notes that the Byzantine influence is quite obvious in the first general synod of the Persian church in 410, held during the patriarchy of Isaac.[39] A Byzantine imperial envoy jointly presided over the synod with the Persian patriarch, and the synod both endorsed the faith of Nicaea and recognized the eminence of the See of Constantinople.[40] It also represented the extension of toleration to Christians in Persia, however, and the independence of the patriarch of Seleucia-Ctesiphone from the bishop of Antioch as well. By the third synod in 424, which met after a period of renewed persecution, no representative from Constantinople was present, and the patriarch of the Persian church was declared equal to any other patriarch East or West, free from the administrations of any Western bishop. Such a declaration of administrative independence became necessary for the survival of the Persian church after the formal conversion of the imperial Roman order to Christianity in the fourth century, for Rome was the imperial enemy of Persia. By the fifth century, the political suspicion of Christians within the Persian empire combined with the theological legacy of Theodore of Mopsuestia to give the eastern church its distinctive contours.

The Persian church's long experience of being a minority religion and opposed by the officially recognized imperial religion was in many ways an impediment to its life of faith. On the other hand, the Persian church did not experience a radical change in its political fortunes with the Islamic defeat of the Sasanid dynasty and the resulting establishment of the Islamic caliphate in the middle of the seventh century. Many Christians eventually converted to Islam, but overall the Persian churches successfully adapted and survived the next six centuries under Islamic rule. If the burden of minority and oppressed status was difficult for the church within the new Islamic empire, it was not necessarily a new experience.

Things were somewhat different for the churches in North Africa following the rise of Islam and its spread across the continent. There the rise of Islam in the seventh century brought about more radical changes for the Christian churches. In many areas of Roman North Africa at the western end of the Mediterranean Sea, Christianity all but ceased to exist as the population was converted to Islam. In Egypt, however, the Coptic church did survive, and continues today as a sizeable church, albeit as a distinctive and often oppressed minority community within Egyptian society.[41] Islam did not conquer Ethiopia, where the church continues to trace its heritage to the earliest days of the Christian movement. In some sense then Ethiopia stands symbolically for the direct connectedness of African Christianity with the time of the Apostles and the early Christian movement and a reminder that the Christian religion is no stranger to the African continent, which is no empty claim for many today.

In Matthew's Gospel narrative of the birth of Jesus, Persian Magi come and worship him, while Egypt provides the place of refuge from Herod's planned destruction (Matt. 2:1-20).[42] Like Persian Christians and others from the East who found their identities represented in Jerusalem on the Day of Pentecost remembered in Acts 2, ancient African Christians found their compatriots numbered among those who heard their tongue spoken by the Apostles that day. The churches of Persia might have looked back at the extra-canonical story of the letter from Jesus sent to King Abgar, and the coming of Thaddaeus, sent by St. Thomas in the years immediately following the resurrection. But the African churches, and especially the church of Ethiopia, could trace the coming of the Christian message into their domain directly to the biblical story of Acts 8:26-40, which recounts the conversion of the Ethiopian royal treasurer through the ministry of the Apostle Philip.

Clarice J. Martin has examined the ethnographic identity of this Ethiopian traveller in Acts 8, noting the scant attention paid to this story by commentators on the book of Acts. The term Ethiopian indicated dark-skinned peoples in classical literature, and was often used to identify peoples to the south of Egypt in the Mediterranean world.[43] Martin points out that modern maps of the biblical world often do not even include Africa south of Egypt, from which this royal visitor to Jerusalem hailed. Yet the biblical traditions regularly refer to peoples of Cush, Nubia, and South Arabia.[44] Given the inclusion of the story in Luke's narrative of the church, one must include the peoples of Ethiopia within the circle of the Second Testament's apostolic traditioning of the faith. This particular person in Acts' narrative of early Christian tradition would most likely have historically been an official of the Nubian kingdom of Meroë.[45]

First-century readers of Luke's work would have recognized the parallel between the chamberlain in Acts 8:27 who is called "an Ethiopian eunuch, a court official of the Candace, queen of the Ethiopians, in charge of her entire treasury" (NRSV) and the Queen of Sheba who came to visit Solomon in I Kings 10:1-10.[46] Both came to Jerusalem; the Queen of Sheba to test Solomon's wisdom, whose fame had spread throughout civilization; the Ethiopian eunuch to worship in Jerusalem, but who had questions for the Apostle Philip concerning the prophet Isaiah. Significantly, Acts tells the story of this conversion of a Gentile prior to the story of Cornelius, a Roman centurion of the Italian Cohort, which points the reader of the book toward the West.

Historically verifiable details of the development of the Christian church in the regions of Nubia, Cush, and Ethiopia are scant prior to the arrival of the Syrian Christian brothers Frumentius and Aedesius in the Axumite kingdom south of the city of Meroë, in the fourth century.[47] Victims of shipwreck, they were brought to the court as slaves and rose in power, finally serving as regents to the infant king of Axum. Around the year 350, Frumentius journeyed to Alexandria, where he was ordained by Athanasius and assigned the bishopric of the Axumite kingdom.[48] The church was greatly strengthened in its missionary outreach at the end of the fifth century when Syrian monks, fleeing from the aftermath of Chalcedon in the Roman world, took refuge in the regions of Ethiopia and Nubia which were beyond the Roman imperial domain and sympathetic to the Monophysite form of Orthodoxy which the Syrian and Egyptian churches also embraced. These two latter regions became predominantly Islamic after the seventh century, while the Ethiopian empire remained predominantly Christian. Theologically, on the other hand, after the fifth century both the Egyptian and the Syrian churches were more closely related to the Ethiopian church, which today remains in communion with the Coptic bishop of Alexandria.[49]

The Monophysite doctrine, which emphasized the singular nature and personhood of Jesus Christ after the incarnation, was strongly defended by the theological school of Alexandria, and the wider church in Egypt.[50] It is to Alexandria, then, that the genealogist of early Christian history turns to understand better the theological identity of the Ethiopian and Egyptian churches.

This is not the Alexandria of the master narrative of Western Christendom, however, for that Alexandria turns "heretical" after Chalcedon and is "lost" to Islam. Rather, it is the Alexandria that is African and hybrid which is a resource for theological retraditioning today. The city of Alexandria, like Egypt as a whole, was a meeting place for religions and cultures in the ancient world. In the first century, Judaism, Hellenism, Hermeticism, and other streams of indigenous Egyptian tradition all flowed there. Later, Gnosticism and Manichaeism flourished, often blurring the boundaries between orthodoxy and heterodoxy.

Early Christian tradition credits St. Mark the Evangelist with being the first bishop of Alexandria, and indeed there are historical arguments for the possibility (if not veracity) of the tradition.[51] The city itself is often called the leading intellectual center of the Hellenistic world at that time. Its theological (or catechetical) school developed under Pantaenus, Clement, and Origen likewise was arguably the most influential Christian educational institution of the first centuries of the Christian movement.[52] The city gave the early Christian church movement some of its most important and most influential theologians: Origen, Clement, Athanasius, and Cyril, to name only a few. Following the intellectual lead of the Alexandrian Jewish theologian Philo, the city's Christian teachers became noted theologically for their doctrinal emphasis on the *logos*, and exegetically for their allegorical interpretations of Scriptures. But even where Alexandria's theological emphases were not shared, its ecclesial impact was keenly experienced.

Alexandria affected the theological configuration of Christianity in Egypt, but the monastic movement in the desert to the south gave distinctive shape to its Christian spirituality. These two streams of Egyptian Christianity developed in a critical relationship to each other, even when they followed different pathways or trajectories of practice. The desert monasteries often harbored criticism of the excesses and impieties of the church and its hierarchy in Alexandria. Yet it was Athanasius, the bishop of Alexandria and one of the most important defenders of the Nicaean trinitarian orthodoxy, who wrote the *Life of Anthony*, "[t]he most widely read text on early Egyptian monasticism."[53] At that time the desert monasteries appear to have been the refuge of theological beliefs which came to be suppressed by the church hierarchy as heterodox, as the discovery of the Nag Hammadi manuscripts buried in the Egyptian desert for 1,500 years suggests.[54] Nevertheless, the spirituality of the desert fathers and mothers remains a widespread and enduring contribution to all branches of world Christianity.[55]

Perhaps even more important for the genealogist of early Christian tradition, the theological stance of Egyptian monasticism of Antony, Pachomius, and Shenoute represented expressions of Egyptian Christianity that were opposed to the excessive Hellenization of Alexandrian theology.[56] In the final analysis, Egypt was a colonized land, and the Egyptian or "Coptic" language and culture were those of a colonized people. Under Greek and then Roman rulers, the people of Egypt suffered under heavy tributes and agrarian exploitation, which is why the coming of Islam was seen by many as a movement of liberation and not a conquest. But even prior to the rise of Islam, from their location in the Upper Nile region the spiritual teachers of the desert embarked on an Egyptian movement of Christian resistance and reconstruction, one which would reach deeply into the Latin and Greek church traditions as well.[57] The political importance of Egyptian monastic teachers has sometimes been obscured by suspicions raised against their heterodoxical beliefs. Interpreted through the lens of their cultural identity, however, the rigorist monastic life they promulgated can be seen as a form of protest and resistance against the growing accommodation of Christianity to the dominant culture and politics of the Greco-Roman world.

A similar theology and praxis of resistance can be seen in the indigenous theological movements of North Africa west of Cyrenaica, an area which was also under Roman imperial rule but more closely related to the Latin-speaking church of Rome. This section of Africa, referred to as the Maghrib, was during the period prior to Islam one of the more Christianized regions of the Roman Empire. Theologians of the stripe of Augustine, Tertullian, and Cyprian all claimed it as their home. As a region under colonial domination, it was also a place of resistance against Rome, politically as well as ecclesially.[58] The history of Christianity in the Maghrib abounds with movements and groups considered heretical from the dominant Catholic perspective, but many of these were motivated by resistance to imperial domination. W. H. C. Frend has called one such North African movement the "Champions" (called "Circumcellions" by Catholic opponents), who emerged around the middle of the fourth century (just after Constantine the Great), "a movement of protest reflecting a tradition of martyrdom that harked back to Maccabean examples [from Second Temple Judaism]" and "the first Christian group to aim openly at the overthrow of the existing social order and a complete reversal of its values."[59] They formed in effect the "left wing" of the larger Donatist movement, which was likewise anti-imperial in its focus.

The Donatists emerged in the fourth century out of the controversy over the church's policy toward readmission of *traditores*, or those who had appeared to betray their confession of Christian faith during periods of imperial persecution. Donatus, who was from the southern part of Numidia near the Sahara, was elected as an alternative bishop of Carthage in 311 by a dissenting party opposed to readmission of *traditores* to the ranks of the clergy. The Donatists refused to recognize the legitimacy of the sacraments dispensed by such *traditores*, leading to full schism between Catholic and Donatist churches. This is at least the usual theological reasoning given for the division of the North African church. Frend's work suggests other reasons as well, however. The rigorism of the Donatist church regarding the readmission of traitors to the faith is part of a wider ethical rigorism characteristic of North African Christianity, not unlike the monasticism of Egypt. In the case of the Donatists, Frend argues, this rigorism was closely linked to local cultural resistance against Roman colonialism, and the protests of peasants and the urban poor against the ruling classes of the Latinized cities.[60]

Frend's argument has not been without its critics, among them the historian Peter Brown who has sought to demonstrate the cultural diversity within the tradition of Catholic Christianity in its early centuries.[61] Nevertheless a genealogist of early church history cannot help but be tempted by the conclusions he draws, not only concerning the North African Donatist church, but concerning the wider history of "heretical" movements among the early Christian churches in general. I quote Frend at length, to catch the full impact of his point:

> It is interesting to note, in conclusion, that Donatism does not stand alone as an example of a dissenting form of Christianity which found acceptance in the villages and among a population little affected by classical culture. In Asia Minor, for instance, contrary to the general practice among the Catholics, the Novatian bishops often had their sees in villages, while their councils, at Pazos in 368 and Mylukomé in 515, met in villages also. The epitaph of a Catharist priest Eugenius, at Bash Hüyük, speaks of the deceased as a "tower of courage to the poor, and in the village pre-eminent over all." The tradition of dissent from the Catholic religion in some parts of the country seems to have been continuous. A prophetic Church was succeeded by a Montanist, and a Montanist by a Novatian. In Egypt, too, the centre of a similar tradition of dissent against the official religion of the Empire was in the Thebaid, in the villages of the Upper Nile, and its leaders, as Schnoudi [Shenoute], were Copts who knew of Greek civilization only in order to hate it. In Egypt and Asia Minor, as well as in North Africa, the "heretical" form of Christianity struck deepest root where native linguistic and cultural traditions were most vigorous.[62]

The political and cultural dimensions of Frend's genealogy of dissent are important to note, for otherwise these "heretical" movements appear to be simply fallings away from the one, true faith. The places we have looked at briefly in considering the diversity of early (Apostolic) traditions—Edessa, Persia, India, Ethiopia, Egypt, and the Maghrib—plotted along a map form an arc around the eastern and southern boundaries of the Roman Empire. They offer early Christian traditions from the periphery of the Roman imperial Christendom, and thus are not only generative traditions in their own right, but offer resources for resistance against the master narrative of imperial Christendom. Much of their oppositional character against Roman imperial Christianity was taken over by Islam in the seventh century of the common era, which swept a major portion of these regions of the world into its new imperial order. In Egypt and Persia in particular, Christian churches assumed a new minority status which they continue to hold today. Nevertheless, the demise of these churches, and the erasure of their memory from master narrative of Christendom, does not preclude their return in the contemporary postmodern world of global Christianity. In our own situation the genealogy of early Christian traditions invites us to develop a more positive understanding of their witness of resistance over against the master narrative of Christendom.

My quick survey of the multiple traditioning of Christianity during its first six centuries pointed to the development of Christian churches and significant traditions in Persia, India, Ethiopia, Egypt, and the Maghrib. What we see at the beginning of the sixth century of the common era is not a Christendom flowing through the twin streams of Greek and Latin traditions, but Christendom which is already embodied in multiple trajectories of tradition. Several of these were within the domain of Roman imperial power. But others appropriated aspects of Greco-Roman religious and cultural traditions, yet were themselves located outside (and sometimes in a political world hostile to) Rome's dominion. Christianity was a transregional religious faith, long before the modern missionary movement of the West. In Peter Brown's vivid description of the ancient world:

> Like identifiable beads, found scattered from a single, broken necklace, archeologists have discovered fragments of Christian texts that speak of basic Christian activities pursued from the Atlantic to the edge of China. Both in County Antrim, in Northern Ireland, and in Panjikent, east of Samarkand, fragmentary copy-books—wax on wood for Ireland, broken potsherds for Central Asia—contain lines copied from the Psalms of David. In both milieux, in around AD 700, something very similar was happening. Schoolboys, whose native languages were Irish and Soghdian, tried to make their own, by this laborious method, the Latin and the Syriac versions, respectively, of a truly international, sacred text.[63]

Moffett draws the ecclesial implications even more explicitly: "The pattern at the end of the fifth century between Christianity in Asia and the West was not schism, but diversity in unity."[64] If we were to locate the date earlier, say in the fourth century before Constantine and the legal adoption of Christianity by the imperial state, we could of course include much of North Africa in this pattern of diversity in unity. Nor was such diversity only experienced among churches outside the Latin or Greek cultural contexts. An equally great diversity could have been experienced among Christians who resided in the western regions of the Roman Empire as among those beyond the imperial boundaries. Indeed, the diversity of Christianity within Western Christendom by the eighth century is the major theme of Peter Brown's book just cited. The linguistic and cultural distances that separated Noricum, Ireland, Francia, Frisia, and Germany from Rome were as great, or greater, than those that separated Rome from North Africa, Syria, and Egypt.

Genealogical Ruptures in the European Tradition(s)

Earlier in this chapter I noted that a genealogy seeks to uncover multiple origins and sources of a tradition, in this case interpreting the multiple trajectories of the early Christian movement in terms of their resistance to the formation of a Roman imperial Christendom. A genealogy also seeks to uncover the ruptures in history which narratives tend to bridge, undermining the transcendent trajectory of a singular historical narration. It looks for the places where the narrative has been told in such a way as to cover the fractures of family histories. The genealogist is interested in the historical fissures and breaks, in this case the ruptures in the unwavering succession of the One Holy Catholic Church which comes to be identified with Western European history. Locating these historical ruptures serves to uncover the dimensions of power at work in historical narration, exposing the construction of what appears to be a transcendent identity out of local narratives. It also emphasizes the contextual nature of theological traditioning as well, as new contextual social and cultural situations are engaged dialogically in and by churches seeking to inherit (or pass on) tradition.

The rise of Christianity itself was announced by its first generation of apostles as a radical rupture or break with what had gone before in history. The early Christian messengers self-consciously proclaimed the community following Christ to be living in a new messianic era, an apocalyptic age which expressed the fullness of time (*kairos*). The Apostolic message proclaimed that a radical break between the aeons had taken place, brought about by the inauguration by God of a new age. What was effected by this break was not the annulment of the covenant and promise given in the past to Israel, however, but their fulfillment or realization. "This is that which the prophets of Israel had proclaimed" was the message the Apostolic movement sought to communicate.

This new eschatological age lengthened in time, however, and the promised return of the Messiah appeared delayed, requiring teachers within the movement to articulate a more subtle connectedness between the ages. The first instances of this are found in the pages of the Second Testament itself, with the fuller connection with Israel's past and the scriptures of Israel seen in both the Gospels and the Epistles. As the Christian movement spread beyond its initial Jewish adherents into the Gentile community of the Roman world, a generation of apologists emerged to forge the intellectual connections that linked Christ and the Apostolic movement with the history and tradition of classical Greek and Roman cultures as well. This became a standard rhetorical practice of the Christian community within the Roman world. Indeed, the rapid growth of Christianity within the Roman Empire is partially explained, according to historian Averil Cameron, by

> the capacity of the great Christian preachers and writers to accommodate themselves to the modes of discourse that already prevailed, and thereby almost to take their audience by stealth, in particular by laying claim to past history.[65]

Through these strategies of proclamation and discourse, Christian teachers brought about a break with the cultural past among their hearers (through the practice of conversion), at the same time they reformed a connection with the cultural past of their hearers (Justin Martyr's doctrine of the universal *logos*, for instance, or Augustine's use of Rome to symbolize the eternal city of God). The effect of such teaching was to create a sense of rhetorical continuity where historical discontinuity was being experienced. This historical rupture took place not at once, but over the course of several centuries, giving time for the writers and teachers of the Christian movement to work out the details of their strategies. By the time the break between the classical and the Christian periods of history around the Mediterranean became obvious in the fourth century, a full historical and theological discursive tradition was in place to articulate the change in providential terms.

Another such break began in both the Greco-Roman and the Persian worlds in the seventh century with the rise of Islam. While it is beyond this book to undertake a genealogy of Islam, certainly the rhetorical strategies demonstrated in the Holy Quran, in relation to other "peoples of the Book," in later Muslim teaching regarding Christians and Jews, and in the absorption by Islam of much of classical Greco-Roman learning suggest discursive parallels with the earlier Christian movement. In both instances, the power of religious narratives of revelation and conversion gave meaning to historical change and discontinuities, recovering the pre-revelation and pre-conversion past, and integrating it meaningfully within the new faith as its working history.

In these two cases the change was one of religious faith, and the rhetorical narrative strategies employed seek at once to ameliorate and articulate the disruptive effects of conversion. Furthermore, both of these major historical events—the conversion of the classical Greco-Roman world to Christianity, and the conversion of a major portion of Christendom to Islam—are figured within the grand narrative of Christendom itself as radical moments of change— as beginning point and as end-point for at least a portion of the Christian world (the so-called "loss" of North Africa to Islam). A no less significant historical break, or series of breaks, occurred within the history of Christendom, however, yet one that is figured as considerably less discontinuous by the grand narrative of Christendom. The manner in which this latter historical fissure has been bridged by the narrative of Christendom has had considerable ideological consequence, for it has given Europe its historical identity in the inheritance and continuation of classical Roman culture.

Early in his text on *Christianity in European History*, Herbert Butterfield alerted us to the disjuncture within the narrative. Christianity, he wrote, spread into the Mediterranean world "in the days before a 'Europe' in the historian's sense of the world had as yet come into existence at all."[66] The civilization of this Mediterranean world into which the early Christian movement spread joined together Greek, Roman, Egyptian, and West Asian political and cultural forms. One cannot easily advance the claim that Alexandria and Antioch were European cities, nor that Athanasius and John of Damascus were European theologians. One can readily argue that the church of Rome played a significant—if not a central—role in shaping the Christian faith as it developed in its first centuries. But to speak of ancient Rome as "European" in this period is anachronistic. The city of Rome was the political capital of the Mediterranean world until the fourth century when the capital was shifted to Constantinople and the empire was divided into two. Even after the fourth century Rome continued to hold a great deal of religious, if only symbolic political, power within the Mediterranean world. But this Greco-Roman civilization was not European.

Nor was the civilization that eventually came to be known as Europe the only one to claim descent from the Greco-Roman world. The heritage of the Greco-Roman civilization eventually was claimed by three separate empires: Byzantium, Western Europe, and Islam. We cannot speak meaningfully about a historical entity called Europe until at least the beginning of the ninth century, or the time of Charlemagne, Judith Herrin has argued:

> The term *Europa* is indeed used for the first time at the turn of the eighth/ninth century for the area over which Charles was nominally sovereign, an area quite restricted, therefore, compared to its modern geographical usage ... Traditional approaches, which often assume that the distinct character of modern Europe was already present in embryonic form in Charles's realm, are distorted by hindsight. A more accurate historical reading will set the "western" development within a Mediterranean context, where it becomes evident that it was one part of a much larger process, whose centre of gravity lay in the East.[67]

Herrin's point is not that political, cultural, and religious institutions that were forged together under Charlemagne did not exist prior to the ninth century. Rather, her point is that the civilization that developed in Western Europe under the spiritual direction of the religious institution headed by the bishop of Rome was a new synthesis drawing on the ancient Mediterranean world, and it shared its claim to inheritance of the Greco-Roman world with two other contenders. She goes so far as to argue that the problematic character of the claims to inheritance by both Islam and Western Europe is revealed in both societies' efforts at "inventing tradition," *hadith* for Islam and the *Donation of Constantine* for Rome.[68] But even the stronger claims for direct inheritance of Greco-Roman civilization in the Byzantium Empire does not constitute an adequate basis for asserting the European character of the ancient Mediterranean world. In each of the three cases a distinctive successor of the Greco-Roman world claimed its inheritance while undertaking the construction of a new civilization.

Certainly the emergence of a new civilization centered in northern Europe was facilitated by the cultural cohesion provided by the Christian religion, and especially by the commonality facilitated by the Latin language. The linguistic-cultural translation that Peter Brown described above, sometime around the year 700 when a schoolboy whose native language was Irish tried to make the Latin version of the Bible his own, was a part of a much larger literal and symbolic transfer of books and beliefs northward. Like the Latin language, they moved from the Mediterranean world northward and westward, to a new civilization emerging from what had previously been the periphery of the Roman world.[69] The church of Rome played a major role in communicating the classical heritage of the Mediterranean world to this new civilization, whether wittingly or unwittingly providing its ideological justification and intellectual heritage. In the long run, the effect of this transposition was to render the north European countries Christian and identify them with the classical tradition of the Mediterranean world.

Nevertheless, this does not justify asserting the unbroken continuity of a European Christian civilization which emerged after 900 with the Roman and Mediterranean world of the classical age. One is even historically hard-pressed to locate such a unified civilization called Europe prior to the modern age. The term was used essentially as a geographic term prior to the modern period when it began to serve the ideological function of providing a unified political-cultural identity. The contours of this ideology emerged at the beginning of the modern period in the colonial enterprise for which the concept of Europe served to demarcate the boundary between civilization and its periphery.[70] However great the differences and divisions were among the emergent modern nation-states of the region, the common identity of Europeanism proved to be a stronger ideological force for constructing a new center within the world political arena.

At the rise of the modern era, Christianity was already firmly established as the dominant religion of the peoples within the region that would become the ideological domain of Europe. Christian churches likewise had already had a long experience of collaboration with the dominant political powers of the region. The identification of Christian history with the history of Europe thus seemed natural for many, especially those within the dominant social classes. To be a member of a European nation was to be Christian, or so it seemed from within the constructed horizons of this religio-cultural ideology. As we have already seen, it is still the ideological perspective held by many Christian theologians and church historians, which is why a historian of Christianity can call the effort to de-Europeanize Christian history ridiculous.[71]

The historian's ridicule notwithstanding, the notion that the history of Christianity prior to the modern age is mainly European is being challenged not only by non-European Christian churches but also by churches and communities of faith within the political and cultural boundaries of Western European society. One finds challenges to the exclusivism of the dominant Christian tradition arising in many places. The homogeneous historical character suggested by the phrase, "*the* Western Church," is not an accurate description of historical reality. European Christian history is quite diverse, and was so long before the Protestant Reformation and the rise of modern denominationalism. Significant communities of opposition and resistance opposed the universal claims put forth by the dominant churches of Rome, and later those of the magisterial (or state-supported) Protestant Reformation, long before the revolutions of the modern period. This is a major objection which needs to be raised against the notion of Christianity having a European heritage: it renders singular what is in fact a diversity of European historical streams, traditions, and experiences interacting over centuries. Some of these traditions were lost to particular regions of the continent for long periods of history. Others continued to be persecuted and suppressed without being exterminated. Even in Europe, there has not been one church, one history, or one historical essence of Christianity.[72]

Many historical strands were woven together to form the fabric of the history now commonly called European. Significant among these are Jewish, Muslim, and indigenous as well as Christian religious vectors of tradition. Christianity itself came as a foreign religion to different regions of what is now considered Europe, as members of various tribes and classes professed allegiance to differing degrees. At the same time many pre-Christian traditions survived the process of conversion to Christianity, some to become integrated into local expressions of faith and theology, and others to continue as sources of resistance and dissent.

Some of these latter indigenous religious and cultural practices have survived into the modern period despite being persecuted as pagan. Even after the Christian religion had achieved near-total domination in Western Europe under the institutional head of the bishop of Rome, forces from beyond Europe's borders continued to influence churches on the continent, Islam representing the most visible such force acting on the history of Europe. The far more subtle diffusion of religious and cultural influences from further east represents another instance of forces from beyond the boundaries of Europe becoming effective in its history. Within Europe the enduring existence of Jews continues to challenge the tendency to identify European religious history exclusively with Christianity, and more recently to reform the dominant Christian community. The synthesis that Christians in churches in Europe have achieved over many centuries has prompted Raimundo Panikkar to refer to European Christianity as:

> the ancient paganism, or to be more precise the complex Hebrew-Helleno-Greco-Latino-Celtico-Gothico-Modern religion *converted* to Christ more or less successfully.[73]

What then is one to do with such a fractured, complex, syncretistic historical heritage of European Christian identity? If we acknowledge the fundamental hybridity not only of European Christian tradition, but of Christianity on a global scale, are we then left without a meaningful history, a coherent identity, which can be called one's own? What does anyone do with a genealogy that has turned up diversity where assumptions of a unitary historical past once reigned, or with a genealogy that has subverted the transcendental pretense of an uninterrupted historical heritage that could be described as a unified or unbroken "blood-line"?

To begin, the genealogy of world Christianity invites us to stop narrating the history of Christianity as the sole preserve of Europe, or the West. We should continue to narrate European church history, but only as the history of the churches of Europe. We should become more intentional about narrating the diversity of this history in Europe, paying particular attention to the narratives of the underside of history, of women, of minority communities which suffered oppression at the hands of the dominant classes and their ecclesial supporters.[74] The genealogy sketched above of the Christian churches in the first six centuries of the common era suggests resources for a more focused historical critique of the pretensions of imperial power with which the dominant churches (Catholic or Orthodox) in the Roman Empire came to be identified. In other words, the genealogy provides intra-ecclesial resources for the critique of imperial ideology and power in the emergence of the Christian tradition itself, showing such a critique not to be extraneous to tradition, but close to the very heart of its formation.

Second, the genealogy suggests that one must learn to narrate several family stories in order to represent one's historical heritage or identity. It is not enough to tell one narrative or pursue one trajectory of history to understand fully the meaning and heritage of Christian faith. The student of Christian history and the student of Christian theology alike are challenged by the genealogy of Christian tradition to learn several histories, to be able to tell several narratives, to engage several historical identities. The genealogy shows Christianity to be at its inception already a hybrid, and its diversifications to have increased with the passage of time. More options for faith, not less, are the results of church traditioning. But then the multiple configurings of history which the genealogy of tradition uncovers might be, after all, what God intends for the churches to experience. Perhaps diversification and revelation are not as antithetical as simple formulations of truth versus error, or orthodoxy versus heterodoxy and heresy have made them to appear. The process of traditioning can be one that enables us to live with two or more truths at once, to live with the differences of history as well as with the differences of global Christian community.

7 | The Grace to Renew the Past

For the critic must attempt to fully realize, and take responsibility for, the unspoken, unrepresented pasts that haunt the historical present.
—Homi K. Bhabha[1]

When they were satisfied, he told his disciples, "Gather up the fragments left over, so that nothing may be lost."
—John 6:12 (NRSV)

I began this book with the observation that the ground has shifted in world Christianity, and that these changes have implications for how we understand the Christian past. With others I share the conviction that we are moving beyond the modern age. What exactly will come after, no one is sure. Ours is a period of transitions, and one that is yet open-ended. Calling it a "post" era (postmodern, postcolonial) indicates the predicament of being beyond the end, but not quite past the beginning of something new.[2] It can alert us as well to the need to be deepening historical consciousness, not abandoning it.

The irony of remembering a modernist past that is not yet exactly past is compounded when we consider the modernist impulse itself. Modernism defined itself as *sui generis* and "just now," the age of the New which is perpetually present. The modernist credo declared it to be an age without precedent or tradition.[3] The postmodern refuses to do the same by the act of taking the modern as its past.[4] This is not to say that the postmodern is destined simply to repeat its past, or is bound irrevocably to the singular trajectory of historical fact projected by the unifying and totalizing impulses of modernity. Postmodern ways of thinking seek to be free from the transcendental pretense of modernity, articulated through their turn to the particular and the many. Postcolonial ways of remembering seek to subvert the colonial memory imposed from the metropolis.[5]

In both cases, the subversive historiographical work of localizing and remembering takes the form of a genealogy, whether or not one employs such a term. Rather than constructing a singular narrative of history, going beyond means opening up multiple memories of the past as much as multiple options for the future. On its own the "post" in postcolonial, postmodern discourses can only be considered provisional and paradoxical: provisional insofar as it marks a period of transition, and paradoxical insofar as that which is its past defined itself as the criticism of all that was past.[6]

Regarding the modernist criticism of the past, we have come to suspect that modernism did not so much live without a past as it remade the past to suit its own interests. Regarding the colonial criticism of the past, we have come to realize that by attempting to displace the cultural memory of the other, colonialism succeeded in altering the cultural memory of itself. Of particular concern for this book is the manner in which modernism and Western colonialism configured a European Christian past, which the modern West itself then sought simultaneously to abandon in the practice of Enlightenment and reproduce in practices of colonial missions. The complex social, political, religious, and cultural forces that historically formed Christendom were in the modern period reduced to a singular narrative trajectory. The resulting identification made it appear that the history of Europe was only Christian, and the history of Christianity was only European.

We could regard this, of course, as being just one more expression of European colonial hegemony, which indeed in one sense it was. Christendom represented a dominant form, or cluster of forms, of cultural and national churches, a form of the Christian religion which was entirely accommodated to the social, economic, and political power of a dominant North Atlantic civilization. But to do so would be to miss the further irony that Christendom, the dominant form of global Christianity, was itself being marginalized by the forces of modernity insofar as it continued to embody tradition, and thus continued to mediate a living past.

The shifting ground brought about by the end of modernism and colonialism has now provided us with the opportunity, if not the imperative, to reexamine the Christian past in order to reconfigure its meanings for the future. This is the renewing practice of faith called traditioning, or handing over. The content of any tradition is the past, its historical form, while its life is in the handing on. A postmodern/postcolonial rendering of tradition must of necessity move beyond the mere negation of the past that is brought about by criticism, to a new embrace of the past that is accomplished through traditioning. The practice of traditioning acknowledges that the past is not over, even if the past is different. It seeks to remember a past that is different in order to make a difference in the future. Christian theology after colonialism and modernism in particular needs to remember the Christian past (including its modern and colonial forms), precisely to make a difference for the Christian future, if not the future of all humankind.

The modern period witnessed a determined attempt to remember the Christian past through the political and cultural construct of Christendom. Throughout this book I have argued that European Christendom does not encompass the whole of the history of Christian religion, only one of its more dominant forms. The domination was expressed through hegemonic forms, leaving many still to equate Christianity with its dominant (mainline) European-American incarnations. The modern period witnessed an acceleration of the centralizing forces at work in representing this social-religious-cultural construction. In the process, the complex historical experience of world Christianity was reduced to the medieval European *Corpus Christianum*, and the latter was in turn itself reduced to a unified, and unifying, myth.[7] The westward-directed momentum of the narrative itself facilitated its easy adaptation to the dominant Anglo-Saxon ethos of the United States, situating the United States as the inheritor, end, and goal of Western Christendom.[8]

The preceding pages have argued that the historiography of Christendom gave rise to the ideological construction of a master narrative which reduced the Christian past to a singular march of history through European time. Theologically, it reduced the meaning of Christian faith, whose historical mediation was previously recognized through multiple traditions, to a single cultural form situated entirely within the history of Western Europe.[9] By reducing the traditions to tradition, a modern "Babylonian captivity" of Christian theology ensued, impressing church doctrines and dogmas into the service of a dominant cultural ideology. In the end, the history of European Christendom became normative and revelatory for world Christian identity.[10]

Fortunately for the argument of this book, this ideological captivity is not the sole heritage of Christianity in the modern period. The modern Christian archive is replete with examples of ecclesial resistance and dissent, from inside and outside the gates of Western Christendom. While the argument of this book has been that Christianity in the modern period has been dominated by a particular historiography, it has also shown that minority perspectives endured and can be reclaimed for a heritage of resistance. They survived in communities that resisted the grand schemes of being swept up into modernism's totalizing narratives in a Hegelian moment of *Aufhebung*, thereby offering resources for openings in new theological directions.[11]

In its majority form (majority not necessarily meaning greater numbers, only greater power), Christianity in the modern period sought to sustain or reforge an alliance between churches and European social-cultural life. But the synthesis was never total, nor did it completely extinguish the movements of dissent, many of which it helped to create. Minority perspectives grew like weeds in the field of Christian modernity; one loses count of the independent churches and movements that are scattered throughout the history of world Christianity and continue to flourish around the world today. They have resisted by their very indeterminacy, which has, at the same time, led them into indeterminate and unexpectedly new, rhizomatic formations.

By the end of the last century it was clear to a number of observers, even in the West, that the cultural synthesis of modern European and North American Christendom, Protestant or Catholic, had collapsed. The myth of the European *Corpus Christianum* continued to exert a strong pull on theological and historical studies through the twentieth century. But the handwriting was already on the wall for any to read in the critiques of modern Christendom being advanced in the nineteenth century. These were epitomized by Karl Marx and Sören Kierkegaard, both of whom attacked the alliance between Christianity and the new ruling social class of Europe, the bourgeois.[12] It is no mere coincidence that the master narrative of Christian history emerged within European and North American historical circles at the time the critique of Christendom was being advanced so vigorously from within the same intellectual community, for in many ways the master narrative sought to address the crisis in historical representation brought about by the critique of Christendom.

The critique of the master narrative of Christendom has not brought about the end of Christianity, nor the end of the history of the Christian churches. It has, however, brought about a crisis in the representation of Christian history through a particular narrative mode. The crisis of Christendom has brought about a crisis of the representation of Christian history and identity through a singular narrative of tradition. The power to represent, like the power to speak, was denied to those marginalized by the master narrative of Christian history whom it situated outside the boundaries of legitimacy. Outside the boundaries of orthodoxy, of Christendom, of the mainline churches of the West, theirs was an unspoken, unrepresented past—what Albert J. Raboteau calls "the invisible institution" of slave religion, for instance.[13] The crisis of European Christendom is equally a crisis of representation.[14] Representing a more adequate Christian past remains the task of the postmodern and postcolonial Christian critic.

One response to the crisis has been to fall into the trap of abandoning representations of tradition, seeking to jump back immediately across 2,000 years of history, and rejecting the mediation of tradition. The primitivist or restorationist option continues to be especially attractive to a large number of Christians in the United States, where the cultural myth of new beginnings has been particularly influential. Ironically, primitivism and restorationism in the United States have now themselves become something of a viable tradition within Protestant Christianity, with a history that stretches back more than a century into American religious life. Unfortunately, these theological responses do little to resolve the crisis of representation and tradition, other than continuously to close the eyes of believers to the crisis that confronts them. Their attraction is understandable: given the manner in which the dominant historical tradition of Christendom has succeeded in representing itself as encompassing the totality of the legitimate Christian past, those who would reject the domination and oppressions of Christendom would seem to have no other option but to reject its totalizing representations of the past.

Over against this tendency, however, I have argued throughout this book for a way of traditioning that opens up the Christian past to being remembered in common, without remembering a common history. I have argued that one need not abandon a longer memory of Christian history and tradition in order to abandon the past of Christendom that has been oppressive. There are alternatives for history and tradition from within the history and tradition of the past itself. What once appeared fixed, closed, and entirely given, can then be seen to be open, altering, and the basis for re-creating Christian tradition. For Christian communities of faith today, this insight brings with it the imperative to seek after those alternative histories, and those altering ways of remembering through scriptures and traditions. One might be so bold as to say that renewal of the Christian churches requires not forgetting the past, but a more faithful remembering of the past. In this case, the challenge would be to locate theological memories in such a way that Christians would be enabled by their past to make new futures.

Theologically, the crisis of representation can be seen as an invitation to what the gospels call *metanoia*, or repentance. The possibility of repentance is always understood biblically to be a moment of grace, an opening by God to a new mode of life which enables humankind to renew its community. In this sense the call to repentance is always also an offering of grace, the grace of conversion or change. Christians have long called on others inside and outside their churches to conversion and change. But Christians must also be open to their own change, on the basis of their own biblical and theological heritage of *metanoia* and grace. So Christian tradition must always remain open to its own conversion, inasmuch as it is to remain Christian.

These pages have sought to respond to the call for historical *metanoia* by turning from the master narrative of Christendom toward a new remembering of un- or underrepresented Christian pasts, and a more diversified accounting of church history. Admittedly the previous chapter hardly begins to do full justice to the call for a more adequate historical accounting that is faithful to the multiplicity of Christian pasts. It has only sought to point the way toward a fuller comprehension of the diversity of origins in Christian history and traditioning. It points the way toward a fuller representation of Christian tradition in its first centuries through multiple histories and historical trajectories. The cultural diversification of early Christian experience is emblematic, and not conclusive. The multiple directional movements away from Jerusalem indicate the open-ended character of early Christian self-understanding and identity, an open-endedness that continuously subverts the closures of Christendom and imperial Christian faith.

Even such a brief historical glance at early Christian history and tradition within and beyond the geographic boundaries of what would eventually become Christendom undermines the exclusivist reduction of Christianity to its dominant, imperial forms. It suggests broader cultural and historical horizons of experience than those represented by the master narrative of Christian history. The Christian movement did not reach the ends of the earth during the first several centuries of its existence, as Paul or the author of Acts might have hoped. It has yet to reach the ends of the earth today. But the ongoing awareness of Christians living beyond the cultural and political borders of each local church community effectively locates the cutting edge of identity and the borderland of their existence in the midst of their local, ecumenical community. True ecumenical consciousness marginalizes every center by moving the center of Christian identity to the margins, or periphery, of history.[15]

More adequate historical investigation of the diversity of early ecumenical Christian experiences is still needed, as is a fuller historical accounting of the multiplicity of Christian traditions from the days of the Apostolic movement. A more adequate accounting would certainly shed more light on the various ecclesial communities of descent which claim direct theological inheritance from the various ancient ecumenical churches—Chalcedonian, Armenian, Coptic, Ethiopian, Assyrian, and Indian Orthodox, for instance. It would also shed light on Christian communities of assent for whom Christianity is a relatively recent phenomenon, and whose religious and cultural memories reach beyond the borders of the Christian movement. What is needed is an ecumenical historiography that facilitates a fuller appropriation of these histories among communities in dissent, gathering up their various fragmented parts, seeing that none is lost. Such a historiography seeks justice through redemption of minority historical memories, and opens up new options for the practice of Christian faith. Representing the diversity of the Christian past, such fuller accountings of Christian history would offer alternatives in the service of renewing its future.

History as that which is past, we have already noted, has in one sense a rigidity or fixed character insofar as it is that which has already been given. The past has happened and cannot be changed. Precisely because it is past, it has a shape that cannot be altered. But history as a meaningful recounting or accounting of the past—its other sense—is neither given nor fixed by the past itself, as I have likewise argued above in the opening chapters. And it is in this interpretive dimension of the past as something which has yet to be fully constructed that the alterity of history reveals itself, precisely in its capacity for being altered. It is in this dimension of history as recounting and accounting for the past that we discovered the past to be a tradition, an effective history which is capable of being effective only if it is being handed over.

The task of effective remembering does not go on apart from the task of practicing justice. Both the past and the present are evaluated through the lens of ethical judgment. Along these lines we would do well to note once more that individual Christians and churches have before them the task of engaging in historical solidarity, that is, in committing themselves to practices of solidarity in their historical engagements. We connected with a Christian past that is wider than the one that has been represented by the dominant historiography and ecclesial tradition. There are also numerous episodes of injustice and oppression from this past which were not rectified in their own time, or which remain unsettled. They cry out for faithful remembering and call for a witness against the oppression, as part of the continuing practice of seeking justice

THE GRACE TO RENEW THE PAST 129

and peace in the world today. Indeed, the task of solidarity through faithful remembering is one that will endure until the time of the eschaton.

Furthermore, it is not just a Christian past that we must seek to remember for handing on the Christian faith. Solidarity with those who have suffered and alternative remembering both lead us to ask whether it is enough for a Christian community to study and embrace only an explicitly Christian past as its own. Here we see the historiographical significance of our theological affirmation that God has been working throughout all time and history, in the whole world (the *oikoumene*). The divine revelation of such presence in action (God's presence always being an activity) has not been confined to the geographic location where Christian churches have lived and proclaimed the good news of God's once-for-all incarnation in Jesus Christ. The work of God in creation and history has not been confined to the boundaries of the churches, or among the lives of persons who are Christian. Theologically we can affirm divine illumination through Christian proclamation and the Christian past, without asserting the divine limitation to this past. The past that shapes Christian tradition need not be exclusively a Christian past. Indeed, the study of Christian history and tradition must not be confined to studying a Christian past. Faithful study of Christian tradition *must* be open to the whole human past. An effective sense of Christian tradition has more to do with a Christian reading of the past than it does with an exclusive reading of the Christian past. Christianity is a world religion, living amidst a world community of religions, faiths, and ideologies; to understand the Christian past we must understand the histories of its relatives and neighbors.

The theological question which is often raised at this point from within the Christian circle of faith concerns the relative value or authority we ascribe to a past that is not explicitly Christian. Christianity, one often hears, is a historical religion or faith. That is to say, its fundamental truth claims rest upon historical events which took place during the first century of the common era beginning with the life, ministry, death, and resurrection of Jesus Christ. These events, and their subsequent meaning for those who experience the Spirit of Christ, are recounted as the Gospel, the good news of God's salvation. In the years following the events in Galilee and Jerusalem, followers of Jesus carried the message of his life and death, and of their experience of his resurrected presence, to new cultural environments across the world. The history of those enduring communities which formed around that message provides the basic substance for church history. The theological questions of faith and practice they sought to address provide the substance for the study of the history of Christian doctrine or dogma today.

As the message of the gospel and the communities which formed around it adapted to new cultural and political contexts, new theological configurations took shape. Looking back at these various periods and configurations of church history, we certainly benefit in our understanding by attending to the formative questions and determining influences which were brought into the church from these various cultural and historical situations. It is helpful, for instance, in understanding the complexities of Nicene orthodoxy to have a better understanding of the Hellenistic philosophical context from which the church's theologians drew much of their interpretive terminology. One need not necessarily advance claims for the divine inspiration of Plato, Aristotle, the Stoics, and other Hellenistic philosophers (although many certainly have done so) in order to demonstrate their relevance for understanding early Christian theology.[16] In such a case we would not have to argue for the Stoics to be regarded as a source of divine revelation, but for their thinking to be a means by which some in the early Christian churches illuminated the revelation they experienced in Jesus Christ. The same would then be true for any number of new religious and cultural influences which have challenged and shaped—and continue to challenge and shape—Christian traditions in other times and places.

Throughout this book I have spoken of the Christian movement and at times of the Christian church in a way that implies a more or less coherent historical subject. Through time, this subject has taken different form through local or particular churches, related to the various material and historical contexts in which they have lived. Because a church must live in its own particular age, it is related to that age, and to those who live alongside it in a common world. A church speaks the language(s) of others in a particular historical and cultural context. Its members sustain themselves through the material forms of life which others in that age share. Those within the church are prone to the same diseases and temptations that afflict others around them. At the same time, within any particular age we can meaningfully identify a historical entity called "a church" that is distinguishable from the wider world that forms its particular context. We can do so because these particular communities of faith also share in the context of Christian memory, naming the name of Jesus. They gather in his memory and experience his Spirit, taking for themselves through time the identifying name of being "Christian."

The particularities of these different churches' historical and cultural identities are of interest for Christian theological reflection, but often they are so only because they are related to Christ and the Spirit which are their defining theological reference points. Of course the historical dimensions of church life cannot be entirely obscured by their christological and pneumatological referents. Where these particularities are minimized, obscured, or abstracted from their contexts, the historical embeddedness of Christian theology and tradition is lost. On the other hand, where we have taken the intermixing of the divine and the human to be fully realized in ecclesial life, we have found a history that reveals truths which in turn gives to these histories a certain revelatory authority as tradition.

The logic here seems simple and straightforward: the study of church history is by definition the study of the history of those entities called the church or churches. It might even appear that such study would not be properly directed toward historical times and places in which Christian churches were not found. The study of church history could be considered most profitable if directed toward those historical times and places where churches had achieved political, social, or cultural dominance, or had achieved a sustained theological (that is, dogmatic) consensus across several periods or geographical locations. Church history, we might even be tempted to assert, entails the study of Christian churches in their contexts, and these contexts have been predominantly the Greco-Roman, then Roman, then modern European worlds prior to the last century. How Christ has been understood and remembered in the theologies and liturgies of these churches provides the proper study of Christian theology and the history of Christian doctrine.

Before we succumb too easily to such historiographical reasoning, however, we need to look more carefully at its theological assumptions. To begin with, this historical model poses a distinction between divine and human dimensions of ecclesial life that then allow one to speak of the church of Jesus Christ in a transhistorical way. But actual ecclesial life is more incarnational than this, and often it is impossible to separate what those in the churches themselves have considered to be of divine or transcendent importance and what are historical, sociological, or economic realities. The assumption that all Christian churches share a common theological set of referents, or have a common theological core which forms the essence of the church, is just that—an assumption, but one that is not easily supported by historical investigation. Studying the history of Christian churches does not uncover a common essence among them so much as it does differences across historical times and places. Christological, pneumatological, and even soteriological doctrines are certainly shared among many of these churches, but they provide more intertextual points of reference than they do a common essence for the church.[17]

Furthermore, historical theological reflection on tradition has often implicitly, if not explicitly, asserted that God's self-revelation, or salvific acceptance of God's self-revelation, has taken place only in those historical locations where Jesus Christ is explicitly known or remembered. The theological assertion *extra ecclesiam nulla salus* (outside the church there is no salvation) has tended to restrict Christian historical reflection as well to its institutional confinement in the church. In the last century this dogmatic assertion has been challenged by a great number of theologians from different perspectives, to the point now where few would hold it without some form of qualification.[18] A more inclusive understanding of God's offering of salvation, of God's universal involvement in the arenas of human historical experience, and of God's intentions for human community have been advanced by a wide spectrum of theologians within the churches.[19] We have already considered some of the historical implications of the theological affirmation of God's saving presence and self-revelation outside the history of Christendom. If God has been active in all human affairs, however hidden such activity has remained, the fuller investigation of human affairs through their various histories is required of Christian historical study.

Churches have pursued theological reflection and dialogue in concrete social and cultural situations through history precisely because they have been guided by the belief that the resurrected Christ goes before them into the world, and because the Spirit of the living God blows throughout all human history. Christians have sought out historical dialogue partners, including persons of other living religious faiths, often out of the conviction that the God whom they have encountered in the church is universally present throughout all human history and in all creation. Christian historical reflection might well follow a similar universal direction today, seeking to examine the insights of Buddhist history and doctrine alongside those of Hellenism.[20] A more universal approach to church history might discover that African historical experience of community is informative for understanding the early Christian interpretation of the Trinity and needs to be investigated along with that of the Latin and Northern European experiences in order to gain a fuller understanding of that doctrine.[21]

This is not to say that church history ought to be dissolved into a more general study of world history, or the history of world religions. Of course there is great value in the study of world religions and world history in their own right, apart from any explicitly Christian theological consideration or concern.[22] At the same time, church history as a discipline occupies a particular place within the community of faith that defines itself as Christian, whether or not the historians who pursue the discipline claim such a place. It is reasonable that the particularities of a community of faith's identity would significantly inform the historical scope of investigation. But focusing one's scope is not the same as limiting it.

Given the great diversity among churches in the world, one might suppose that the history of the churches, focused through their particular experiences and interests in relation to other churches and to broader historical forces around them, would give rise to a greatly decentered historiography. A full survey of church history, taking its cue not from the master narrative of Christendom but from the diversity of world Christian ecclesial experiences, would necessarily broaden to encompass the totality of global history. There would be points of common ecumenical historical experience among these different communities of Christian faith, although such points might be marked more by the disagreement they produced than by the agreement they achieved. Moreover, there would be points or experiences within each of these various communities' histories where divergent historical forces intersected to create new configurations of community life and faith. The study of the histories of these churches could not proceed without attending to the separate historical forces or trajectories that intersected at various locations, places where breaks with the past occurred and new forms of consciousness crystallized, challenging later generations to find new continuity with them. Genealogical investigation of these different communities of Christian faith through their various sites of history and memory requires of the historian a fuller articulation of the several historical trajectories or pathways which converged at such sites to (re)form a particular community of faith.[23]

For such a genealogist, it does not necessarily matter that a particular ecclesial location can claim a relatively short time of Christian faith identity. The history of Christianity in Korea, for instance, is often depicted as being only one or two centuries old—not a long narrative as far as church histories go. To tell a longer Korean Christian narrative, church historians have often opted for a mission history, which takes the history of Korean Christianity primarily to be an extension of church history from Europe and North America. A more genealogical approach to Korean church history, however, takes the events of the formation of a believing Christian community one or two centuries ago in Korea to be the site of memory at which several histories intersected. The dynamic for this event lies as much within the history of Korea as it does within the history of Western missions. Narrating the history of Korean Christianity requires that one tell the longer narrative of Korean history, in its full religious and cultural formations.

Genealogies become broader, not narrower, as they move backwards in time. The genealogy of Korean church history, or of any church history for that matter, cannot be reduced to the narrative of a single trajectory or line (in this case the history of the missionary expansion of churches in Europe) and claim to be doing justice to the overall historical experience. A more adequate historical accounting by this measure requires a fuller investigation of the various histories which were previously separate, if temporally parallel, but which intersected in the particular church's formation.[24] This we have seen exemplified by the work of the *minjung* theologians and historians in Korea, who take the history of the Korean *minjung* in their wider Asian cultural context as the subject of their work.

At the global ecumenical level, the geographical spread of Christianity in its early years serves as much as emblem or sacrament of world Christian diversity as it does the history of its realized achievement. Churches in Asia and Africa today do not often trace direct historical descent from their ancient ecumenical predecessors in these regions, some of whom were historically circumscribed or even cut off. Yet even the histories of those cut off are not prevented from being symbolically or sacramentally significant for diverse communities of faith today, who are able to embrace such histories through contemporary acts of assent. Traditions considered insignificant by the historiography of modern Christendom might become significant building blocks of the postmodern Christian world, not unlike the Christ they remember who was also abandoned only to become the cornerstone of a new age. The minority status of Christian churches such as found in the history of Persia is particularly relevant in this case, for it offers an alternative paradigm from early Christian experience in which the expansion of churches into new situations did not become absorbed by the forces of dominant imperial power. Christian churches that experience minority status today might find in this history ecumenical precedent for renewing their witness.[25]

As one would expect, the meaning of European and North American missionary expansion is greatly reconfigured in such a frame of historical reference. The movement of churches across cultural boundaries is not ignored, but the meaning of the European aspect of the heritage of these churches is reconfigured. What has appeared to many to be simply the story of the conversion of people in Asia to Christianity becomes more explicitly the story of the conversion of European forms of Christianity to an Asian religion. The same would be true for African and Latin American forms of modern Christianity. But would it not also be true even for the dominant churches of the North? Have they not also been continuously engaged in reconfiguring the meanings of the faith in response to new situations around them in the modern (and now postmodern) worlds?

Regarding the narrative accounting of European Christianity (even admitting its manifold historical forms): is it not the proper object of study for those who are of European descent? Even if Christianity in European history is understood to be subsidiary to what God is doing in the whole of the world, and if the history of European Christendom is not understood to be the exclusive domain of God's grace, is it not still possible for people of the European tribes to tell their own history from a perspective within their own boundaries? Why should those within the churches of the North Atlantic world be concerned to tell their church history differently? Even if what they previously took to be a universal history now is demonstrated to be a local or tribal history, is it not nevertheless legitimately considered to encompass the history of their tribes? Why then should the historical mediations of Christian tradition *outside* Europe be considered critical for contemporary reconstruction of Christian tradition *inside* Europe?

The histories of at least some of these other churches are often already included in some manner in the dominant historical accountings, although they are often configured as being dependent on European Christianity and therefore a function of its own historical existence. Within the construction of European Christian historical identity (including the history of Christianity in the dominant North American churches which embrace the European heritage of faith), could not the otherness of Asian, African, and African American, Native American, and Latin American histories legitimately be dissolved?

It is at this point that the importance of the wider historical existence of Christian identity prior to and apart from its European contextualization, and especially prior to the modern colonial expansion of Christianity from Europe and North America, is critical for the dominant churches of the North Atlantic world itself. The Swedish missiologist Carl F. Hallencreutz points out that while it is important for the churches of the North to recognize that the history of Christianity outside Europe does not begin with the arrival of Cristobal Colon in the Caribbean in 1492, and that Christianity outside Europe is not confined to being the underside of European history; nevertheless it has provided critical voices that are challenging European churches.[26]

Furthermore, Europe not only extended itself into Asia, Africa, and Latin America, but actively transported Africans, Asians, and Latin Americans into its own European cultural domains, often in chattel slavery and forced labor. Europe's others built the empires European churches lived amidst. The long history of African-American cultural influences in North America makes it impossible to understand European-American Christianity apart from the African influences. The increase in migrations into cities and countries of the North increases the multicultural influences that continue to affect churches there. In the end, it is impossible to understand European and North American church history in tribal terms; these histories are complex and multicultural. Certainly a more adequate history of world Christianity would serve as a critical corrective to the domination and oppression fostered by the teaching of the history of Christendom within the dominant North Atlantic world. The migrant and the postcolonial perspective are not far apart.[27]

Christianity from the North Atlantic world did become vital and revitalizing in contexts beyond Christendom through being translated into the vernacular of new times and places. Translation is not simply repetition, but a form of transformation, as many who have struggled with the task have noted. The movement of Christianity into vernacular situations, the "localizing" process that Robert J. Schreiter has pointed toward, requires such translation.[28] As Bhabha notes regarding the translations of postcolonial thought, such translation "desacralizes the transparent assumptions of cultural supremacy, and in that very act, demands a contextual specificity, a historical differentiation *within* minority positions."[29] The critical insights translation brings about in situations of minority perspectives and desacralizing politics are not necessarily confined to the communities from which they originate. Their critical effect needs to be felt within the dominant cultural tradition as well.

A more adequate accounting of church history will examine such translations, and their critical effect on the dominant traditions. Taking its cue from the multi-directional perspective of the book of Acts, it will see the language and faith of the church being translated. Rome, the endpoint of the book of Acts, is simply the next localization of the faith for the New Testament writer. Beyond Rome, the movements to Constantinople, Chalcedon, Paris, Moscow, Wittenburg, Geneva, and even New York entailed new, local translations of the faith. The multiple endpoints of contemporary world Christianity are an invitation to study a variety of translations of church history across the globe, offering parallel trajectories of faith intersecting in critical and mutually constructive ways.

The history of the translation of the faith is not yet complete, because the history of the Christian churches is not yet complete. And this in turn means that the fullest realization of the meaning and content of divine revelation even within the churches is not yet achieved.[30] The eschatological dimension of church history opens its study to the widest possible horizon of human historical experience and requires us to consider all historical experiences in the church as provisional and anticipatory.[31] This eschatological horizon relativizes all of our historical and theological affirmations about what is and is not essential to church history, and about what is and is not a part of the divine mystery of salvation. It makes the churches, in their history as well as their theologies, relative to something else, which is the widest horizon of God's self-revelation. This horizon, asserts Pannenberg on biblical grounds, is the widest horizon of human history which is yet to be completed and remains therefore open to the fullness of global human experience.

Christian churches in any given historical moment find themselves living in a relativized situation, one in which their experience remains incomplete and open to the dimensions of otherness embodied by other churches and by God (and especially God's multitudinous self-revelation). Their historiography needs to be open-ended in order to be able to render a more adequate account of this experience. This is not to say that churches ought to practice an uncritical acceptance of each and every history, or that one's own history is necessarily beyond the critique of others. Churches need to be open to criticism of their own histories and identities from beyond themselves, for none is pure. "The struggle today is for open communities," writes K. C. Abraham.

> The question is how can we build a global solidarity of open communities. A community of communities that accepts a plurality of identities in a non-threatening, but mutually affirming way is the core of our vision.[32]

Solidarity and openness to one another are modeled, K.C. Abraham argues, on God's trinitarian openness to the world. As such, the mutual submission that is characteristic of trinitarian understanding of God's love is operative at a historiographical level of church history as an openness to one another's ecclesial memory or tradition. Churches need to be different from one another in order for them to be in community with one another. Since, unlike the Trinity, human beings are also sinful, the openness of mutual submission must also be accompanied by an openness to mutual correction. On this point the words of the African theologian Fabian Eboussi Boulaga are eloquent:

> Because they are frankly given as particular and plural, each church posits the need for the others, by which and thanks to which each is passé, by

which each transcends itself. The deficiency of all the churches is that they are so far from being the origin and principle. None can claim to possess the fullness of truth. Thus it is in reciprocal recognition and acknowledgment, in exchange and confrontation, that they will discover the principle of unity and an active universality, in the sense of a process of universality and unification whose fulfillment will be the end of history.[33]

This concept of universality through reciprocity and mutual acknowledgment is quite distanced from the conception of *una sancta catholica* that would seek to blend perspectives together to create a uniform or unified historical memory of tradition.[34] A unified memory of tradition can only work to suppress the diversifying elements that are at work in exchanges and confrontations among churches. However much we might insist upon the mystery of Holy Tradition being unified and one, the history of the incarnation introduces differences: this has been the long insistence of those who would deny that the Father was incarnate, or that the Spirit is the Son. In a similar trinitarian manner, we cannot suppress the historical facticity of the incarnational differences of traditions in the churches which are diversified and many.[35]

Admittedly the situation of continuing disunity among churches of the world constitutes a scandal. The scandal lies in their lack of charity, however, not in their differences. Ecumenical dialogue needs to recognize, and theorize, more clearly the importance of the multiple histories among world Christian communities. Otherwise, efforts to reduce their multiplicity to a common historical memory can only be repressive.[36] On the other hand, this is not to argue that the concept of catholicity is to be jettisoned in favor of an unaccountable diversity and unremitting historical polarization. Churches can be mutually accountable to one another even on the basis of their differing memories of the same historical events. We need not reduce their diversities to a singular expression of tradition for them to extend mutual recognition, reception, and correction.

Throughout this book I have been arguing for mutual acknowledgment and correction among churches through, not in spite of, their multiple histories and traditions. The goal of ecumenical dialogue might better be expressed as seeking not the unity of the Christian tradition, but the community of Christian traditions. In place of the Apostolic tradition we might then better speak of Apostolic traditions, recalling the diversity known among churches in the past and the diversity we encounter in the Christian scriptures. To this end Christian theology stands to benefit from recent historical studies which have reconceptualized history (or History) as a field of multiple histories.[37] The text/textile of history is woven of strands and networks of human experiences which are themselves already strands of smaller, multiple, woven histories.[38] What might have appeared to the modernist historian to be a grand narrative of History moving single-mindedly and irrevocably toward its unifying goal

138   THE GRACE TO RENEW THE PAST

now appears to be an assemblage of multiple larger and smaller histories.

Various traditions of Christian faith are likewise woven texts or tapestries, composed of multiple strands of historical experience which are in turn made possible and carried along by the fabric of the whole. Many of these incorporate strands which in the past were suppressed by dominant communities as heretical. Many incorporate strands of religious and cultural traditions which lie otherwise outside the boundaries of dominant, orthodox traditions. The task of ecumenical dialogue might be re-weaving, without losing, these strands of traditions. I would immediately note that this is not the multiplicity of denominationalism. Denominations are voluntary associations that compete with one another in the "marketplace" of religions, transforming Christianity into a consumer product along the way.[39]

The critical pluralism of Christian traditions I am seeking lies beyond both the history of a singular, universal tradition and that of separate, denominational traditions. Beyond the absolute one and the isolated many is a conception of traditions mutually shaping one another and mutually entering into one another in critical and creative ways.[40] The influences running back and forth among various historical traditions are multiple and complex.[41] Traditions interact along many fronts at once, composing fields of multiple, intersecting planes. By situating our vision of tradition amidst the pluralism of the community of traditions of faith in the world today, we can better understand the manner in which they change and undergo renewal in times of crisis.

Were we to think historically and theologically not of tradition as an isolated or singular phenomenon, but always of traditions in the plural, inextricably bound together in complexes and assemblages, we would find ourselves seeking to uncover the relation among them and the manner in which each tradition incorporates within itself memories and experiences from beyond itself, related through externalized historical processes that lead to change. There is, of course, the danger that we lose sight of the enduring characteristics within these various traditions, or fail to see their structured continuities which persist over time. We might also fail to attend clearly to the dynamics of power by which new items are incorporated into existing structures of tradition. As liberation theologians have argued, we must be diligent in undertaking an analysis of the mechanisms of power and counter-power—symbolic and material—by which the rhizomes of traditions are formed. Such questions lead us historically to ask why African Americans clustered around the Baptist and Methodist traditions? Or what forces are being manifest in the emergence of diverse Pentecostal traditions in Africa and Latin America? To this end we are in need of the narratives of forming, or an analysis at the open-end.

What benefits or gains for the study of traditions does such a conceptualization offer? Here in brief summary form I will suggest only three by way of conclusion. The first is that reconceiving Christian tradition as a community of traditions in dialogue enables us to locate within the field of the

THE GRACE TO RENEW THE PAST 139

traditions themselves a *self-corrective* capacity for criticism and renewal. Traditions encompass multiple options within themselves, often including oppositional voices and voices that are inscribed by being silenced. Over against the dominant voices or strands of the tradition (which can come to represent the whole metonymically through their power takeovers) oppositional voices often take the form of counter-traditions. Despite the metonymic reductions that seek to delegitimize such voices of counter-tradition, these alternatives remain as sources of criticism and challenges to unity effected through power. As Pelikan has noted,

> Tradition has the right to vindicate itself by appropriating much of what its critics say, for it was said, not only against the tradition but within the tradition, long before.[42]

Those perpetrating power takeovers (past or present) have often succeeded in silencing the internal voices of counter-traditions, representing the voices of dissent as an alien other, striving to erase them from the collective memory. Yet even where such violence has been accomplished, voices of dissent remain, present in their silence and represented within and by the very memory of their elimination. They remain inscribed in the memory of the very acts that sought to erase them. Silenced, they nevertheless continue as alternative memories offering hope for change. Ironically, in its acts of exclusion, a dominant or hegemonic tradition must often remind itself and others of what in the past it sought to eliminate. Past options and opportunities remain inscribed within traditions in the narratives of the silencings, as heresies that remain inscribed within the actions that excommunicated them. As historical study begins again to trace the itineracy of these silencings through the dominant records, the counter-traditions of history continue to open up the possibility of their return in the memory and identity of present or future generations.

This latter point I believe to be a significant argument for the study of the histories of heresy and dissent. (And quite often the history of heresy is the history of dissent.) It is precisely because parties who would eventually be able to claim the mantle of orthodoxy fought so bitterly in earlier generations to eradicate what they regarded as heresies that today we find the same heresies worth recovering, if only to understand what the "orthodox" defined themselves over against. So we pursue the study of Gnostics, Donatists, and Montanists in Christian theology today. Quite often what has been defeated in one generation as heresy offers another generation legitimation for change, as the Waldensians and Hussites did for the later European Protestant Reformation.

In these cases, the memory of such heresies has served as a reminder that the tradition can be otherwise. Amidst the contentions of the past we find a more critical identity and directions for change, for it is from within the historical range of multiplicities in the past that the new arises.[43] It is in the play of multiplicities, especially over against the totalizing and unifying trends that have characterized modernity, that the diversity of the historical past (that is, of traditions) re-emerges. We do not need to take flight to pure transcendence in order to discern the emergence of what is new; the notion of multiplicity forestalls too-easy recourse to an absolute "beyond." It is from the midst of history, from the interstitial that the infinite possibilities of multiplicity emerge, that the new overspills.

The second benefit derived from conceiving of Christian tradition in terms of its multiplicity is to see *new options opening for the churches' future(s)*. The very concept of the multiplicity of tradition invites us to expect the future of Christian churches to be different than what has been in their past. We are invited to expect the new, recognizing the process of revelation itself to be open-ended. Alongside the historiographical reduction of the diversity of Christian traditions to tradition, the modern period witnessed a more general reduction of religion to material or cultural terms. The processes of explanatory causation became all-encompassing within the modern paradigm, and expectations for the new or surprising accordingly came to be severely restricted. Both on the primary level of historical experience, and on the secondary level of historical explanation of experience, the totalizing forces and structures of modernity exerted a centripetal effect on religion as well.

Now, however, we see numerous occasions where the very conditions of postmodern historical experience are calling into question reductionistic understandings of the world and centralizing expectations for religion. Even as the centripetal forces of modernity have been at work, equally centrifugal forces were at work to break open the iron cage and challenge the totalizing effects of modern life. Not only have the theories of reductionism failed to satisfy conditions of satisfactory explanation, but the experiences of innovation and the new in modernity have opened up more diversity than uniformity in corporate and individual experiences. Diversity and multiplicity return in the form of remainders that escape the totalizing net of explanation and experience. Through them, differences continue to be reborn, through new convergences and clusterings which are neither predictable nor precedented. The implications for Christian theology are that the future of its traditions will be even more diverse than its past. Rather than conform to the boundaries set for it by the past, the future of Christian theology will continue to outstrip the historical past, reconstituting and expanding the multiplicity of its meanings as it does so.

The diversity of the past, and the open-ended nature of the future, of revelation, and faith in turn invite us to explore *new modes of Christian community*, the third gain from a more pluralistic conception of tradition. In the multiplicity of traditions we find permission to risk failure, which we find bound together with the successes of our pasts. Churches need not abandon their pasts, only exclusive and excluding remembrances of them. At the same time, churches need not be bound by their pasts, because a fuller remembrance of history and tradition can open up options from the past to which they can newly assent. Such new modes of Christian community which open up before us, we are reminded by Philip Potter, are fitting for a pilgrim church.

> The diasporic nature of the church is also a sign of its provisional character—always being renewed, recalled, and sent. We are learning afresh the insight of the Reformers that the church should be the *ecclesia reformanda*, the church always in the process of being reformed.[44]

Potter then quotes the report from the Third Assembly of the World Council of Churches in 1961 which urged churches of the world to examine afresh the structures of their lives with an eye toward facing the challenges of their day.

> In a spirit of penitence and of willingness to be led by the Spirit of God into new ways of witness, the whole church must recognize that its divine mission calls for the most dynamic and costly flexibility . . .[45]

In this invitation to "costly flexibility" we find an invitation to live dangerously in order to open new horizons, and ultimately to experience the holy in new and diverse ways. The cost is not the loss of the past or tradition, but rather the loss of the idols of ecclesial life which resist redemptive change and renewal. Yet in the multiplicities of our traditions we discover a plenitude of options for faithful living and innumerable precedents for change. Through a deeper remembrance of the past, we can discover both freedom from the tyranny of mere repetition of form and the authority to create anew. We find them within our traditions themselves because these bear witness to the creative energy of the new which was at work among past generations.

We can also discover new forms of mutuality and solidarity with the past when we take seriously the diversity, creativity, and uniqueness of the generations that have gone before us. Contemporary theologies have begun to explore more intentionally the meaning of mutuality and dialogue as theological praxes crossing the boundaries of community today. A greater appreciation for diversity has begun to replace the reactive ethnocentrisms and liberal tolerance that maintained the boundaries of separatism and dominance. In a similar manner renewed appreciation for the lived diversity of the past can facilitate our mutuality and solidarity with those who have inhabited the past. When we heed the imperative to live beyond the rigid boundaries constructed by the forces of repression in the modern era we can extend our solidarity to cross the boundaries of time as well.[46]

The empowerment of tradition is a collective practice achieved in community. It is never an individualized affair. So traditioning involves building the webs of relationships that sustain community. The best spun webs of relationships support difference-in-community, in the present and with the past. In a concrete manner, solidarity with the past and difference-in-community mean that we are not confined to a past that looks like us, confined only to the past that is directly antecedent to our community in the present. Through the boundary-breaking acts of solidarity and community, the ancestors and saints, the heritages and legacies of multiple historical pasts, become available to our diverse communities of the present. We have already pointed out that no tradition has existed in historical isolation. There have long been significant overlapping, interaction, and mutual shaping. As we become more attentive to the diversity of historical pasts today, we need to become more intentional about learning to tell two or more narratives well within a framework that provides for commonality and difference.[47] Perhaps those who inhabit dominant traditions can begin to dehegemonize themselves by learning of alternative pasts. Those who inhabit traditions on the margins can, in the words of Spivak, "shuttle between the center (inside) and the margin (outside) and thus narrate a displacement."[48] Or, alternately, those on the margins can create new networks of solidarity and mutuality by linking the traditions of the margin in new alliances and coalitions.

In all of these cases living among the multiplicity of traditions requires skills and resources which have not always been nurtured well within the various dominant Christian traditions themselves. They have been more likely to repress difference than to welcome it; more likely, in Mikhail Bakhtin's terms, to move toward a unitary language of centralization than to open toward the centrifugal forces of "heteroglossia" (tongues of difference).[49] Repression of difference conjoined with material interests or a sheer Nietzschean will to power have given rise in the past in too many instances to the oppressions of racism, classism, patriarchy, or cultural genocide. In religious form they have led to practices of proselytism that barely disguise their tendencies toward ethnocide and religiocide, seeking to render the religiously different religiously the same. In all these various forms, repression of difference and of the other/Other has aimed toward totalizing history and absolutizing tradition, practices which must now be abandoned.

If we must confront the repressive character of totalized history or absolutized tradition, it seems to me that at the same time we must avoid the error of absolutizing difference itself. Traditions are not absolute in their incommensurability, closed to influences from outside themselves historically. They overlap considerably, and are continuously engaging and engaged through historical processes and relations which give rise to decentered totalities. The alterity of a tradition, its Otherness, is not an absolute difference but a differentiation. The difference of a tradition is difference-in-relation. The narratives of traditions themselves tell us this in the way they encompass continuities and change.

So reinventing tradition begins with listening to the dialogue that tradition already is, in the dialogical context of a community of traditions within which we are located. It leads from listening to re-telling, that is, to re-narrating or re-doing the narratives of tradition and history, in order for our communities of faith to be telling more stories, not less. Our traditions thereby become more intentionally replete with multiple memories as we learn to narrate multiplicity in radically (rhizomatically) different ways. At the same time, we need to attend to telling the narratives that undergird a critical perspective or stance, the narratives of the marginalized or of those who have borne the brunt of oppressions in the modern world. We must do so in order to bring into clearer focus the imperatives for change and for living dangerously beyond the end of the modern era. We realize that our re-traditioning is often like carrying on a dialogue in the midst of a cacophonous world. We think it is worth reinventing them, however, traditioning anew amidst the hopes of a faith not yet finished.

Notes

Preface

[1] From his address to the Tenth International Congress of Historians, September 7, 1955, quoted by Hubert Jedin in his "General Introduction to Church History," in *History of the Church*, H. Jedin and John Dolan, eds., vol. 1: *From the Apostolic Community to Constantine*, by Karl Baus (New York: Crossroad, 1982), 6.

1. Faithful Histories

[1] The institution in which I have been teaching, New York Theological Seminary, has for several decades been committed to making theological education accessible to communities of faith for whom the resources of such formal education are not readily available in the metropolitan New York region. The story of New York Theological Seminary is told in George W. Webber, *Led by the Spirit: The Story of New York Theological Seminary* (New York: Pilgrim Press, 1990), and Robert W. Pazmiño, *The Seminary in the City: A Study of New York Theological Seminary* (Lanham, MD: University Press of America, 1988).

[2] See Kosuke Koyama, *Mount Fuji and Mount Sinai: A Critique of Idols* (Maryknoll, NY: Orbis Books, 1985); and Dale T. Irvin and Akintunde E. Akinade, eds., *The Agitated Mind of God: The Theology of Kosuke Koyama* (Maryknoll, NY: Orbis Books, 1996), especially Part II.

[3] Perhaps no Christian theologian of the last century has argued the case for the transcendent seeking the categorical more forcefully than the Roman Catholic theologian Karl Rahner, for whom this principle forms the cornerstone of his entire theological corpus. So while I do not agree with much of Rahner's eventual theological development of the transcendental concept, and especially with his conviction concerning its supreme self-expression through the history of the Western (Latin, or Roman Catholic) church, I nevertheless find compelling his argument for the historicity of its self-revelation. See especially Karl Rahner, *Hearers of the Word*, Michael Richards, trans. (New York: Herder and Herder, 1969); and idem, *Spirit in the World* (New York: Herder and Herder, 1968).

[4] Ernst Troeltsch, *Christian Thought: Its History and Application*, Baron F. von Hügel, trans. (London: University of London Press, 1923), 103-129, especially 123 on the pluralism of churches.

[5] Philip Schaff, *The Principle of Protestantism*, translated from the German by John W. Nevin, 1845, Lancaster Series on the Mercersburg Theology, Bard Thompson and George H. Bricker, eds. (Philadelphia and Boston: United Church Press, 1964), 115. It should be noted that in this text and in his subsequent work as a church historian in North America Schaff was committed to making the case for a "Protestant Catholicism" in which the churches of the Reformation were seen as the rightful inheritors of the medieval European, and thus ancient ecumenical, Christian faith. Consequently, he was opposed to much of what was becoming the dominant form of evangelical faith in North America, which included restorationist and primitivist views that denied the inheritance of a European past. The construction of this alternative (anti-)tradition of popular religiosity in North America is the subject of Nathan O. Hatch's excellent study, *The Democratization of American Christianity* (New Haven and London: Yale University Press, 1989).

[6] Schaff, *The Principle of Protestantism*, 167.

[7] Schaff, *The Principle of Protestantism*, 176.

[8] Schaff, *The Principle of Protestantism*, 176 (emphasis original).

[9] I.D. Stewart, *The History of the Freewill Baptists for Half a Century*, vol. 1: *From the Year 1780 to 1830* (Dover, NH: Freewill Baptist Printing Establishment, 1862), i.

[10] Quoted in R. H. S. Boyd, *An Introduction to Indian Christian Theology* (Bangalore: The Christian Literature Society, 1969), 107.

[11] Boyd, *An Introduction to Indian Christian Theology*, 109.

[12] See Ulrich Beck, Anthony Giddens, and Scott Lash, *Reflexive Modernization: Politics, Tradition and Aesthetics in the Modern Social Order* (Cambridge: Polity Press, 1994); Anthony Giddens, *Modernity and Self-Identity: Self and Society in the Late Modern Age* (Cambridge: Polity Press, 1994); and Marshall Berman, *All That Is Solid Melts into Air: The Experience of Modernity* (New York: Simon and Schuster, 1982). It is important to note here the intimate connection of the detraditionalization thesis to the emergence of the discipline of social theory; see Karl Marx, *Capital: A Critique of Political Economy*, vol. 1, *The Process of Capitalist Production* (New York: International Publishers, 1967); Max Weber, *Economy and Society: An Outline of Interpretive Sociology*, vol. 1, Guenther Roth and Claus Wittich, eds. (Berkeley: University of California Press, 1978); and Emile Durkheim, *The Elementary Forms of Religious Life*, Joseph W. Swain, trans. (New York: Free Press, 1965).

[13] See Frederic Jameson, *Postmodernism, or, The Cultural Logic of Late Capitalism* (Durham: Duke University Press, 1991).

[14] The disruptive and subversive forces of traditions that might otherwise be considered marginal to the dominant social forces of modern capitalist society have been amply studied and discussed in the emerging discipline loosely termed "cultural studies." For a comprehensive introduction to the field, see Lawrence Grossberg, Cary Nelson, and Paula A. Treichler, eds., *Cultural Studies* (New York: Routledge, 1992).

[15] For an excellent overview of the forces of detraditionalization and retraditionalization, and various expositions of the coexistence thesis, see Paul Heelas, Scott Lash, and Paul Morris, eds., *Detraditionalization: Critical Reflections on Authority and Identity* (Cambridge, MA: Blackwell Publishers, 1996).

[16] Here I am making use of the provocative insights of Paul Morris, in his essay "Community Beyond Tradition," in *Detraditionalization*, 223-249, especially 239-245.

[17] Morris, "Community Beyond Tradition," 227.

[18] Juan Luis Segundo, *Liberation of Theology*, John Drury, trans. (Maryknoll, NY: Orbis Books, 1982), 10.

[19] Segundo, *Liberation of Theology*, 81.

[20] Segundo, *Liberation of Theology*, 9, 78-80.

[21] Aloysius Pieris, *Love Meets Wisdom: A Christian Experience of Buddhism* (Maryknoll, NY: Orbis Books, 1988), 87, emphasis original.

[22] Pieris, *Love Meets Wisdom*, 87.

[23] Pieris, *Love Meets Wisdom*, 121.

[24] Friedrich Nietzsche, *On the Genealogy of Morals*, Walter Kaufmann and R. J. Hollingdale, trans. (New York: Random House, 1969), 77.

[25] Philip Schaff, *What Is Church History? A Vindication of the Idea of Historical Development* (Philadelphia: J. B. Lippincott, 1846), 9-10.

[26] Herbert Butterfield, *Christianity in European History* (London: Collins, 1952), 24; see also 5-7.

[27] Herbert Butterfield, *Christianity in European History*, 45.

2. History and Tradition: From Crisis to Re-Creation

[1] "Dualism: In Ralph Ellison's Invisible Man," *New and Collected Poems* (New York: Atheneum/Macmillan Publishing Co., 1988), 50.

[2] H. Richard Niebuhr, *The Meaning of Revelation*, (New York: MacMillan Publishing Co., 1960 edition).

[3] Niebuhr, *The Meaning of Revelation*, 35-36 (emphasis added).

[4] Paul Ricoeur, *Time and Narrative*, vol. 1, Kathleen McLaughlin and David Pellauer, trans. (Chicago: University of Chicago Press, 1984), 31-35.

[5] See Timothy Bahti, *Allegories of History: Literary Historiography after Hegel* (Baltimore and London: The Johns Hopkins University Press, 1992), 7.

[6] The phrase is that of Jacques Le Goff, *History and Memory* (New York: Columbia University Press, 1992), 108. In a section subtitled, "Paradoxes and Ambiguities of History," 106-111, Le Goff explores in greater detail the question of whether history is a science that takes as its object a past that is independent of the historian, or if in the words of Croce, "all history is contemporary history."

[7] John Huizinga, "A Definition of the Concept of History," *Philosophy and History: Essays Presented to Ernst Cassirer*, Raymond Klibansky and H. J. Paton, eds., (Oxford: Clarendon Press, 1936), 7 (emphasis original).

[8] Huizinga, "Concept of History," 5.

[9] Huizinga, "Concept of History," 9 (emphasis original).

[10] "Africans in the Diaspora," *Princeton Theological Seminary Bulletin* 7:2 (1986): 115.

[11] *Heterologies: Discourse on the Other* (Minneapolis: University of Minnesota Press, 1986), 218.

[12] Quoted by Legoff, *History and Memory*, 89.

[13] Le Goff, *History and Memory*, 124.

[14] Le Goff, *History and Memory*, 216 (emphasis original).

[15] Le Goff, *History and Memory*, 99.

[16] On the structure of temporality and change, see Paul Ricoeur, *Time and Narrative*, vol. 3, Kathleen Blamey and David Pellauer, trans. (Chicago: University of Chicago Press, 1988), "Section I: The Aporetics of Temporality," 11-96; and Reinhart Koselleck, *Futures Past: On the Semantics of Historical Time* (Cambridge, MA: The MIT Press, 1985), 274-277.

[17] The designations "North Atlantic" and "the West" are used here synonymously to denote the historical and cultural communities of predominantly Western European descent, including those in North America, Australia, and New Zealand.

[18] On the "crisis of history," see Harvey J. Kaye, *The Powers of the Past: Reflections on the Crisis and the Promise of History* (Minneapolis: University of Minnesota Press, 1991), 12-64.

[19] On the nature of modernity, and its severing effects, see Peter L. Berger, *Facing Up to Modernity: Excursions in Society, Politics, and Religion* (New York: Basic Books, 1977), especially 70-80, which provides a critique of five basic dilemmas modernity has imposed on social life. David Frisby, *Fragments of Modernity: Theories of Modernity in the Work of Simmel, Kracauer and Benjamin* (Cambridge, MA: MIT Press, 1986) investigates the transitory character of modernity as manifest in the discontinuities of the modern metropolis and capitalism. A more positive assessment of modernity as a liberating vision of progress is provided by Marshall Berman, *All That Is Solid Melts into Air: The Experience of Modernity* (New York: Simon and Schuster, 1982).

[20] "Theses on the Philosophy of History," *Illuminations: Essays and Reflection*, Hannah Arendt, ed. (New York: Schocken Books, 1969), 257-258.

[21] Reinhart Koselleck, *Futures Past: On the Semantics of Historical Time* (Cambridge, MA: The MIT Press, 1985), 200. See also Timothy Bahti, *Allegories of History: Literary Historiography after Hegel* (Baltimore: The Johns Hopkins University Press, 1992), 25-51.

[22] Koselleck, *Futures Past*, 203.

[23] ". . . einer allgemein das Recht verwaltenden *bürgerlichen Gesellschaft* . . ." Immanuel Kant, "Idee zu einer allgemeinen Geschichte in weltbürgerlicher Absicht," *Werke*, vol. 4, Ernst Cassirer, ed. (Berlin: Bruno Cassirer, 1912), 156 (emphasis original). I have chosen not to follow the translation of Lewis Beck in Immanuel Kant, *On History* (Indianapolis: Bobbs-Merrill Co, 1963), 16, where the crucial phrase is translated "civic society." Marx was essentially correct in

arguing that the bourgeois class had laid claim to universality, concealing the particularity of the claim under the cloak of a universal civil society.

[24] See Charles H. Long, *Significations: Signs, Symbols, and Images in the Interpretation of Religion* (Philadelphia: Fortress Press, 1986), especially ch. 6, "Primitive/Civilized: The Locus of a Problem," 79-96.

[25] Immanuel Kant, "Idea for a Universal History from a Cosmopolitan Point of View," *On History*, 16 (emphasis original).

[26] Kant, "Idea for a Universal History," 24.

[27] For a fuller discussion of historicism, see Georg G. Iggers, *The German Conception of History: The National Tradition of Thought from Herder to the Present* (Middletown, CT: Wesleyan University Press, 1983).

[28] See Leonard Krieger, "Elements of Early Historicism: Experience, Theory, and History in Ranke," *History and Theory: Studies in the Philosophy of History*, Beiheft 14, *Essays on Historicism* (1975): 1-14.

[29] Ernst Troeltsch, *The Absoluteness of Christianity and the History of Religions* (Richmond, VA: John Knox Press, 1971), 89 (emphasis added).

[30] Ernst Troeltsch, *Gesammelte Schriften III, Der Historismus und seine Probleme: Erstes Buch, Das logische Problem der Geschichtsphilosophie* (Tubingen: J.C.B. Mohr [Paul Siebeck], 1922), especially 12-17, 695-710.

[31] Troeltsch, *Der Historismus und seine Probleme*, 12.

[32] Troeltsch, *Der Historismus und seine Probleme*, 32-35.

[33] "Es is so bequem, unmündig zu sein." Kant, "Was is Aufklärung?" 169.

[34] Martin Heidegger, "The Age of the World Picture," *The Question Concerning Technology and Other Essays* (New York: Harper and Row, 1975), 128.

[35] Troeltsch, *Der Historismus und seine Probleme*, 709 (translation mine).

[36] Troeltsch, *Der Historismus und seine Probleme*, 707. On the European Christian dogmatic concept of history prior to Europe's modern age, see Klaus Scholder, *The Birth of Modern Critical Theology*, John Bowden, trans. (London: SCM Press, 1990), 65-87.

[37] On the particular question of an Islamic universal historical perspective, Hichem Djait has written: "It is false to confine historical tradition first to the Greek and then to the Western mind. Islamic culture has been, together with Europe, the culture manifesting the strongest sense of the past, made concrete in history on the grand scale, with all the rigor, critical thinking, and cold objectivity which that implies, beside the striking sense of color we find in the first historians, those of the archaic period. In the case of both Europe and Islam we are dealing with two great cultures that constantly refer to history, plunged as deeply as they are into the stream of historical evolution. (Hichem Djait, *Europe and Islam: Cultures and Modernity*, Peter Heinegg, trans. [Berkeley: University of California Press, 1985], 164.)

[38] Robert C. Solomon, *History and Human Nature: A Philosophical Review of European Philosophy and Culture, 1750-1850* (New York: Harcourt Brace Jovanovich, 1976).

[39] The contradiction has continued to characterize Western theology, argued Joseph Cahill, bringing it to a point of exhaustion today. See his article, "Theological Studies, Where Are You?" *Journal of the American Academy of Religion* 52:4 (1984), 746.

[40] Huizinga, "Concept of History," 8.

[41] *The Postmodern Condition: A Report on Knowledge* (Minneapolis: University of Minnesota Press, 1984), 37.

[42] Long, *Significations*, 9.

[43] Long, *Significations*, 85.

[44] Long, *Significations*, 9.

[45] William J. Bouwsma, *A Usable Past: Essays in European Cultural History* (Berkeley: University of California Press, 1990), 348, 361, has called the narrative of universal progress "the traditional dramatic organization of Western history," and "the dramatic scheme ... with its concept of linear history moving the human race ineluctably to its goal in the modern world." It

has collapsed, Bouwsma asserted in his 1978 presidential address before the American Historical Association. In its wake he proposed that historiography adopt a pluralistic cultural and historical consciousness, which he argues has its own historical precedent in Western culture in the Renaissance. The Renaissance vision of pluralism, Bouwsma concluded, "implies the possibility of a multiplicity of historical dramas, both simultaneous and successive . . . Above all, since it insists on no particular outcome for the dramas of history, it leaves the future open" (361-362).

[46] The "Final Statement" from the inaugural conference of the Ecumenical Association of Third World Theologians in Dar es Salaam, 1976, spoke of "a radical break in epistemology" in turning intentionally toward the historical situations of the Third World for (re)generating theological knowledge. The break was from dominant Western theologies, and by extension the historical consciousness employed within them. See Sergio Torres and Virginia Fabella, eds., *The Emergent Gospel: Theology from the Developing World* (London: Geoffrey Chapman/Maryknoll, NY: Orbis Books, 1978), 269. For a fuller discussion of the "epistemic" shift in liberation theologies, see Sharon D. Welch, *Communities of Resistance and Solidarity: A Feminist Theology of Liberation* (Maryknoll, NY: Orbis Books, 1985).

[47] This was an insight Ernst Troeltsch pursued throughout his career, as he sought a new cultural synthesis for Christian faith in the European context. See further Toshimasa Yasukata, *Ernst Troeltsch: Systematic Theologian of Radical Historicality* (Atlanta: Scholars Press, 1986). Systematic exploration of such a synthesis from a contemporary Western theological perspective is pursued by Peter C. Hodgson and Robert H. King, eds., *Christian Theology: An Introduction to Its Traditions and Tasks* (Philadelphia: Fortress Press, 1985).

[48] Huizinga, "Concept of History," 5.

[49] Jaroslav Pelikan, in *The Vindication of Tradition* (New Haven: Yale University Press, 1984), 65, writes: "Tradition is the living faith of the dead, traditionalism is the dead faith of the living."

[50] Paul Tillich, *Systematic Theology*, vol. 3 (Chicago: University of Chicago Press, 1963), 300.

[51] T. S. Eliot, *Selected Essays* (San Diego: Harcourt Brace Jovanovich, 1978), 4.

[52] Along these lines Eugen Rosenstock-Huessy once noted, "*each generation has to act differently precisely in order to represent the same thing*" (*The Christian Future, or, the Modern Mind Outrun* [New York: Harper and Row Publishers, 1966], 130 [emphasis original]).

[53] On the concepts of "effective history" and "effective historical consciousness," see Hans-Georg Gadamer, *Truth and Method* (New York: Crossroad, 1986), 267-310.

[54] Eliot, *Selected Essays*, 4.

[55] See Marty E. Marty, "Tradition, Verb (Rare)," *University of Chicago Record* 9:4 (1975): 136-138.

[56] Eric Hobsbawm, "Introduction: Inventing Traditions," *The Invention of Tradition*, Hobsbawm and Terence Ranger, eds. (Cambridge: Cambridge University Press, 1992), 1. Hobsbawm continues on p. 6: "However, insofar as there is such reference to a historic past, the peculiarity of 'invented' traditions is that the continuity with it is largely factitious."

[57] Edward A. Shils, *Tradition* (Chicago: University of Chicago Press, 1981), 5.

[58] Koselleck writes in *Futures Past*, 142: "Historical science, mindful of its temporal location, becomes the study of the past. This temporalization of perspective was certainly advanced by the swift change of experience embodied in the French Revolution. The break in continuity appeared to uncouple a past whose growing foreignness could only be illuminated and recovered by means of historical investigation." See also Shils, *Tradition*, 6.

[59] Yves M. J. Congar, *Tradition and Traditions: An Historical and a Theological Essay* (New York: Macmillan Co., 1967), 20; and *The Meaning of Tradition* (New York: Hawthorn Books, 1964), 19-24.

[60] "Tradition and Traditions," *In the Image and Likeness of God* (Crestwood, NY: St. Vladimir's Seminary Press, 1985), 151.

[61] Writes Lossky, on p. 154 of *In the Image and Likeness of God*: "If it is necessary to distinguish what is transmitted (the oral and written traditions) and the unique mode according to which this transmission is received in the Holy Spirit (Tradition as the principle of Christian

knowledge), it will nonetheless be impossible to separate these two points; hence the ambivalence of the term 'tradition,' which designates simultaneously the horizontal line and the vertical line of the Truth possessed by the Church."

[62] R. P. C. Hanson, *Tradition in the Early Church* (Philadelphia: Westminster Press, 1962), 7.

[63] Letty M. Russell, *Church in the Round: Feminist Interpretation of the Church* (Louisville, KY: Westminster/John Knox, 1993), 37.

[64] Russell, *Church in the Round*, 201.

[65] Protestant defense of the authority of Scripture over tradition, from the Reformers to conservative evangelicals today, has often made appeal to the historic belief of Christian churches through the ages to supplement the doctrine of *sola scriptura*, an appeal made implicitly to something that resembles orthodox Christian tradition. For an example of such an appeal to the historic belief of the Church (tradition) as supportive of the doctrine of the inerrancy of Scripture, see John D. Woodbridge, "Some Misconceptions of the Impact of the 'Enlightenment' on the Doctrine of Scripture," *Hermeneutics, Authority, and Canon*, D. A. Carson and John D. Woodbridge, eds. (Grand Rapids: Zondervan Publishing House, 1986), 237-270.

[66] Harold O. J. Brown, "On Method and Means in Theology," *Doing Theology in Today's World: Essays in Honor of Kenneth S. Kantzer*, John D. Woodbridge and Thomas E. McComiskey, eds. (Grand Rapids: Zondervan Publishing House, 1991), 167.

[67] Pelikan, *The Vindication of Tradition*, 11.

[68] See Benjamin B. Warfield, *Revelation and Inspiration* (New York: Oxford University Press, 1927) for his sustained defense of the plenary verbal inspiration of both Testaments. Warfield did not hesitate to state that the Bible is a book of oracles, containing "the crystallized speech of God" (390). On the threat posed by historical criticism to such absolutist conceptions of the Bible, and the ensuing controversy in Anglo-American biblical scholarship at the end of the nineteenth century, see Mark S. Massa, *Charles Augustus Briggs and the Crisis of Historical Criticism* (Minneapolis: Fortress Press, 1990).

[69] See James M. Robinson and Helmut Koester, *Trajectories through Early Christianity* (Philadelphia: Fortress Press, 1971), 270.

[70] Pelikan, *The Vindication of Tradition*, 50, points out the irony that historical criticism has now become itself a tradition, one I would now add that is being criticized by a number of postmodern biblical scholars as ineffective in mediating a living past.

[71] Troeltsch, *Der Historismus und seine Probleme*, 772.

3. The Accountability of Handing Over

[1] Walter Benjamin, *Illuminations*, Hannah Arendt, ed. (New York: Schocken Books, 1969), 255.

[2] Lucille Clifton, "why some people be mad at me sometimes," *Next: New Poems* (Rochester, NY: BOA Editions, 1987), 20.

[3] See Dominick LaCapra, "Rethinking Intellectual History and Reading Texts," *Rethinking Intellectual History: Texts, Contexts, Language* (Ithaca: Cornell University Press, 1983), 30. While LaCapra refers in this essay specifically to the dialogical character of the discipline of intellectual history in this essay, his engagement with Heidegger's hermeneutics opens up his theoretical exploration of the dialogical relationship between present and past for consideration regarding the broader concept of tradition.

[4] Jürgen Moltmann, *The Crucified God: The Cross of Christ as the Foundation and Criticism of Christian Theology* (New York: Harper and Row, 1974), 7.

[5] On the historical emergence of modern secularism in the North Atlantic world, see Franklin L. Baumer, *Modern European Thought: Continuity and Change in Ideas, 1600-1950* (New York: Macmillan, 1977); Owen Chadwick, *The Secularization of the European Mind in the Nineteenth Century* (Cambridge: Cambridge University Press, 1975); and James Turner, *Without God, Without Creed: The Origin of Unbelief in America* (Baltimore: Johns Hopkins University Press, 1985). Alasdair MacIntyre, *Whose Justice? Which Rationality?* (Notre Dame: University of

Notre Dame Press, 1988), which explores the manner in which justice and rationality are defined by a tradition, regards secular European Enlightenment as one of several distinctive traditions to be examined.

[6] The concept of accountability in contemporary Christian ethics was introduced by H. Richard Niebuhr in *The Responsible Self* (New York: Harper and Row, 1963). Darryl M. Trimiew, in *Voices of the Silenced: The Responsible Self in a Marginalized Community* (Cleveland: The Pilgrim Press, 1993), has developed Niebuhr's concept significantly in the direction of multiple social accountabilities to marginal communities of the oppressed. In a similar vein, Beverly Wildung Harrison, *Our Right to Choose: Toward a New Ethic of Abortion* (Boston: Beacon Press, 1983), has argued that the Christian tradition is to be held ethically accountable to women's lives.

[7] The ethical and aesthetic conception of answerability was explored by M. M. Bakhtin in early writings which were only discovered by his students in the 1970s. Bakhtin sought to develop a philosophy of the answerable act which achieved the unity of the deed and its content or meaning (representation). In doing so he sought to challenge the abstract universality of Kant's categorical imperative with participatory thinking which poses our "non-alibi in being" in order to ground the ethical imperatives (the ought) in concrete actuality. See M. M. Bakhtin, *Toward a Philosophy of the Act*, Michael Holquist and Vadim Liapunov, eds. (Austin: University of Texas Press, 1993).

[8] Most incidents in which charges of heresy are leveled against individuals or communities today reflect specific political theological commitments, on the right or left. Thus the world Christian community generally affirmed in the 1980s the conviction that apartheid in South Africa constituted a Christian heresy, while in the 1990s a number of conservative evangelicals in North America regarded as heresy feminist theology's use of the female image of *sophia* as a representation for the divine.

[9] See Isaac Gottlieb, ed., *Jerusalem to Jabneh: The Period of the Mishnah and Its Literature* (Tel Aviv: Everyman's University, 1981), Units 8-10.

[10] See s.v. *didomi*, *Theological Dictionary of the New Testament*, vol. 2, Gerhard Kittel, ed., 172; for a fuller, and more positive, discussion of the Pharisee tradition(s) that are the object of the Gospel polemic, see Jacob Neusner, *From Politics to Piety: The Emergence of Pharisaic Judaism* (New York: KTAV Publishing House, 1979).

[11] Along these same lines one should note that the Latin word *traditio* is the etymological root for both tradition and traitor in English.

[12] Christopher Morse, *Not Every Spirit: A Dogmatics of Christian Disbelief* (Valley Forge: Trinity Press, 1994), 47-48, has pointed out the theological significance of the New Testament resistance of the mode of traditioning exemplified by Judas. For a dissenting perspective regarding both Judas and the translation of *paradidomi* as betrayal, see William Klassen, *Judas: Betrayer or Friend of Jesus?* (Minneapolis: Augsburg Fortress, 1996).

[13] See Letty Russell, "Tradition as Mission: Study of a New Current in Theology and Its Implications for Theological Education," unpublished Th. D. dissertation, Union Theological Seminary, New York, 1969, 109-115. Anton Wessels, *Images of Jesus: How Jesus Is Perceived and Portrayed in Non-European Cultures* (Grand Rapids: Wm. B. Eerdmans, 1990), 13-17, has noted the ambiguity of *paradidomi*/ tradition in reference to the imperial images of Jesus Christ that one finds in the later history of Byzantine and Latin Christianity.

[14] See M. M. Thomas, *Risking Christ for Christ's Sake* (Geneva: WCC, 1987).

[15] Benjamin, *Illuminations*, 255.

[16] See Paul Tillich, *Systematic Theology*, vol. 1 (Chicago: University of Chicago Press, 1951), 83-86.

[17] On re-inventing the past, see V. Y. Mudimbe, *The Invention of Africa: Gnosis, Philosophy, and the Order of Knowledge* (Bloomington: Indiana University Press, 1988).

[18] Benjamin, *Illuminations*, 255.

[19] Ernst Troeltsch, *The Absoluteness of Christianity and the History of Religions*, David Reid, trans. (Richmond: John Knox Press, 1971), 95-98.

[20] See Craig Dykstra, "Reconceiving Practice," in *Shifting Boundaries: Contextual Approaches to the Structure of Theological Education*, Barbara G. Wheeler and Edward Farley, eds.

(Louisville: Westminster/John Knox, 1991), 35-66. Dykstra draws explicitly on the definition of practice found in Alasdair MacIntyre, *After Virtue* (Notre Dame: Notre Dame University Press, 1981), 187. I would add Marx's insight that critically-conscious human activity directed specifically toward socially transformative engagement be distinguished as *praxis*.

[21] See Matthew L. Lamb, *Solidarity with Victims: Toward a Theology of Social Transformation* (New York: Crossroad, 1982); Johannes B. Metz, *Faith in History and Society: Toward a Practical Fundamental Theology* (New York: Seabury, 1980); and Edmund Arens, "Internationale, ekklesiale und universale Solidarität," *Orientieung* 53 (1989): 216-220. Realization of the manner in which practice or praxis provides the norms for theological discourse has been a major insight of liberation theologies as seen in Gustavo Gutiérrez, *A Theology of Liberation: History, Politics and Salvation* (Maryknoll, NY: Orbis Books, 1973), 6-13. See also Susan Thistlethwaite and Mary Potter Engel, *Lift Every Voice: Constructing Christian Theology from the Underside* (San Francisco: Harper and Row, 1990; rev. ed. Maryknoll, NY: Orbis Books, 1998).

[22] Juan Luis Segundo, *Liberation of Theology* (Maryknoll, NY: Orbis Books, 1976), 7-13.

[23] Helmut Peukert, *Science, Action, and Fundamental Theology: Toward a Theology of Communicative Action*, James Bohman, trans. (Cambridge, MA: The MIT Press, 1986), 208; Peukert cites as his source Christian Lenhardt, "Anamnestic Solidarity: The Proletariat and Its Manes," *Telos* 25 (1975): 133-155.

[24] Peukert, *Science, Action, and Fundamental Theology*, 209.

[25] Peukert, *Science, Action, and Fundamental Theology*, 237.

[26] Peukert, *Science, Action, and Fundamental Theology*, 244.

[27] The charge that liberation and contextual theologies have abandoned their Christian identity, a charge made by some opponents, does not stand up to serious investigation. Gustavo Gutiérrez demonstrated this in his dialogue with the theological faculty of the Catholic Institute of Lyons in 1985, which took place as a traditional doctoral defense for which he submitted his body of published theological works as a dissertation in theology. He was granted the doctorate in theology *summa cum laude*. For the proceedings of the defense, and for insight into Gutiérrez's own relationship to the European Catholic theological tradition, see Gutiérrez, *The Truth Shall Make You Free* (Maryknoll, NY: Orbis Books, 1990).

[28] On the structural *metalepsis* involved in Benjamin's argument for the present's redemption of the past, see Bahti, *Allegories of History*, 183-203.

[29] Judith Plaskow, *Standing Again at Sinai: Judaism from a Feminist Perspective* (San Francisco: Harper Collins, 1990), 204.

[30] See Edward E. Sampson, *Celebrating the Other: A Dialogical Account of Human Nature* (Boulder, CO: Westview Press, 1993).

[31] Sampson, *Celebrating the Other*, 125.

[32] See Ronald F. Thiemann, "Piety, Narrative, and Christian Identity," *Word and World* 3:2 (1983): 148-159.

[33] The study of multiple origins is a critical component of Michel Foucault's genealogical method which seeks history in the "details and accidents" that accompany every beginning, which finds in the "vicissitudes of history" what he calls "the face of the other" (*Language, Counter-Memory, Practice: Selected Essays and Interviews*, Donald F. Bouchard, ed. [Ithaca, NY: Cornell University Press, 1977], 144).

[34] Gilles Deleuze and Félix Guattari, *A Thousand Plateaus: Capitalism and Schizophrenia*, Brian Massumi, trans. (Minneapolis: University of Minnesota Press, 1987), 3-25.

[35] Deleuze and Guattari, *A Thousand Plateaus*, 11. "A rhizome ceaselessly establishes connections between [sic] semiotic chains, organizations of power, and circumstances relative to the arts, sciences, and social struggles" (7).

[36] Quoted in Lawrence Grossberg, *We Gotta Get Out of This Place: Popular Conservatism and Postmodern Culture* (New York: Routledge, 1992), 48.

[37] Ihab Hassan, *The Postmodern Turn: Essays in Postmodern Theory and Culture* (Columbus: Ohio State University Press, 1987), 160.

[38] Deleuze and Guattari, *A Thousand Plateaus*, 8.

[39] Deleuze and Guattari, *A Thousand Plateaus*, 8.

[40] On the social dimensions of the economic doctrine of the Trinity, see Catherine Mowry LaCugna, *God for Us: The Trinity and Christian Life* (San Francisco: HarperCollins, 1993); Jürgen Moltmann, *The Trinity and the Kingdom: The Doctrine of God* (San Francisco: Harper and Row, 1988); Ted Peters, *God as Trinity: Relationality and Temporality in Divine Life* (Louisville: Westminster/John Knox, 1993); Colin E. Gunton, *The Promise of Trinitarian Theology* (Edinburgh: T & T Clark, 1991); and Okechukwu Ogbonnaya, *On Communitarian Divinity: An African Interpretation of the Trinity* (New York: Paragon House, 1994).

[41] Julia Kristeva, *Revolution in Poetic Language*, Margaret Waller, trans. (New York: Columbia University Press, 1984), 60. Kristeva writes: "If one grants that every signifying practice is a field of transpositions of various signifying systems (an inter-textuality), one then understands that its 'place' of enunciation and its denoted 'object' are never singular, complete, and identical to themselves, but always plural, shattered, capable of being tabulated." For a fuller exploration of the implications of Kristeva's theory for constructive contextual theology, see Dale T. Irvin, "Contextualization and Catholicity: Looking Anew for the Unity of the Faith," *Studia Theologica* 48:2 (1994): 83-96.

[42] Concerning the representation of continuity/discontinuity in narrative, see Paul Ricoeur, *Time and Narrative*, vol. 1, Kathleen McLaughlin and David Pellauer, trans. (Chicago: University of Chicago Press, 1984). On the narrative and theological studies in general, see Stephen Crites, "The Narrative Quality of Experience," *Journal of the American Academy of Religion* 39:3 (1971): 290-307; Hans W. Frei, *The Eclipse of Biblical Narrative: A Study in Eighteenth and Nineteenth Century Hermeneutics* (New Haven: Yale University Press, 1974); idem, *The Identity of Jesus Christ* (Philadelphia: Fortress Press, 1975); George W. Stroup, *The Promise of Narrative Theology: Recovering the Gospel in the Church* (Atlanta: John Knox Press, 1981); Ronald F. Thiemann, *Revelation and Theology: The Gospel as Narrated Promise* (Notre Dame: University of Notre Dame Press, 1985); Mary Ann Tolbert, *Perspectives on the Parables: An Approach to Multiple Interpretation* (Philadelphia: Fortress, 1979); Michael Goldberg, *Jews and Christians, Getting Our Stories Straight: The Exodus and the Passion-Resurrection* (Nashville: Abingdon Press, 1985); Frank Kermode, *The Genesis of Secrecy: On the Interpretation of Narrative* (Cambridge: Harvard University Press, 1979); and Stanley Hauerwas and L. Gregory Jones, *Why Narrative? Readings in Narrative Theology* (Grand Rapids: Wm. B. Eerdmans, 1989).

[43] Hayden White, *Tropics of Discourse: Essays in Cultural Criticism* (Baltimore: The Johns Hopkins University Press, 1978), 88 (emphasis original).

[44] Plaskow, *Standing Again at Sinai*, xvii.

[45] Plaskow, *Standing Again at Sinai*, xvii (emphasis mine).

[46] Plaskow, *Standing Again at Sinai*, 134.

[47] Plaskow, *Standing Again at Sinai*, 124.

[48] Among the initial texts that pointed in this direction, see James H. Cone, *A Black Theology of Liberation* (Philadelphia: Lippincott, 1970); Carol P. Christ and Judith Plaskow, eds., *Womanspirit Rising: A Feminist Reader in Religion* (New York: Harper and Row, 1979); and Enrique Dussel, *A History of the Church in Latin America: Colonialism to Liberation (1492-1979)*, Alan Neely, trans. (Grand Rapids: Eerdmans, 1981; original in Spanish, 1974).

[49] For an introduction to the historiographical initiatives begun by the Ecumenical Association of Third World Theologians in the 1980s, and a more general survey of Latin American, Asian, and African church historiography in the direction of developing alternatives to missions historiography, see G. M. Verstraelen-Gilhuis, "The History of the Missionary Movement from the Perspective of the Third World," in *Missiology: An Ecumenical Introduction: Texts and Contexts of Global Christianity*, A. Camps et al, eds. (Grand Rapids: Eerdmans, 1995), 253-264.

[50] See especially Aloyisus Pieris, *An Asian Theology of Liberation* (Maryknoll, NY: Orbis Books, 1988).

[51] See Manuel M. Marzal, Eugenio Maurer, Xaverio Albó, and Bartomeu Melià, *The Indian*

Face of God in Latin America (Maryknoll, NY: Orbis Books, 1996).

[52] Virgilio Elizondo, *Galilean Journey* (Maryknoll, NY: Orbis Books, 1982); and idem, *The Future Is Mestizo: Life Where Cultures Meet* (Bloomington, IN: Meyer-Stone Books, 1988).

4. Theology of History

[1] A. M. Allchin, *The Living Presence of the Past: The Dynamic of Christian Tradition* (New York: Seabury Press, 1981), 22.

[2] Albert J. Raboteau, "Africans in the Diaspora," *Princeton Theological Seminary Bulletin* 7:2 (1986): 115.

[3] See Hans W. Frei, *The Eclipse of Biblical Narrative: A Study in Eighteenth and Nineteenth Century Hermeneutics* (New Haven: Yale University Press, 1974).

[4] Paul Ricoeur, *Time and Narrative*, vol. 1, Kathleen McLaughlin and David Pellauer, trans. (Chicago and London: University of Chicago Press, 1984), 95-120, critically examines the antinarrativist historiographical arguments advanced by the French Annales school, and the "covering law" theory of analytic philosophy. Against the former, Ricoeur demonstrates the narrative structure of the Annales historiography's concept of the *longue duree*; against the latter, he demonstrates the narrative interpretive character of the covering laws employed by analytic philosophers.

[5] James E. Bradley and Richard A. Muller summarize this point nicely in their recent textbook, *Church History: An Introduction to Research, Reference Works, and Methods* (Grand Rapids: Wm. B. Eerdmans, 1995), 35: "The past does not exist, and all we have is a set of surviving traces of the past. All traces of evidence already reflect some level of interpretation—perhaps in the character of the documentation, the style, or the design." Here I also find Peter Gay's concise summation compelling: "Historical narration without analysis is trivial, historical analysis without narration is incomplete" (Peter Gay, *Style in History* [New York: McGraw-Hill Book Co., 1974], 189).

[6] See Marc Bloch, *The Historian's Task* (New York: Vintage Books, 1953), 60-62; and Paul Ricoeur, *Time and Narrative*, vol. 3, Kathleen Blamey and David Pellauer, trans. (Chicago: University of Chicago Press, 1988), 116-126.

[7] See Michel de Certeau, *Heterologies: Discourse on the Other* (Minneapolis: University of Minnesota Press, 1986), 200; and Reinhart Koselleck, *Futures Past: On the Semantics of Historical Time* (Cambridge: The MIT Press, 1985), 112.

[8] Leon J. Goldstein, "History and the Primacy of Knowing," *History and Theory* Beiheft 16 (1977), *The Construction of the Historical Past*, 33.

[9] Robert L. Heilbroner, *The Future as History: The Historic Currents of Our Time and the Direction in Which They Are Taking Us* (New York: Harper and Brothers, 1960), 193.

[10] Robert L. Heilbroner, *The Future as History: The Historic Currents of Our Time and the Direction in Which They Are Taking Us* (New York: Harper and Brothers, 1960), 193.

[11] See Mark A. Noll, " 'And the Lion Shall Lie Down with the Lamb': The Social Sciences and Religious History," *Fides et Historia* (1988): 5-30.

[12] Here I am arguing explicitly against another historiographical position held by Bradley and Muller, *Church History*. They write: "Church historians should aim at objectivity even as they acknowledge that it demands as broad and comprehensive a perspective in the analysis of ideas as it does in the depiction of complex events in the institutional or political life of the church" (3). It is hard to avoid the suspicion, however, that such an allegiance to the cult of objectivity conceals unexamined ideological commitments, a suspicion born out several pages later where they write: "Western intellectual history provides a foundation for studying the history of the church, the history of Christian thought, and systematic theology as well" (10). It is precisely such ideological wedding of Western thought and church history that I am challenging throughout this book.

[13] Karl Barth, *Church Dogmatics* III.1, 78.

[14] Barth, *Church Dogmatics*, III.1, 78.

[15] Barth gives this an explicitly theological formulation early in *Church Dogmatics*, I.1, 163,

when he writes: "The Word of God in the highest sense makes history."

[16] On the consistency of Barth's dialectical theology, see Bruce L. McCormack, *Karl Barth's Critically Realistic Dialectical Theology: Its Genesis and Development 1909-1936* (Oxford: Oxford University Press, 1995).

[17] Thus McCormack writes concerning his subject's response to Calvin's conception of biblical history being sacred history: "For Barth, *historia sacra* is the eschatological history of God which stands over against all history, biblical and profane. 'Biblical history too can only *proclaim* the "*historia sacra*," the history of *salvation*, the history of *God*. And, on the other hand, "*historia sacra*" is the hidden meaning and content of *all* history; it is *the* history which wants to speak and above and beyond so-called profane history as well' " (*Karl Barth's Critically Realistic Dialectical Theology*, 305).

[18] Along the lines of sacred history, Barth wrote in *Church Dogmatics* III.1, 60: "The history of salvation is *the* history, the true history which encloses all other history and to which in some way all other history belongs to the extent that it reflects and illustrates the history of salvation ... No other history can have any independent theme in relation to this history, let alone be a general and true history in the context of which the history of salvation can only be one among others."

[19] William Stacy Johnson, *The Mystery of God: Karl Barth and the Postmodern Foundations of Theology*, Columbia Series in Reformed Theology (Louisville: Westminster John Knox Press, 1997), 33.

[20] Karl Rahner, *Hearers of the Word*, Michael Richards, trans. (New York: Herder & Herder, 1969), 140-165.

[21] Karl Rahner, "History of the World and Salvation-History," *Theological Investigations*, vol. 5 (London: Darton, Longman and Todd Ltd., 1966), 99.

[22] Rahner, "History of the World and Salvation-History," 107.

[23] Rahner, "History of the World and Salvation-History," 109.

[24] Admittedly my brief remarks on these two theologians hardly do justice to their theological endeavors. I refer to their thinking primarily to illustrate the tendency of Protestant and Catholic theologies to maintain ecclesiocentric conceptions of salvation history. To a certain degree they can be said to represent the dominant ecclesial expressions of Protestant and Roman Catholic orthodoxy this century. Precisely because Barth and Rahner have had such a profound influence on twentieth-century world Christian theology, their reflections on salvation in history draw our attention.

[25] For a historical definition of the Orthodox churches, see John Meyendorff, *The Orthodox Church: Its Past and Its Role in the World Today*, John Chapin, trans. (Crestwood, NY: St. Vladimir's Seminary Press, 1981).

[26] See Archbishop Iakovos Koukoujis, "The Contribution of Eastern Orthodoxy to the Ecumenical Movement," *The Orthodox Church in the Ecumenical Movement: Documents and Statements 1902-1975*, Constantin G. Patelos, ed. (Geneva: World Council of Churches, 1978), 217.

[27] See the insightful article by Kallistos Ware, "Tradition and Traditions," *Dictionary of the Ecumenical Movement*, Nicholas Lossky et al., eds. (Geneva: World Council of Churches / Grand Rapids: Wm. B. Eerdmans, 1991), s.v. Ware writes: "While Tradition is indeed the dynamic movement of God in history, it is to be seen also in a metahistorical or eschatological perspective. It is not so much a long line stretched out in time as the gathering of time itself into God's eternity, the irruption into this present age of the eschaton, or age to come," 1017.

[28] The Seven Ecumenical Councils regarded by the Eastern Orthodox (or Chalcedonian) churches are named for the cities in which they were held: Nicaea I (325), Constantinople I (381), Ephesus (431), Chalcedon (451), Constantinople II (553), Constantinople III (680), and Nicaea II (787). After Nicaea II, bishops of the Greek-speaking East and Latin-speaking West no longer met in ecumenical councils recognized by both communities. Hence the Eastern Orthodox accept only the decisions of these first seven as ecumenically (universally) authoritative. Coptic, Ethiopian, Armenian, Syrian, and Indian Orthodox churches accept only the authority of the first

156 NOTES

three councils, rejecting the two-nature Christology officially defined by the canons of Chalcedon. Assyrian Orthodox churches (known in the West as Nestorian) accept only the first two of these councils. Beginning with the Synod of Isaac (410), the Assyrian Church held a series of general synods which shaped its own theological heritage. The Roman Catholic church, on the other side of the world, continued after 787 to convene councils of bishops and cardinals which it considers to be ecumenical insofar as they represent the fullness of the Roman Catholic church, which is dogmatically for Roman Catholic theology the one true church of Jesus Christ on earth. For more on the history and impact of the Ecumenical Councils, see *Dictionary of the Ecumenical Movement*, s.v.

[29] Regarding the political nature of the first ecumenical council at Nicaea, Robert M. Grant, "Religion and Politics at the Council at Nicaea," *Journal of Religion* 55:1 (1975): 5, writes: "Some of the earliest witnesses call the council [at Nicaea in 325 A.D.] 'ecumenical,' but the term means no more than 'Roman-imperial.' What the council actually represented was the area [of the eastern half of the Roman empire] formerly controlled by Licinius." On the relation of the actual political life of Orthodox churches to the concept of being "ecumenical," see Willem A. Visser't Hooft, "The Word 'Ecumenical'—Its History and Use," *A History of the Ecumenical Movement, 1517-1948*, Ruth Rouse and Stephen Charles Neill, eds. (Geneva: WCC, 1986), 737. Concerning the political status of the Orthodox churches within Islamic society after the fall of the Byzantine empire, see Meyendorff, *The Orthodox Church*, 88, where he writes: "In his role as *millet-bachi*, 'head of the Christian nation,' or 'ethnarch' in Greek, the [Orthodox ecumenical] patriarch was now virtually the regent of an enslaved people."

[30] Patelos, ed., *The Orthodox Church in the Ecumenical Movement*, 226.

[31] Geiko Müller-Fahrenholz, "Salvation History," s.v. *Dictionary of the Ecumenical Movement*.

[32] H. G. Wood et al, *The Kingdom of God in History* (Chicago: Willett, Clark & Co., 1938), 111. See also Paul Tillich, *Systematic Theology*, vol. 3 (Chicago: University of Chicago Press, 1963), 308-311.

[33] Tillich, *Systematic Theology*, vol. 3, 309-311.

[34] Tillich, *Systematic Theology*, vol. 3, 311.

[35] Tillich, *Systematic Theology*, vol. 3, 311.

[36] Tillich, *Systematic Theology*, vol. 3, 363.

[37] Tillich, *Systematic Theology*, vol. 3, 364.

[38] Tillich, *Systematic Theology*, vol. 3, 374-377.

[39] Tillich, *Systematic Theology*, vol. 3, 378.

[40] Tillich, *Systematic Theology*, vol. 3, 381.

[41] Wolfhart Pannenberg, ed., *Revelation as History*, David Granskou, trans. (New York: Macmillan Co., 1968), 3-4.

[42] Pannenberg, ed., *Revelation as History*, 133.

[43] Pannenberg, ed., *Revelation as History*, 154-155.

[44] See the report of the Faith and Order Commission of the World Council of Churches, *New Directions in Faith and Order Bristol 1967: Reports—Minutes—Documents* (Geneva: WCC, 1968), 25: "So God's history must sooner or later give birth to the conception of universal history, in the sense that all groups, tribes, nations, imperia, races, and classes are involved in one and the same history."

[45] *New Directions in Faith and Order Bristol 1967*, 25 (emphasis mine).

[46] See Georg G. Iggers, *The German Conception of History: The National Tradition of Historical Thought from Herder to the Present* (Middletown, CT: Wesleyan University Press, 1983, rev. ed.); and Stuart H. Hughes, *Consciousness and Society: The Reorientation of European Social Thought, 1890-1930* (New York: Alfred E. Knopf). The connection between historical consciousness and the so-called "human sciences" is made by Wilhelm Dilthey; see his *Introduction to the Human Sciences: An Attempt to Lay a Foundation for the Study of Society and History*, Ramon J. Betanzos, trans. (Detroit: Wayne State University, 1988). Georg Lukacs,

History and Class Consciousness: Studies in Marxist Dialectics, Rodney Livingstone, trans. (Cambridge, MA: The MIT Press, 1971), argued for the primacy of history for Marxism. On the historical consciousness of Max Weber, in relation to social theory and his concept of rationalization, see Guenther Roth and Wolfgang Schluchter, *Max Weber's Vision of History: Ethics and Method* (Berkeley: University of California Press, 1979).

[47] See Hichem Djait, *Europe and Islam: Cultures and Modernity*, Peter Heinegg, trans. (Berkeley: University of California Press, 1985); and Robert Young, *White Mythologies: Writing History and the West* (London: Routledge, 1990). On the Eurocentric historical consciousness of Marx and Engels, see Diane Paul, " 'In the Interests of Civilization': Marxist Views of Race and Culture in the Nineteenth Century," *Journal of the History of Ideas* 42:1 (1981): 115-138.

[48] Ben C. Ollenburger, "From Timeless Ideas to the Essence of Religion: Method in Old Testament Theology before 1930," *The Flowering of Old Testament Theology*, Ben C. Ollenburger, Elmer A. Martens, and Gerhard F. Hasel, eds. (Winona Lake, IN: Eisenbrauns, 1992), 11.

[49] G. Ernest Wright, *God Who Acts: Biblical Theology as Recital* (London: SCM Press, 1952), 115.

[50] Wright, *God Who Acts*, 121.

[51] Wright, *God Who Acts*, 58.

[52] Gerhard von Rad, *The Problem of the Hexateuch and Other Essays* (New York: McGraw Hill, 1966), 144.

[53] Von Rad, *The Problem of the Hexateuch*, 164-165.

[54] See James Barr, *Old and New in Interpretation: A Study of the Two Testaments* (London: SCM Press, 1966); Bertil Albrektson, *History and the Gods: An Essay on the Idea of Historical Events as Divine Manifestations in the Ancient Near East and Israel* (Lund: Gleerup, 1967); J. J. M. Roberts, "Myth *versus* History," *Catholic Biblical Quarterly* 38:1 (1976), 1-13; John van Seters, *In Search of History: Historiography in the Ancient World and the Origins of Biblical History* (New Haven: Yale University Press, 1983). Further background discussion is provided in Henning Graf Reventlow, *Problems of Old Testament Theology in the Twentieth Century* (Philadelphia: Fortress Press, 1985), especially ch. 3, "The Problem of History."

[55] See Langdon Gilkey, *Reaping the Whirlwind: A Christian Interpretation of History* (New York: Seabury Press, 1981). Concerning the impact of historical method in North American theology and biblical studies in particular, see Mark S. Massa, *Charles Augustus Briggs and the Crisis of Historical Criticism* (Minneapolis: Fortress Press, 1990), 3-23.

[56] Gerhard Ebeling, *Word and Faith* (Philadelphia: Fortress Press, 1963), 336.

[57] Ebeling, *Word and Faith*, 370. Ebeling is certainly not alone in his claim regarding the Christian origins of modern historical consciousness. Regarding the range of twentieth century Euro-American thinking on the issues, see C. T. McIntire, ed., *God, History, and Historians: Modern Christian Views of History* (New York: Oxford University Press, 1977). The classical exposition of direct linkage between Christian faith and modern historical-mindedness is Karl Löwith, *Meaning in History* (Chicago: University of Chicago Press, 1949). Bernard Lonergan identifies the transition from classicism to historical consciousness in *Method in Theology* (New York: Seabury Press, 1972); see also his essay, "The Transition from a Classicist World-View to Historical-Mindedness," *A Second Collection: Papers of Bernard J. F. Lonergan*, William F.J. Ryan and Bernard J. Tyrrell, eds. (London: Darton, Longman and Todd, 1974), 1-10. An argument for modern historical consciousness itself being the European "other" to Christian faith in the modern era is made by Trutz Rendtorff in "The Modern Age as a Chapter in the History of Christianity: or, The Legacy of Historical Consciousness in Present Theology," *Journal of Religion* 65 (1985); and idem, *Church and Theology: The Systematic Function of the Church Concept in Modern Theology* (Philadelphia: Westminster Press, 1971).

[58] Peter Hodgson, *God in History: Shapes of Freedom* (Nashville: Abingdon Press, 1989), 205.

[59] Hodgson, *God in History*, 194.

[60] Hodgson, *God in History*, 249.

[61] Hodgson, *God in History*, 47.

158   NOTES

[62] Hodgson, *God in History*, 205.

[63] Hodgson, *God in History*, 209.

[64] It needs to be pointed out here that Hodgson responds almost primarily to one of them, Mark C. Taylor. His criticism is surprising in that much of what he accuses the postmodernist of embracing—"intellectual games and hedonistic play," " 'carnival, comedy, and carnality' in lieu of historical purpose," and even "the nihilistic play of the elite" (Hodgson, *God in History*, 40-41), he himself practices in different forms later in his text. Hodgson too engages in the play of figures and tropes, playing on etymologies and puns which very much resemble the postmodernist's intellectual games of hedonistic play (ibid., 83, 94, 97). Certainly the "we" that forms the discursive community of his text is no less elite than that of the postmodernist discourse he criticizes, despite whatever commitments to solidarity with the poor and oppressed that might be expressed through either forms of discourse.

[65] Hodgson, *God in History*, n. 184.

[66] Mark C. Taylor, *Erring: A Postmodern A-Theology* (Chicago: University of Chicago Press, 1984), 55.

[67] Hodgson, *God in History*, 93-95.

[68] Taylor, *Erring*, 72.

[69] Taylor, *Erring*, 68-72.

[70] Taylor, *Erring*, 108.

[71] Taylor, *Erring*, 76.

[72] Taylor, *Erring*, 76.

[73] Martin Heidegger, "The Word of Nietzsche: 'God is Dead,'" *The Question Concerning Technology and Other Essays* (New York: Harper and Row, 1977), 63-64.

[74] Need we be reminded again of Hegel's words concerning African history? "Africa proper, as far as History goes back, has remained—for all purposes of connection with the rest of the World—shut up; it is . . . the land of childhood, which lying beyond the day of self-conscious history, is enveloped in the dark mantle of Night . . . The peculiarly African character is difficult to comprehend, for the very reason that in reference to it, we must quite give up the principle which naturally accompanies all *our* ideas—the category of Universality . . . At this point we leave Africa, not to mention it again. For it is no historical part of the World; it has no movement or development to exhibit" (Georg Wilhelm Friedrich Hegel, *The Philosophy of History*, J. Sibree, trans. [New York: Dover Publications, 1956], 91, 93, 99).

[75] See Eric R. Wolf, *Europe and the People without History* (Berkeley: University of California Press, 1982).

[76] Choan-Seng Song, "New China and Salvation History: A Methodological Enquiry," *South-East Asian Journal of Theology* 15:2 (1974): 52-67; "From Israel to Asia: A Theological Leap," *Mission Trends III: Third World Theologies*, Gerald H. Anderson and Thomas F. Stransky, eds. (New York: Paulist Press, 1976), 211-233; and *Third-Eye Theology: Theology in Formation in Asian Settings* (Maryknoll, NY: Orbis Books, 1979).

[77] Song, "New China and Salvation History," 57.

[78] Song, "From Israel to Asia," 216.

[79] D. Preman Niles, "Toward a Framework for Doing Theology in Asia," *The Human and the Holy*, E. Nacpil and D. Ellwood, eds. (Maryknoll, NY: Orbis Books, 1980), 276.

[80] D. Preman Niles, "Report of the Executive Secretary of the Commission on Theological Concerns (CTC) 1979-1980," *CTC Bulletin* 2:1-2 (1981): 10. Niles wrote in a footnote, p. 13: "José Míguez Bonino . . . from whom I have taken the model of two stories, speaks rather of two histories—the Biblical and the Gentile histories—and the 'double historical reference' for Gentile Christians. I prefer the term 'story' since we are dealing with several different forms of historical and cultural expressions of the self-understanding of people."

[81] D. Preman Niles, "Story and Theology—A Proposal," *East Asian Journal of Theology* 3 (1985): 121. See also Suh Nam-dong, "Theology as Story-Telling: A Counter-Theology," *CTC Bulletin* 5:3 (1984): 4-11. Regarding "bracketing" Western history, see Carlos Abesamis, "Doing Theological Reflection in a Philippine Context," *The Emergent Gospel: Theology from the*

Developing World, Sergio Torres and Virginia Fabella, eds. (Maryknoll, NY: Orbis Books, 1978), 119.

[82] Kim Yong-bock, *An Introduction to the Asian Reality*, WSCF Dossier (Geneva: WSCF, 1975), 2. See also *Minjung Theology: People as the Subject of History*, Commission on Theological Concerns of the CCA, ed. (Maryknoll, NY: Orbis Books, 1981); and Jung Young Lee, ed., *An Emerging Theology in World Perspective: Commentary on Korean Minjung Theology* (Mystic CT: Twenty-Third Publications, 1988).

[83] See also Hyun Youn-hak, "Minjung Theology and the Religion of Han," *East Asia Journal of Theology* 3:3 (1985): 354-359; and Suh Nam-dong, "Historical References for a Theology of Minjung," *Minjung Theology*, 155-182.

[84] Samuel Rayan, "Indian Theology and the Problem of History," *Society and Religion*, Richard W. Taylor, ed. (Madras: Christian Literature Society, 1976), 167-193.

[85] Rayan, "Indian Theology and the Problem of History," 175.

[86] Aloysius Pieris, *An Asian Theology of Liberation* (Maryknoll, NY: Orbis Books, 1988), 74. See also A. Mathias Mundadan, *Indian Christians: Search for Identity and Struggle for Autonomy* (Bangalore: Dhamaram Publications, 1984); Hormice C. Perumalil, *Christianity in India: A History in Ecumenical Perspective* (Alleppey: Prakasam Publications, 1973); and Robin H. S. Boyd, *An Introduction to Indian Christian Theology* (Madras: CLS Press, 1975).

[87] On the emergence of a self-consciously postcolonial movement of African theology, see *Drumbeats from Kampala: Report of the First Assembly of the All Africa Conference of Churches* (London: Lutterworth Press, 1963); and Gwinyai Muzorewa, *The Origins and Development of African Theology* (Maryknoll, NY: Orbis Books, 1985).

[88] Mercy Amba Oduyoye, *Hearing and Knowing: Theological Reflections on Christianity in Africa* (Maryknoll, NY: Orbis Books, 1986), 15-28, explores the importance of Egyptian, Ethiopian, and Donatist traditions for contemporary Africa.

[89] J. F. Ade Ajayi, "The Continuity of African Institutions under Colonialism," *Emerging Themes of African History*, Terrence O. Ranger, ed. (Dar es Salaam: East African Publishing House, 1968), 194.

[90] Emmanuel A. Ayandele, *African Historical Studies* (London: Frank Cass and Co., 1979), 230.

[91] Ayandele, *African Historical Studies*, 211.

[92] Ogbu U. Kalu, "African Church Historiography," *African Historiography: Essays in Honour of J. A. Ajayi*, Toyin Falola, ed. (London: Longman, 1993), 170. Significantly, Kalu quotes David Livingstone, who said: "Already Africa is God's. God did not wait for me to bring Him. I found Him in every village."

[93] Kalu, "African Church Historiography," 170.

[94] See M. R. Spindler, "Writing African Church History (1969-1989): A Survey of Recent Studies," *Exchange* 19:1 (1990): 70-87.

[95] V. Y. Mudimbe, *The Invention of Africa: Gnosis, Philosophy, and the Order of Knowledge* (Bloomington, IN: Indiana University Press, 1988), 195. See also V. Y. Mudimbe and B. Jewsiewicki, eds., *History Making in Africa, History and Theory: Studies in the Philosophy of History* Beiheft *32* (1993).

[96] Quoted by Mudimbe, *The Invention of Africa*, 169. On the African historical practice of renewing tradition, see Kenneth O. Dike and J.F. Ade Ajayi, "African Historiography," *International Encyclopedia of the Social Sciences*, David L. Sills, ed., vol. 6 (New York: Macmillan Co., 1967), 395; and E. A. Ruch, "Philosophy of African History," *African Studies* 32:2 (1973): 117.

[97] Fabien Eboussi Boulaga, *Christianity without Fetishes: An African Critique and Recapture of Christianity* (Maryknoll, NY: Orbis Books, 1984), 168-170.

[98] On the conception of history as an open-ended, interactive field of forces, and the possibility of articulating hidden histories within it, see Jane Schneider, "Introduction: The Analytic Strategies of Eric R. Wolf," in *Articulating Hidden Histories: Exploring the Influences of Eric R. Wolf*, Jane Schneider and Rayna Rapp, eds. (Berkeley: University of California Press, 1995), 3-30. On the concept of opacity, see Charles Long, *Significations*.

5. Narratives of Church History

[1] William A. Clebsch, *Christianity in European History* (New York: Oxford University Press, 1979), 3.

[2] Charles H. Long, *Significations: Signs, Symbols, and Images in the Interpretation of Religion* (Philadelphia: Fortress Press, 1986), 196.

[3] Ogbu U. Kalu, "African Church Historiography," *African Historiography: Essays in Honour of J. A. Ajayi*, Toyin Falola, ed. (London: Longman, 1993), 170.

[4] Christopher Morse, *Not Every Spirit: A Dogmatics of Christian Disbelief* (Valley Forge: Trinity Press International, 1994), 288.

[5] Morse, *Not Every Spirit*, 310.

[6] Morse, *Not Every Spirit*, 313.

[7] Marianne Sawicki, *Seeing the Lord: Resurrection and Early Christian Practices* (Minneapolis: Fortress Press, 1994), 264.

[8] Andrew F. Walls, "Old Athens and New Jerusalem: Some Signposts for Christian Scholarship in the Early History of Mission Studies," *International Bulletin of Missionary Research* 21:4 (1997): 149.

[9] Walls, "Old Athens and New Jerusalem," 148.

[10] Morse, *Not Every Spirit*, 313.

[11] For an overview of the movement of narrative theology, see Stanley Hauerwas and L. Gregory Jones, *Why Narrative? Readings in Narrative Theology* (Grand Rapids: Wm. B. Eerdmans, 1989). William C. Placher, *Narratives of a Vulnerable God: Christ, Theology, and Scripture* (Louisville: Westminster John Knox Press, 1994), demonstrates to my mind the success of narrative theologies. I would note, however, that the question of God's identity being narrated through the biblical texts is more complex than most narrative theologians have acknowledged, as Frank Kermode has argued in *The Genesis of Secrecy: On the Interpretation of Narrative* (Cambridge, MA: Harvard University Press, 1979).

[12] See A. M. Mundadan, *History of Christianity in India, vol. 1: From the Beginning* (Bangalore: Church History Association of India, 1984).

[13] W. E. B. Du Bois, *The Souls of Black Folk* (New York: Penguin Press, 1982; originally published, 1903).

[14] Long, *Significations*, 107.

[15] Long, *Significations*, 185-199.

[16] See Hans Küng and David Tracy, eds., *Paradigm Change in Theology* (New York: Crossroad, 1984).

[17] While the literature on theology and culture is too vast to include here, a start can be found in Ans J. van der Bent, "Christianity and Culture: An Analytical Survey of Some Theological Approaches," *The Ecumenical Review* 39:2 (1987): 222-227. Consideration of cultural diversity has long occupied the discipline of missiology where it continues to receive considerable attention, as can be seen in David J. Bosch, *Transforming Mission: Paradigm Shifts in Theology of Mission* (Maryknoll, NY: Orbis Books, 1991), 420-456. A clear indication of the interrelatedness of social, political, and cultural factors emerged for liberation theologies through the Ecumenical Association of Third World Theologians, as can be seen in Virginia Fabella and Sergio Torres, eds., *Irruption of the Third World: Challenge to Theology* (Maryknoll, NY: Orbis Books, 1983). See also Dale T. Irvin, "Contextualization and Catholicity: Looking Anew for the Unity of the Faith," *Studia Theologica* 48:2 (1994).

[18] See David Lowenthal, *The Past Is a Foreign Country* (Cambridge: Cambridge University Press, 1985). Lowenthal's arguments are those of a historic preservationist, and pertain mostly to the monuments and material artifacts of the past which are changed by their being recontextualized in social life; whereas I am more interested in the changes in patterns of culture and identity which are manifested in the material artifacts of the past. Nevertheless, material and cultural dimensions of the past are not unrelated, and his phrase is a telling one, whether we apply it to the preservation

NOTES   161

of monuments or the realization of the difference represented by the heritage of the past.

[19] Among the many excellent surveys of this period of church history, few have successfully integrated critical social historical methods into what was in the past often confined to being a narrative of the history of doctrine. See, for instance, W. H. C. Frend, *The Rise of Christianity* (Philadelphia: Fortress Press, 1984), and Justo L. González, *The Story of Christianity, vol. 1: The Early Church to the Dawn of the Reformation* (San Francisco: Harper & Row Publishers, 1984). For the narrower narrative of the history of doctrine itself, see Jaroslov Pelikan, *The Christian Tradition: A History of the Development of Doctrine, vol. 1: The Emergence of the Christian Tradition (100-600)* (Chicago: University of Chicago Press, 1971), and Justo L. González, *A History of Christian Thought, vol. 1: From the Beginnings to the Council of Chalcedon in A.D. 451* (Nashville: Abingdon Press, 1970).

[20] I use the term "so-called" following Alexander Kazhdan, who writes in his article "Byzantium: The Emperor's New Clothes?" *History Today* 39 (September 1989): 26, "The state of Byzantium, the so-called Byzantine empire, has never existed; the term was invented in the sixteenth century to designate the empire the capital of which was Constantinople, the city on the Bosphorus, which was supposedly founded in 330 and destroyed by the Ottoman Turks in 1453 ... throughout the Middle Ages the Byzantines were the citizens of Constantinople only, not the subjects of the emperor who reigned in Constantinople. These subjects did not even notice that they stopped being Romans and began being Byzantines—they considered themselves Romans until they woke up under the rule of the sultans."

[21] Harvey J. Kaye, *The Powers of the Past: Reflections on the Crisis and the Promise of History* (Minneapolis: University of Minnesota Press, 1991), 40-41.

[22] Jean-François Lyotard, *The Post-Modern Condition: A Report on Knowledge* (Minneapolis: University of Minnesota Press, 1984). Lyotard sets large-scale interpretations of history purportedly of universal significance in opposition to multiple local narratives and anti-narratives, or stories of resistance. In the paragraphs that follow I will use "grand narrative" and "master narrative" interchangeably to refer to the content of the dominant historiography of Church history, and "meta-narrative" to emphasize the interpretive frameworks for which such grand narratives are put to use. For a fuller discussion and defense of the narrative character of history-writing, see Paul Ricoeur, *Time and Narrative*, vol. 1, by Kathleen Blamey and David Pellauer, trans. (Chicago: University of Chicago Press, 1984); Paul Veyne, *Writing History: Essays on Epistemology* (Middletown, CT: Wesleyan University Press, 1984); H. Stuart Hughes, *History as Art and as Science: Twin Vistas on the Past* (Chicago: University of Chicago Press, 1964); and Peter Gay, *Style in History* (New York: McGraw-Hill Book Co., 1974).

[23] Adolf von Harnack, *History of Dogma*, 7 vols., Neil Buchanan, trans. (New York: Dover Books, 1961).

[24] Educated in the United States and Germany, Walker was for many years professor of Ecclesiastical History at Yale University. His church history textbook was originally published in 1918, but since then has been updated and revised a number of times. The contributors to the successive revisions have all been themselves significant church historians in their own right, making *A History of the Christian Church* a unique text insofar as it bears the signature of a significant community of historical discourse. I will be quoting from the third edition (New York: Charles Scribner's Sons, 1970).

[25] Butterfield, *Christianity in European History*, (London: Collins, 1945), 7.

[26] Walker, *A History of the Christian Church*, 102.

[27] Walker, *A History of the Christian Church*, 3-4. This quote appears in the first three editions (1918, 1959, and 1970) but does not appear in the completely rewritten first chapter of the 1985 edition.

[28] Herbert Butterfield, *Christianity in European History*, 45.

[29] A full, positive defense of this thesis can be found in Kenneth Scott Latourette, *The Emergence of a World Christian Community* (New Haven: Yale University Press, 1949).

[30] Karl Rahner, "Towards a Fundamental Theological Interpretation of Vatican II," *Theological Studies* 40:4 (1979): 716-727. In its first historical phase, Rahner argued, the Christian church

was for a short time a Jewish movement. The second phase that followed was a long period of European church history that lasted until the twentieth century. With Vatican II a third phase in the history of the Christian church became apparent, one in which it is becoming truly a world church.

[31] Hubert Jedin and Karl Baus, "Preface," *History of the Church*, vol. 1, *From the Apostolic Community to Constantine* (New York: Crossroad, 1982), ix.

[32] Jedin, "General Introduction to Church History," *Church History*, vol. 1, 9.

[33] Jedin, "General Introduction," *Church History*, vol. 1, 5.

[34] Jedin, "General Introduction," *Church History*, vol. 1, 6.

[35] H. Jedin and Konrad Repgen, "Preface," *History of the Church*, vol. 10, *The Church in the Modern Age* (New York: Crossroad, 1981), xi.

[36] John P. Dolan, "Preface to the English Edition," *Church History*, vol. 4, *From the High Middle Ages to the Eve of the Reformation* (New York: Crossroad, 1980), xiii.

[37] Jedin, "Preface," *Church History*, vol. 4, xi.

[38] Jedin, "Preface," *Church History*, vol. 4, xii.

[39] Justo González, "Globalization in the Teaching of Church History," *Theological Education* 29:2 (1993): 55.

[40] For an excellent historical exploration of the genealogy, development, and effects of the myth of this westward narrative, see Jan Willem Schulte Nordholt, *The Myth of the West: America as the Last Empire*, Herbert H. Rowen, trans. (Grand Rapids: Wm. B. Eerdmans, 1995).

[41] The strangeness of this effect can be seen in the opening pages of what is otherwise an excellent contextual theological text, Robert E. Hood's *Must God Remain Greek? Afro Cultures and God-Talk* (Minneapolis: Fortress Press, 1990). In the opening page of his text Hood stated an alternative version to Harnack's Hellenization thesis: ". . . over 1500 years, the core notions of Christian life and thought . . . were forcefully if not always gracefully hammered into the Greek mold." Missionaries from Europe in the nineteenth century brought to Africa "their almost visceral faith in the Greek way of thinking" (xi). The assumption of direct lineage from the Greeks to modern Europe on the one hand leads him in the introduction to assume that persons who are within the cultural circle of European ethnicity have greater access or acceptance of ancient Greek metaphysical and orthodox Christian theological ideas, an assumption which begs the question; and on the other, it leads him to ignore the fact that the New Testament was originally Greek, and that North Africans contributed extensively to the theological heritage of the ancient church. Nowhere in his text does he acknowledge the possibility that modern Africans may well be able to understand and appropriate ancient Greek and Latin theologians (Athanasius and Augustine, for instance) more readily than modern Europeans can, on cultural as well as historical grounds of identity, a possibility which will be raised in more detail below.

[42] References to the "younger" churches are more numerous in missionary and ecumenical discourse from earlier in this century, but the terminology has not ceased to be used to designate the relationship between European and non-European churches. See, for example, Walbert Bühlmann, *The Coming of the Third Church: An Analysis of the Present and Future of the Church* (Maryknoll, NY: Orbis Books, 1978), 3-4.

[43] Ulrich Koepf, "A European View of the Problems of Dividing Church History into Periods," *Towards a History of the Church in the Third World: The Issue of Periodisation*, Lukas Vischer, ed. (Bern: Evangelische Arbeitsstelle Oekumene Schweiz, 1985).

[44] Koepf, "A European View," 97.

[45] Koepf, "A European View," 103.

[46] Koepf, "A European View," 101.

[47] Koepf, "A European View," 103 (emphasis original).

[48] Owen Chadwick, "Kirchengeschichte—Weltgeschichte: Europa und die Weltchristenheit," *Europäische Theologie: Versuche einer Ortsbestimmung*, Trutz Rendtorff, ed. (Gütersloh: Gütersloher Verlagshaus Mohn, 1980), 97.

[49] Latourette, *The Emergence of a World Christian Community*, 3 (emphasis added).

6. A Genealogy of Christian Histories and Traditioning

[1] Quoted in Harvey J. Kaye, *The Powers of the Past: Reflections on the Crisis and the Promise of History* (Minneapolis: University of Minnesota Press, 1991), 40.

[2] David Rhoads, *The Challenge of Diversity: The Witness of Paul and the Gospels* (Minneapolis: Fortress Press, 1996), 138.

[3] *Unitatis Redintegratio* 14, in *Vatican Council II: The Conciliar and Post Conciliar Documents*, Austin Flannery, O.P., ed. (Northport, NY: Costello Publishing, 1980), 464.

[4] *Vatican Council II: The Conciliar and Post Conciliar Documents*, 464.

[5] See Dale T. Irvin, *Hearing Many Voices: Dialogue and Diversity in the Ecumenical Movement* (Lanham, MD: University Press of America, 1994), 1-34.

[6] See, for instance, Patricia Wilson-Kastner et al., *A Lost Tradition: Women Writers of the Early Church* (Washington, DC: University Press of America, 1981).

[7] Charles H. Long, *Significations: Signs, Symbols, and Images in the Interpretation of Religion* (Philadelphia: Fortress Press, 1986), 9.

[8] Friedrich Nietzsche, *On the Genealogy of Morals*, Walter Kaufmann and R. J. Hollingdale, trans. (New York: Random House, 1969), 77.

[9] Michel Foucault, *Power/Knowledge: Selected Interviews and Other Writings 1972-1977*, Colin Gordon, ed. (New York: Pantheon Books, 1977), 83.

[10] Foucault, *Power/Knowledge*, 83.

[11] Michel Foucault, *Language, Counter-Memory, Practice: Selected Essays and Interviews*, Donald F. Bouchard, ed. (Ithaca: Cornell University Press, 1977), 145.

[12] See Judith N. Shklar, "Subversive Genealogies," *Myth, Symbol and Culture*, Clifford Geertz, ed. (New York: W. W. Norton, 1971), 129-154.

[13] Johannes Baptist Metz, *Faith in History and Society: Toward a Practical Fundamental Theology* (New York: Seabury Press, 1980), 66-68, 200-204.

[14] See James H. Cone, *The Spirituals and the Blues* (New York: Seabury Press, 1972).

[15] See Albert J. Raboteau, *Slave Religion: The "Invisible Institution" in the Antebellum South* (New York: Oxford University Press, 1978); and Sterling Stuckey, *Slave Culture: Nationalist Theory and the Foundations of Black America* (New York: Oxford University Press, 1986).

[16] Homi K. Bhabha, *The Location of Culture* (London: Routledge, 1994), 139-46, 171-173.

[17] "The Epistle to Diognetus," *Ancient Christian Writers: The Works of the Fathers in Translation*, vol. 6, Johannes Quasten and Joseph C. Plumpe, eds. (Westminster, MD: The Newman Press, 1961), 139.

[18] Edward W. Said, *Culture and Imperialism* (New York: Alfred A. Knopf, 1993), 335.

[19] Said, *Culture and Imperialism*, 335.

[20] See Rhoads, *The Challenge of Diversity*.

[21] See Lamin Sanneh, *Translating the Message: The Missionary Impact on Culture* (Maryknoll, NY: Orbis Books, 1990), 9-48; and Andrew F. Walls, "Old Athens and New Jerusalem: Some Signposts for Christian Scholarship in Early History of Mission Studies," *International Bulletin of Missionary Research* 21:4 (1997): 146-149.

[22] See Bhabha, *The Location of Culture*, 212-228.

[23] See Martin Hengel and Anna Maria Schwemer, *Paul between Damascus and Antioch: The Unknown Years*, John Bowden, trans. (Louisville: Westminster John Knox Press, 1997); James H. Charlesworth and Loren L. Johns, eds., *Hillel and Jesus: Comparative Studies of Two Major Religious Leaders* (Minneapolis: Fortress Press, 1997); and Marianne Sawicki, *Seeing the Lord: Resurrection and Early Christian Practices* (Minneapolis: Fortress Press, 1994).

[24] Edessa was the major city in the kingdom of Osrhoene, an independent buffer state located between the Roman and Persian empires. The fourth-century Christian historian Eusebius preserves an early story of the gospel message coming to this city in the form of a correspondence between Jesus and King Abgar, which Eusebius claimed to have translated from the original

Syriac. Invited by King Abgar to come to Edessa himself, Jesus is reported to have sent back a letter declining the invitation, but promising to send one of his disciples. After the resurrection, Thomas, according to the story, "sent to him as an apostle Thaddaeus, one of the Seventy," presumably those sent out earlier in Luke 10. See Eusebius, *The History of the Church from Christ to Constantine*, G. A. Williamson, trans. (New York: Penguin Books, 1984), 67.

[25] Samuel Hugh Moffett, *A History of Christianity in Asia, vol. 1: Beginnings to 1500* (San Francisco: HarperCollins, 1992), 25-90.

[26] See A. M. Mundadan, *Sixteenth-Century Traditions of St. Thomas Christians* (Bangalore: Dharmaram College, 1971); L. W. Brown, *The Indian Christians of St. Thomas* (Cambridge: Cambridge University Press, 1956); E. Tisserant, *Eastern Christianity in India* (Westminster, MD: Newman Press, 1957); and Placid J. Podipara, *The Thomas Christians* (London: Darton, Longman & Todd / Bombay: St. Paul Publications, 1970).

[27] See J. B. Segal, *Edessa, the Blessed City* (Oxford: Clarendon Press, 1970), and Nina G. Garsoïan, Thomas F. Mathews, and Robert W. Thomson, eds., *East of Byzantium: Syria and Armenia in the Formative Period* (Washington, DC: Dumbarton Oaks Center for Byzantine Studies, 1982). Scott Sunquist has pointed out to me that although the historicity of the traditions of St. Thomas remains difficult to verify, among all of the traditions recalling Thomas, not one recalls him traveling west; all recall him going to the East with the gospel.

[28] See Sebastian P. Brock and Susan Ashbrook Harvey, *Holy Women of the Syrian Orient* (Berkeley: University of California Press, 1987); and S. P. Brock, trans., *The Liturgical Portions of the Didascalia Apostolorum* (Bramcote: Grove Publishers, 1982).

[29] These two theological positions were the Christological positions explicitly rejected in 451 by the Council of Chalcedon which defined Jesus Christ as two natures in one person. What was called by Chalcedonian churches the Monophysite heresy sought to affirm one nature of Jesus Christ after the incarnation; what was called Nestorianism sought to affirm the two (*logos* and humanity) conjoined in the incarnation. For a fuller discussion of the Christological issues involved, see Paulos Gregorios, William H. Lazareth, and Nikos A. Nissiotis, eds., *Does Chalcedon Divide or Unite? Towards Convergence in Orthodox Christology* (Geneva: World Council of Churches, 1981); Paul R. Fries and Tiran Nersoyan, eds., *Christ in East and West* (Macon, GA: Mercer University Press, 1987); and M. K. Kuriakose, ed., *Orthodox Identity in India: Essays in Honour of V. C. Samuel* (Bangalore: Rev. V. C. Samuel 75th Birthday Celebration Committee, 1986).

[30] For a full examination of Theodore's theology, see Richard A. Norris, *Manhood and Christ: A Study in the Christology of Theodore of Mopsuestia* (Oxford: Clarendon Press, 1963).

[31] Stephen Gero, "The See of Peter in Babylon: Western Influences on the Ecclesiology of Early Persian Christianity," in *East of Byzantium*, 49.

[32] One can only speculate what the historiography of world Christianity would look like if the archives of the Persian church, and of other Christian churches in Asia and Africa, had not been lost after the conquests of Islam. Is it possible that we are so much more historically informed by Latin readings of history because the archives of Rome remained relatively unaffected by the crisis of historical disruptions after the year 600 such as those that affected the Byzantine and Persian churches?

[33] Sidney Griffith calls the eighth century Persian text of Theodore bar Kônî's *Scholian* "a Nestorian *Summa contra Gentiles*" from the first century of Islamic rule in Persia, in "Theodore bar Kônî's *Scholian*: A Nestorian *Summa contra Gentiles* from the First Abbasid Century," *East of Byzantium*, 53-72.

[34] Moffett maintains a consistent subnarrative in the text of *A History of Christianity in Asia* on the Persian church's missionary outreach, 207-209. Indeed the Persian church is recognized by many church historians as being a significant missionary tradition, but one suspects in Moffett's case his missiological interest is also due to his own role as a historian of missions.

[35] For the history of the Persian church's mission to China, see Lo Hsiang Lin, *Nestorianism in the T'ang and Yuan Dynasties* (Hong Kong: University Press, 1966). On the history of the

Indian church's eventual turn to the Persian patriarch for assistance and a supply of clergy, see Moffett, *A History of Christianity in Asia*, 265-271.

[36] David B. Barrett, ed., *World Christian Encyclopedia: A Comparative Study of Churches and Religions in the Modern World A.D. 1900-2000* (Nairobi: Oxford University Press, 1982), 23. While this number remains speculative and appears to be somewhat exaggerated, it nevertheless suggests how large the Persian church was prior to the onset of persecutions in the fourteenth century.

[37] See Moffett, *A History of Christianity in Asia*, 480-494.

[38] Moffett, *A History of Christianity in Asia*, 120-122.

[39] Gero, "The See of Peter in Babylon," *East of Byzantium*, 46.

[40] Recognition of its eminence did not mean Constantinople was expected or invited to exercise administrative jurisdiction over the Persian churches, and indeed the patriarch of Constantinople did not exercise such a pastoral office even over the churches of the Roman Empire, or Byzantium. Constantinople was but a city, and its see served as a focus or center for what was conceived of in the eastern Orthodox tradition as an ecumenical commonwealth of churches. At the Persian Synod of 410, recognition of the eminence of Constantinople served a unifying, rather than totalizing, function. See Alexander Kazhdan, "Byzantium: The Emperor's New Clothes?" *History Today* 39 (1989): 26-34.

[41] The word Copt, derived from the Greek *aigyptos* (Egypt), originally denoted the indigenous Egyptian language and culture during the period of Greek rule under the Ptolemies, prior to the birth of Christ. During this period the Greek script began to be used to write the Egyptian language, with seven additional letters. From the period of the early Christian movement in Egypt, theological texts can be found in either or both languages (Greek and Coptic), but the term Coptic can also be used to name persons of indigenous Egyptian culture. Eventually the name was used for the Egyptian church which did not agree with the decisions of the Council of Chalcedon in 451, the council that condemned the teaching of Dioscorus, bishop of Alexandria. After Chalcedon the church in Egypt which was Chalcedonian, or under an alternative bishop who remained in communion with the patriarch of Constantinople, was called "Melkite" (literally, "imperial"). In the paragraphs that follow, when I use the term Egyptian church, I am referring to the indigenous Coptic church.

[42] On the Coptic church's extended tradition of the Holy Family's flight into Egypt with Salome, the midwife, and sojourn through the country, see Otto F. A. Meinardus, *Christian Egypt Ancient and Modern* (Cairo: Cahiers d'Histoire Égyptienne, 1965), 1-4.

[43] Clarice J. Martin, "A Chamberlain's Journey and the Challenge of Interpretation for Liberation," *Semeia* 47 (1989): 105-135.

[44] See Cain Hope Felder, *Troubling Biblical Waters: Race, Class, and Family* (Maryknoll, NY: Orbis Books, 1989), 5-36.

[45] Elizabeth Isichei, *A History of Christianity in Africa: From Antiquity to the Present* (Grand Rapids: Wm. B. Eerdmans / Lawrenceville, NJ: Africa World Press, 1995), 30-32.

[46] Felder, *Troubling Biblical Waters*, 22-35, in reviewing ancient evidences for the identity of the Queen of Sheba notes that Josephus and early Christian writers all took the Queen of Sheba to be Queen of Ethiopia, as Ethiopians still do today.

[47] For a discussion of the political and cultural background of the Axumite kingdom, and its relation to both Arabian and Egyptian kingdoms, see J. D. Fage, *A History of Africa*, 2nd edition (London: Unwin Hyman, 1988), 48-54; and Felder, *Troubling Biblical Waters*, 22-30. For a fuller examination of Ethiopia in both biblical and Greco-Roman worlds, see Frank M. Snowden, Jr., *Blacks in Antiquity: Ethiopians in the Greco-Roman Experience* (Cambridge, MA: Harvard University Press, 1970); Edward Ullendorff, *The Ethiopians* (New York: Oxford University Press, 1961); and idem, *Ethiopians and the Bible* (London: Oxford University Press, 1968).

[48] Harold G. Marcus, *A History of Ethiopia* (Berkeley: University of California Press, 1994), 7; and Steven Kaplan, *The Monastic Holy Man and the Christianization of Early Solomonic Ethiopia* (Wiesbaden: Franz Steiner, 1984), 15.

166   NOTES

⁴⁹ See Mekouria Tekle-Tsadik, *L'église d'Éthiopie* (Paris: Promotion et Édition, 1967).

⁵⁰ See W. H. C. Frend, *The Rise of the Monophysite Movement* (Cambridge: Cambridge University Press, 1972).

⁵¹ Concerning the historical basis for Mark evangelizing in Alexandria, see Birger A. Pearson, "Earliest Christianity in Egypt: Some Observations," *The Roots of Egyptian Christianity*, Birger A. Pearson and James E. Goehring, eds. (Philadelphia: Fortress Press, 1986), 137-145.

⁵² See Isichei, *A History of Christianity in Africa*, 20-23.

⁵³ Samuel Rubenson, *The Letters of St. Antony: Origenist Theology, Monastic Tradition and the Making of a Saint* (Lund: Lund University Press, 1990), 126. For the English translation, see Athanasius, *The Life of Anthony and the Letter to Marcellinus*, Robert Gregg, ed., in the *Classics of Western Spirituality* (New York: Paulist Press, 1980).

⁵⁴ See James M. Robinson, ed., *The Nag Hammadi Library*, 3rd edition (San Francisco: Harper and Row, 1988).

⁵⁵ See Roberta C. Bondi, *To Love as God Loves: Conversations with the Early Church* (Philadelphia: Fortress Press, 1989); and idem, *To Pray and to Love: Conversations on Prayer with the Early Church* (Minneapolis: Fortress Press, 1991). For the sayings of the desert fathers and mothers, see Benedicta Ward, *The Sayings of the Desert Fathers: The Alphabetical Collection* (Oxford: A. R. Mowbray, 1981).

⁵⁶ See James E. Goehring, "New Frontiers in Pachomian Studies," and Janet Timbie, "The State of Research on the Career of Shenoute of Atripe," in *The Roots of Egyptian Christianity*, Pearson and Goehring, eds., 236-270.

⁵⁷ See Peter Brown, *The Rise of Western Christendom: Triumph and Diversity AD 200-1000* (Cambridge, MA: Blackwell Publishers, 1996), 43-44.

⁵⁸ See J. B. Rives, *Religion and Authority in Roman Carthage from Augustus to Constantine* (Oxford: Clarendon Press / New York: Oxford University Press, 1995); and Cecil M. Robeck Jr., *Prophecy in Carthage: Perpetua, Tertullian, and Cyprian* (Cleveland, OH: Pilgrim Press, 1992).

⁵⁹ Frend, *The Rise of Christianity*, 572, 573.

⁶⁰ W. H. C. Frend, *The Donatist Church: A Movement of Protest in Roman Africa* (Oxford: Clarendon Press, 1952).

⁶¹ For his criticism of Frend's position, see Peter Brown, "Christianity and Local Culture in Late Roman Africa," *Journal of Roman Studies* (1968); and idem, "Religious Coercion in the Later Roman Empire: The Case of North Africa," *History* (1963), both quoted in Isichei, *A History of Christianity in Africa*, 37. Peter Brown's own historical narrative in *The Rise of Western Christendom* locates diverse political and cultural formations within the circle of imperial identity in the emergence of distinctive expressions especially of North European Christendom, a thesis which will be drawn on in the discussion below.

⁶² Frend, *The Donatist Church*, 59.

⁶³ Brown, *The Rise of Western Civilization*, 5.

⁶⁴ Moffett, *A History of Christianity in Asia*, 199.

⁶⁵ Averil Cameron, *Christianity and the Rhetoric of Empire: The Development of Christian Discourse* (Berkeley: University of California Press, 1991), 121.

⁶⁶ Herbert Butterfield, *Christianity in European History* (London: Collins, 1952), 6.

⁶⁷ Judith Herrin, *The Formation of Christendom* (Princeton: Princeton University Press, 1987), 295.

⁶⁸ Herrin, *Formation of Christendom*, 297. On the process of inventing tradition in the wake of modernity, see Eric Hobsbawm and Terence Ranger, eds., *The Invention of Tradition* (Cambridge: Cambridge University Press, 1983).

⁶⁹ This is the major thesis of Brown's *The Rise of Western Christendom*, summarized in his final chapter which is subtitled, "Northern Christendom and Its Past."

⁷⁰ On the narrative praxis (re)configuring Europe in the modern colonial era, see Francis Barker et al., eds., *Europe and Its Others: Proceedings of the Essex Conference on the Sociology of Literature, July 1984*, 2 vol. (Colchester: University of Essex, 1985), especially the paper by Jose Rabasa, "Allegories of the Atlas" in vol. 2, 1-16; and Charles H. Long, "Primitive/Civilized:

The Locus of a Problem," *Significations: Signs, Symbols, and Images in the Interpretation of Religion* (Philadelphia: Fortress Press, 1986), 79-96.

[71] Owen Chadwick, "Kirchengeschichte—Weltgeschichte: Europa und die Weltchristenheit," *Europäische Theologie: Versuche einer Ortsbestimmung*, Trutz Rendtorff, ed. (Gütersloh: Gütersloher Verlagshaus Mohn, 1980), 97.

[72] This remains one of the enduring insights of Ernst Troeltsch's *The Social Teaching of the Christian Churches* (Chicago: University of Chicago Press, 1960), explored in greater depth in his essay, "What Does 'Essence of Christianity' Mean?", *Writings on Theology and Religion*, Robert Morgan and Michael Pye, eds. (Atlanta: John Knox Press, 1977), 124-179. One should note the intentional use of the plural in the title of the former book; Troeltsch was arguing for there being Christian *churches* in Europe.

[73] Raimundo Panikkar, "The Relation of Christians to Their Non-Christian Surroundings," *Christian Revelation and World Religions*, Joseph Neuner, ed. (London: Burns and Oates, 1967), 169.

[74] See Carl F. Hallencreutz, "Third World Church History—An Integral Part of Theological Education," *Studia Theologica* 47 (1993): 29-47.

7. The Grace to Renew the Past

[1] Homi K. Bhabha, *The Location of Culture* (London: Routledge, 1994), 12.

[2] Concerning the relation of the "post" of the postmodern to the "post" of the postcolonial, see Kwame Anthony Appiah, *In My Father's House: Africa in the Philosophy of Culture* (Oxford University Press: 1992), 137-157; and Bhabha, *The Location of Culture*, 171-197.

[3] Note that the German term for the modern age is appropriately *die Neuzeit*.

[4] See Peter Ochs, "Compassionate Postmodernism: An Introduction to Rabbinic Semiotics," *Soundings* 76:1 (1993): 139-152.

[5] At this point I would argue that postcolonial and postmodern criticism must be taken together to keep the postmodern from lapsing back into its racist, modernist past. The danger is identified by Cornel West, "Black Culture and Postmodernism," *Remaking History, Dia Ark Foundation Discussion in Contemporary Culture 4*, Barbara Kruger and Phil Mariani, eds. (Seattle: Bay Press, 1989), 92, where he writes: "My own hunch is that oppositional black intellectuals must be conversant with and, to a degree, participants in the debate. Yet until the complex relations between race, class, and gender are more adequately theorized, more fully delineated in specific historiographical studies, and more fused in our concrete ideological and political practices, the postmodernism debate, though at times illuminating, will remain rather blind to the plight and predicament of black America. Therefore I do not displace myself from the postmodernism debate, I simply try to keep my distance from its parochialism and view it as a symptom of our present cultural crisis."

[6] Something of the vast field of the contemporary studies of difference, including postcolonial, antiracist, feminist, subaltern, multiculturalist, and anticapitalist interrogations, can be found in the massive volume on *Cultural Studies*, Lawrence Grossberg, Cary Nelson, and Paula A. Treichler, eds. (New York: Routledge, 1992). A concise statement of what has come to be termed postmodernism is also found in Ihab Hassan, "Toward a Concept of Postmodernism," in *The Postmodern Turn: Essays in Postmodern Theory and Culture* (Columbus: Ohio State University, 1987), 84-96. Fredric Jameson, *Postmodernism, or, The Cultural Logic of Late Capitalism* (Durham: Duke University Press, 1991), provides one of the more exhaustive critical examinations of the material, commercial, aesthetic, and intellectual currents of contemporary North American postmodern culture.

[7] The actual history of European Christendom was never as unified as its representations in the modern memory made it appear to be. Among the more unified of recent historical accounts of medieval European Christendom is Adriaan H. Bredero, *Christendom and Christianity in the Middle Ages: The Relations between Religion, Church, and Society*, Reinder Bruinsma, trans. (Grand Rapids: Wm. B. Eerdmans, 1994), but even his study demonstrates well the various

tensions, traditions, and cultural forces at work in medieval Europe.

[8] See Jan Willem Schulte Nordholt, *The Myth of the West: America as the Last Empire*, Herbert H. Rowen, trans. (Grand Rapids: Wm. B. Eerdmans, 1995).

[9] Yves Congar, *Tradition and Traditions*, 160, points out that the Council of Trent, which so decisively affirmed the authority of tradition for Roman Catholic theology, at the same time acknowledged a multiplicity of traditions. Trent recognized ecclesiastical traditions which, while not identical with Apostolic tradition, could not be methodologically separated from it either. It acknowledged the existence of multiple forms of tradition as modes (not sources) in which the totality of faith was contained. According to Congar: "One fact dominated the discussion [at Trent]: the diversity of opinion among the Fathers and theologians, the lack of any definite idea of 'tradition' ... The council itself speaks of 'traditions' in the plural, but a study of its deliberations shows that the word was used in both singular and plural forms indiscriminately."

[10] This political-ideological "captivity" isn't unique to the modern period. Concerning earlier forms of Constantinian Christendom and the Latin medieval synthesis of church and political life, for instance, see Alistar Kee, *Constantine versus Christ: The Triumph of Ideology* (London: SCM Press, 1982); Brian Tierney, *The Crisis of Church and State 1050-1300, with Selected Documents* (Englewood Cliffs, NJ: Prentice-Hall, Inc., 1964), which includes the Papal Bull of 1302, *Unam Sanctam*; Ernst Hartwig Kantorowicz, *The King's Two Bodies: A Study in Mediaeval Political Theology* (Princeton: Princeton University Press, 1957); and Walter Klaassen, "The Anabaptist Critique of Constantinian Christendom," *The Mennonite Quarterly Review* 55:3 (1981): 218-230.

[11] My criticism of such totalization alludes to the discussion of Jean-Paul Sartre in *Critique of Dialectical Reason*, vol. 1, *Theory of Practical Ensembles*, Alan Sheridan-Smith, trans. (London: Verso, 1976). Sartre concluded that there was totalization without a totalizer in history, leaving intact a notion of totalization or universal history, a theme similar to that being propounded in Fredric Jameson's *The Political Unconscious: Narrative as a Socially Symbolic Act* (Ithaca: Cornell University Press, 1981). For criticism of such visions of totalization in history see Michel Foucault, *Power/Knowledge: Selected Interviews and Other Writings 1972-1977*, Colin Gordon, ed. (New York: Pantheon Books, 1980), 78-92; and Robert Young, *White Mythologies: Writing History and the West* (London: Routledge, 1990).

[12] See Duncan B. Forrester, "The Attack on Christendom in Marx and Kierkegaard," *Scottish Journal of Theology* 25:2 (1972): 181-196; Paul Peachey, "Constantinian Christendom and the Marx-Engels Phenomenon," *The Mennonite Quarterly Review* 55:3 (1981): 184-197; and John W. Elrod, *Kierkegaard and Christendom* (Princeton: Princeton University Press, 1981).

[13] Albert J. Raboteau, *Slave Religion: The "Invisible Institution" in the Antebellum South* (New York: Oxford University Press, 1978).

[14] The concept of a crisis of historical representation I have borrowed from Edward W. Said, whose book, *Orientalism* (New York: Random House, 1978), offers a comprehensive investigation into the problem of historical representation in modern European cultural life.

[15] Here I am very much aware of the dangers of romanticizing marginality, a danger which Gayatri Chakravorty Spivak points to in *Outside the Teaching Machine* (New York: Routledge, 1993), 55, where she writes: "If there is a buzzword in cultural critique now, it is 'marginality' ... When a cultural identity is thrust upon one because the center wants an identifiable margin, claims for marginality assure validation from the center."

[16] Some have even argued that the Greek philosophers had discovered the truth by means of reason, and that the early Christian church's theologians succeeded in that they recast Christian beliefs in the form of Greek philosophy. See, for instance, Harry Austryn Wolfson, *The Philosophy of the Church Fathers, vol. 1: Faith, Trinity, Incarnation*, 3rd edition (Cambridge, MA: Harvard University Press, 1970). Yet here again we do not need to agree with Wolfson's assumptions concerning Hellenistic philosophy to gain from his work valuable insights into the early intellectual history of Christianity.

[17] On the problem of determining a timeless essence for Christianity, see Ernst Troeltsch, "What Does 'Essence of Christianity' Mean?" in *Ernst Troeltsch: Writings on Theology and Religion*, Robert Morgan and Michael Pye, trans. and eds. (Atlanta: John Knox Press, 1977), 124-

181. The notion of theological intertextuality is explored more fully in Dale T. Irvin, "Contextualization and Catholicity: Looking Anew for the Unity of the Faith," *Studia Theologica* 48:2 (1994): 83-96.

[18] Among the more influential theologians this century has been Karl Rahner, whose essays in *Theological Investigations* include: "Membership of the Church According to the Teaching of Pius XII's Encyclical 'Mystici Corporis Christi,' " vol. 2 (Baltimore: Helicon Press, 1963), 1-88; "Anonymous Christians," vol. 6 (Baltimore: Helicon Press, 1969), 390-398; and "Anonymous and Explicit Faith," vol. 16 (New York: Seabury Press, 1979), 52-59. An alternative religious historical framework is found in Raimundo Panikkar, *The Unknown Christ of Hinduism: Towards an Ecumenical Christophany*, revised and enlarged edition (Maryknoll, NY: Orbis Books, 1981). For an overview of contemporary Christian belief regarding the salvific value of other religions, see Gerald H. Anderson and Thomas F. Stransky, eds., *Christ's Lordship and Religious Pluralism* (Maryknoll, NY: Orbis Books, 1983); Paul F. Knitter, *No Other Name? A Critical Survey of Christian Attitudes Toward the World Religions* (Maryknoll, NY: Orbis Books, 1985); Paul F. Knitter and John Hick, eds., *The Myth of Christian Uniqueness: Toward a Pluralistic Theology of Religions* (Maryknoll, NY: Orbis Books, 1987); and John Hick, *A Christian Theology of Religions: The Rainbow of Faiths* (Louisville: Westminster John Knox Press, 1995). Of particular relevance is the essay by C. S. Song, "From Israel to Asia: A Theological Leap," in *Mission Trends 3*, Gerald H. Anderson and Thomas F. Stransky, eds. (New York: Paulist Press / Grand Rapids: Wm. B. Eerdmans, 1976), 211-222.

[19] For a survey of options, including an inclusivist evangelical Protestant perspective, see John Sanders, *No Other Name: An Investigation into the Destiny of the Unevangelized* (Grand Rapids: Wm. B. Eerdmans, 1992).

[20] For the theological gains to be made by such dialogical engagement with Buddhist history and doctrine, see Aloysius Pieris, *Love Meets Wisdom: A Christian Experience of Buddhism* (Maryknoll, NY: Orbis Books, 1988); and Raimundo Panikkar, *The Silence of God: The Answer of the Buddha* (Maryknoll, NY: Orbis Books, 1989).

[21] Okechukwu Ogbonnaya, *On Communitarian Divinity: An African Interpretation of the Trinity* (New York: Paragon House, 1994), has advanced this thesis, specifically arguing that Tertullian's doctrine of the Trinity needs to be understood in light of his North African cultural background, and not only in light of his Roman philosophical inheritance.

[22] I would immediately add that the study of world history and world religions should be kept free from the kind of polemical considerations that often draw Christian theological attention to them, but which have as their objective the extermination of the history of other religions. Unfortunately such a practice of religiocide is often misconstrued as "evangelism."

[23] I have taken the concept of a "site of history and memory" from Nellie Y. McKay's interpretation of the French historiographical theorist Pierre Nora, "Between Memory and History: *Les Lieux de Mémoire*," *Representations* 26:1 (1989): 7-25, as cited by Nellie Y. McKay, "The Journals of Charlotte L. Forten-Grimké: *Les Lieux de Mémoire* in African-American Women's Autobiography," in *History and Memory in African-American Culture*, Geneviève Fabre and Robert O'Meally, eds. (New York: Oxford University Press, 1994), 261-271.

[24] A beginning attempt at such a parallel historiography, in this case of the religious histories of Europe and India, can be found in Trevor Ling, *A History of Religion East and West: An Introduction and Interpretation* (New York: Macmillan, 1974).

[25] This is the direction we have noted above in the historiography of Christianity in India being forged by a number of Indian theologians. For the theological questions this raises for ecclesial self-understanding, see in particular the work of Aloysis Pieris, *An Asian Theology of Liberation* (Maryknoll, NY: Orbis Books, 1988).

[26] Carl F. Hallencreutz, "Third World Church History—An Integral Part of Theological Education," *Studia Theologica* 47:1 (1993), 29-47.

[27] Spivak, *Outside the Teaching Machine*, 243ff.

[28] Robert J. Schreiter, *The New Catholicity: Theology between the Global and the Local* (Maryknoll, NY: Orbis Books, 1997).

[29] Bhabha, *The Location of Culture*, 228.

[30] Along these lines Wolfhart Pannenberg has argued: "According to the witness of the Bible the deity of God will be definitively and unquestionably manifested only at the end of all time and history. At every point in time it is a fact that what is lasting and reliable, and in this sense true, comes to light only in the future." (Wolfhart Pannenberg, *Systematic Theology*, vol. 2, Geoffrey Bromiley, trans. [Grand Rapids: Wm. B. Eerdmans, 1991], 54.)

[31] Pannenberg, *Systematic Theology*, 55, continues: "The limits that are posed with the historicity of human experience apply especially to experience of God because God is never an identifiable object in the world that we all inhabit, and his reality is bound up with experience of the power that we ascribe to him over the world and history, and indeed over the totality of the world in its history. This does not rule out the possibility of provisional experiences of the reality of God and his faithfulness in the course of history, but all the statements that we make about these, in the specific mode of all human talk about God, rest on anticipations of the totality of the world and therefore on the as yet nonexistent future of its uncompleted history. The historicity of human experience and reflection forms the most important limit of our human knowledge of God. Solely on account of its historicity all human talk about God unavoidably falls short of full and final knowledge of the truth of God."

[32] K. C. Abraham, "Globalization and Liberative Solidarity," in *The Agitated Mind of God: The Theology of Kosuke Koyama*, Dale T. Irvin and Akintunde E. Akinade, eds. (Maryknoll, NY: Orbis Books, 1996).

[33] Fabian Eboussi Boulaga, *Christianity without Fetishes: An African Critique and Recapture of Christianity*, Robert R. Barr, trans. (Maryknoll, NY: Orbis Books, 1984), 224.

[34] This point is particularly relevant in light of the efforts of the Faith and Order movement over this last century, which has pursued ecumenical unity and catholicity primarily through a common historical memory. Efforts along these lines, writes the ecumenical theologian Lukas Vischer, are directed to answering questions such as: "How can the separated churches agree on their understanding and presentation of the history of the Church? . . . How is the past to be seen as a common past? How are the different perspectives to blend together into a single perspective?" (L. Vischer, ed., *Church History in an Ecumenical Perspective* [Bern: Evangelische Arbeitsstelle Oekumene Schweiz, 1982], 7.) Vischer provides his own answer to his questions: "The task is to present the history of the *una sancta catholica*. In the presentation an attempt must be made to recall the history of the whole Church" (9). But such an effort to recall the whole history, I have argued, can only result in its overall reduction to a singular, master narrative. See also Dale T. Irvin, *Hearing Many Voices: Dialogue and Diversity in the Ecumenical Movement* (Lanham, MD: University Press of America, 1994).

[35] On this point the Orthodox insistence on Holy Tradition not being reduced to its historical manifestation(s) needs to be noted. Orthodox theology asserts that the fullness of the "mystery" of Holy Tradition cannot be so reduced even if it is incarnationally embodied most fully in the living tradition of the Orthodox Church. This nonreduction introduces a critical distance between theological fullness and historical manifestation(s) which I have above referred to as "eschatological," but which admittedly an Orthodox theologian might be more comfortable referring to as "mystery." See the discussion by Archbishop Iakovos Koukoujis, in his essay, "The Contribution of Eastern Orthodoxy to the Ecumenical Movement," *The Orthodox Church in the Ecumenical Movement: Documents and Statements 1902-1975*, Constantin G. Patelos, ed. (Geneva: World Council of Churches, 1978), 217.

[36] See Dale T. Irvin, *Hearing Many Voices: Dialogue and Diversity in the Ecumenical Movement* (Lanham, MD: University Press of America, 1994).

[37] See Joan Wallach Scott, "History in Crisis: The Other's Side of the Story," *American Historical Review* 94 (1989): 680-692; and Robert Young, *White Mythologies: Writing History and the West* (London: Routledge, 1990).

[38] Gayatri Chakravorty Spivak highlights this text/textile texture of histories in *The Post-Colonial Critic: Interviews, Strategies, Dialogues* (New York: Routledge, 1990), 25.

[39] Far from leaving the future open, denominationalism has tended toward reifying institu-

tional and theological differences, thereby absolutizing each denomination's own life and tradition. For a fuller history of the concept of denominationalism, see Russell E. Richey, ed., *Denominationalism* (Nashville: Abingdon, 1977). A concise statement by Richey can also be found in the *Dictionary of the Ecumenical Movement*, N. Lossky et al., eds. (Geneva: WCC Publications / Grand Rapids: Wm. B. Eerdmans, 1991), s.v.

[40] See James Chukwuma Okoye, " 'Mutual Exchange of Energies' Mission in Cross-Cultural Perspective: An African Point of View," *Missiology: An International Review* 25:4 (1997): 467-479.

[41] This is one of the conclusions reached by Edward W. Said in his book, *Culture and Imperialism* (New York: Alfred A. Knopf, 1993). Said states a major assumption of his study: "If at the outset we acknowledge the massively knotted and complex histories of special but nevertheless overlapping and interconnected experiences—of women, of Westerners, of Blacks, of national states and cultures—there is no particular intellectual reason for granting each and all of them an ideal and essentially separate status. Yet we would wish to preserve what is unique about each so long as we also preserve some sense of the human community and the actual contests that contribute to its formation, and of which they are all a part" (32). Beginning from the assumption that all cultural experiences are heterogeneous, and that the cultural experiences of modern imperialism are so vast that we must speak of intertwined histories on a global scale, Said reads the modern archive contrapunctually (rather than univocally), uncovering the voices from the periphery speaking in the metropolis and the forces in the metropolis collaborating with the opposition in the colonies. Said's "global, contrapunctual analysis" is finally not modeled "on a symphony [that grand art form of modernism] but rather on an atonal ensemble" (318). His final word on the project of creating a new form of tradition in the modern world: "No one today is purely *one* thing . . . No one can deny the persisting continuities of long traditions, sustained habitations, national languages, and cultural geographies, but there seems no reason except fear and prejudice to keep insisting on their separation and distinctiveness, as if that was all human life was about" (336).

[42] Pelikan, *The Vindication of Tradition*, 58.

[43] Jameson, *Postmodernism, or, The Cultural Logic of Late Capitalism*, 310-311, notes that the concept of "new" in modernity is only meaningful when it is related to that which is not new, requiring the presence of the old. When everything is new, the concept loses its meaning and becomes an empty modernist slogan without resonance. See also Bhabha, *The Location of Culture*, 212-235, a chapter entitled "How Newness Enters the World," which explores the emergence of the new from the interstitial spaces between local cultures.

[44] Philip Potter, "Doing Theology in a Divided World," in *Doing Theology in a Divided World*, Virginia Fabella and Sergio Torres, eds. (Maryknoll, NY: Orbis Books, 1985), 16.

[45] Potter, "Doing Theology in a Divided World," 16-17.

[46] See Metz, *Faith in History and Society*, 37-38.

[47] See the insightful review essay by David D. Daniels, "Teaching the History of U.S. Christianity in a Global Perspective," *Theological Education* 29:2 (1993): 91-111.

[48] Gayatri Chakravorty Spivak, *In Other Worlds: Essays in Cultural Politics* (New York: Routledge, 1988), 107.

[49] Mikhail M. Bakhtin, *The Dialogic Imagination: Four Essays*, Michael Holquist, ed. (Austin: University of Texas Press, 1981), 272.

Index

Abraham, K. C., 136
Absoluteness of Christianity and the History of Religions, The (Troeltsch), 24
accountability: ethical concreteness of, 39; retraditioning and, 50–52; tradition's multiple levels of, 47
Africa, 75–77, 110–11, 158n.74, 162n.41
African Americans: commodification of history of, 8; double consciousness of, 84–85; as essential to understanding European-American Christianity, 135; genealogical approach to church history by, 86; postmodernism and, 167n.5
Ajayi, J. F. Ade, 76
Altizer, Thomas J. J., 71
analogia entis, 58
analogia fidei, 58
anamnestic solidarity, 43–44
Annales school, 154n.4
anonymous Christians, 65
Aristotle, 18, 130
Athanasius, 162n.41
Augustine, 69, 109, 117, 162n.41
Ayandele, Emmanuel, 76

Bakhtin, M. M., 142, 151n.7
Barrett, David, 98, 109
Barth, Karl, 58–59, 60, 65, 73, 154n.14, 155n.17, 155n.18, 155n.24
Benjamin, Walter, 22, 42, 44, 45
Berger, Peter L., 147n.19
Berman, Marshall, 147n.19
Bhabha, Homi K., 103, 135
Black theology, 50, 86, 103
Bourdieu, Pierre, 20
Bouwsma, William J., 148–49n.45
Boyd, R. H. S., 6–7

Bradley, James E., 154n.5, 154n.12
Bredero, Adriaan H., 167–68n.7
Brown, Peter, 114, 115, 119, 166n.61
Buddhism, 11, 75, 132
Butterfield, Herbert, 13, 89, 91–92, 118

Cahill, Joseph, 148n.39
Calvin, John, 37
Cameron, Averil, 117
capitalism, 7–8, 29
Chadwick, Owen, 97
Charlemagne, 87
Christendom: the crisis in the representation of, 126–27; critique of the grand narrative of, 87–99; the end of, 72; fissures in the grand narrative of, 117–18; modernism and, 124–25
Christianity in European History (Butterfield), 118
church history: the analogy of faith and, 57–59; critique of the grand narrative of, 86–99; different denominations' view of, 60–61; goals of writers of, 4–7; narratives of, and the hermeneutics of the divine, 82–86; Pannenberg on, 65–66; the problem of the particular and universal in, 79–82; Rahner on, 59–60; the scope of revelation and, 130–32; social scientific methods and, 56; and the study of world religions, 132; the task of, 104; Tillich on, 63–65; translation and, 135–36
Clebsch, William, 85, 92
colonialism, 76, 124
commodification of history, 7–8
Cone, James H., 103
Congar, Yves, 30, 31, 168n.9

174 INDEX

Constantine the Great, 87, 90, 92
consumerism, 7–8
contextual theology, 4, 43, 44, 51, 152n.27
conversion, 9–10, 127
Coptic church, the, 110, 165n.41, 165n.42
councils, ecumenical, 60–61, 155–56n.28
creation, 74, 79–82
Crucified God, The (Moltmann), 37–38

death of God theology, 71
de Certeau, Michel, 20
"Decree on Ecumenism" (Vatican II), 100–101
Deleuze, Gilles, 47, 152n.35
Derrida, Jacques, 71
detraditionalization, 7, 9
Dilthey, Wilhelm, 104
diversity: and confronting the singularity of a Christian past, 1–3; in the early Christian movement, xi, 106–16; historical reinterpretation in light of, 85–86; and the grand narrative of church history, 92–93; postmodernism's concern with, 45–46; as a resource for change, 46–47; the task of church history as uncovering, 104–5. *See also* pluralism
Djait, Hichem, 148n.37
Donatism, 113–14, 139
Du Bois, W. E. B., 84
Dykstra, Craig, 151–52n.20

Ebeling, Gerhard, 68, 157n.57
Eboussi Boulaga, Fabien, 77, 136–37
Ecumenical Association of Third World Theologians, 149n.46, 153n.49, 160n.17
ecumenical councils. *See* councils, ecumenical
ecumenism, 62, 128, 137–38, 156n.29, 170n.34
Egypt, 110, 111, 112–13, 165n.41
Eliot, T. S., 28, 29
Elizondo, Virgilio, 51
Enlightenment, the, 7, 23, 29–30
Ethiopia, 110–11

Eusebius, 163n.24

Faith and Order Commission, 66, 156n.44, 170n.34
Felder, Cain Hope, 165n.46
feminist theology, 31, 43, 49–51, 86, 151n.8
"Finality of Jesus Christ" (Faith and Order Commission), 66
Foucault, Michel, 102, 103, 104, 152n.33
Frend, W. H. C., 113–14
Frisby, David, 147n.19

Gay, Peter, 154n.5
gay/lesbian theology, 43
genealogies (historical): constructing, that reflect the diversity of Christian communities, 103–6; of the early Christian movement, 106–16; examples of, of specific local churches, 133–34; Nietzsche on, 102–3; and ruptures in the European tradition(s), 116–22
Gero, Stephen, 109
Gnosticism, 139
God in History (Hodgson), 69
God Who Acts: Biblical Theology as Recital (Wright), 67–68
Goldstein, Leon, 55
González, Justo, 95
grand narrative: critique of the, of church history, 86–99; fissures in the, of Christendom, 117–18; term discussed, 161n.22
Grant, Robert M., 156n.29
Gregory the Great, Pope, 90, 92
Griffith, Sidney, 164n.33
Guattari, Félix, 47, 152n.35
Gutiérrez, Gustavo, 152n.21, 152n.27

Hallencreutz, Carl F., 135
Handbuch der Kirchengeschichte (Jedin, ed.), 93–95
Hanson, R. P. C., 31, 32
Harnack, Adolf von, 89, 92, 162n.41
Harrison, Beverly Wildung, 151n.6
Hassan, Ihab, 47

INDEX 175

Hegel, G. W. F., 66–67, 69, 70, 71–72, 158n.74
Heidegger, Martin, 72
Heilbroner, Robert, 56
heresy, 39–43, 139, 151n.8
Herrin, Judith, 118
Hinduism, 6, 75
historians: goal of, 3–7; social locatedness of church, 56; the task of, 21. *See also* historiography
historical criticism, 30, 32
historicism, 17, 23–24
historicity, 54, 170n.31
historiography: in Africa, 76; challenge to its grand narrative, 13; and a critique of the grand narrative of church history, 86–99; and hermeneutics of the divine, 82–86; and history as God-bearing, 79–82; implications of its turn from the universal to the particular, 26–27; main principles of, 24; perspective and, 19–20; postmodernism and, 22–23; power and, 102–3; practiced by the oppressed, 102; tendency of, to see the Christian community as European, 12; various views of goal of, 4–7
Historismus und seine Probleme (Troeltsch), 24
history: altering, 128; beginnings of, as a discipline, 66–67; commodification of, 7–8; the crisis of modern, 21–27; diversity and, 1–3; divine revelation and, 57–72; double meaning of term, 18; goal of the historian vis-à-vis, 3–7; intentionality and, 20–21; and the perspective of its narrator, 18–20; revelation and, 17–18; salvation and, 155n.18; Schaff on, 12; a theology of, that encompasses the whole *oikoumene*, 72–78; two dimensions of the term, 55. *See also* church history; historiography; theology of history
History of Dogma (Harnack), 89
History of the Christian Church, A (Walker), 89–91, 92
History of the Church (Jedin, ed.), 93–95

History of the Freewill Baptists, The (Stewart), 5
Hobsbam, Eric, 149n.56
Hodgson, Peter, 69–70, 72, 158n.64
Hood, Robert E., 162n.41
Hugo of St. Victor, 105
Huizinga, Johan, 19–20, 26, 28
Hussites, the, 139

"Idea for a Universal History from a Cosmopolitan Point of View" (Kant), 23
identity, 37–38, 54, 83–84
identity-involvement dilemma, 37–38
intentionality, 35, 49
Isaac of Ninevah, 37
Islam, 87, 110, 114–15, 117, 148n.37

Jameson, Frederic, 7–8, 167n.6, 168n.11, 171n.43
Jedin, Hubert, 93–95
Josephus, 106
Judaism, 49–50, 106
Justin Martyr, 117

kairos, 62–63
Kalu, Ogbu U., 76, 77, 79, 159n.92
Kant, Immanuel, 23, 24–25, 147n.23, 151n.7
Kaye, Harvey J., 88
Kazhdan, Alexander, 161n.20
Kermode, Frank, 160n.11
Kierkegaard, Sören, 126
Kingdom of God, 44, 63–65
Klee, Paul, 22
Koepf, Ulrich, 96–97
Korea, 74–75, 133
Koselleck, Reinhart, 23, 30, 149n.58
Kristeva, Julia, 49, 153n.41

LaCapra, Dominick, 150n.3
latent Christians, 65
Latourette, Kenneth Scott, 98–99
LeGoff, Jacques, 21, 147n.6
Lehrbuch der Dogmengeschichte (Harnack), 89
Lenhardt, Christian, 43

176 INDEX

liberation theology: and commitment to the oppressed, 10; false charge that it has abandoned its Christian identity, 152n.27; retraditioning and, 50–51; roots of, 4; and solidarity with the oppressed who have died, 43, 44; tradition and "treason" in, 43
Ling, Trevor, 169n.24
Livingstone, David, 159n.92
Long, Charles H., 26, 84–85, 102
Lossky, Vladimir, 30, 149–50n.61
Lowenthal, David, 160n.18
Lukacs, Georg, 156–57n.46
Lyotard, Jean François, 26, 88, 161n.22

MacIntyre, Alasdair, 150n.5
Martin, Clarice J., 110–11
Marx, Karl, 126, 147–48n.23, 152n.20
master narrative. *See* grand narrative
Mazrui, A. A., 77
McCormack, Bruce L., 155n.17
Meaning of Revelation, The (H. R. Niebuhr), 17, 18
medieval period of the church, 87–88
mestizo theological identity, 51
metanoia, 9–10, 14, 127
Metz, J. B., 103
Meyendorff, 156n.29
Míguez Bonino, José, 158n.80
mimesis, 18
minjung theology, 74–75, 133
missionaries, 76, 88, 94–95, 96, 162n.41
modernism, 21–27, 123, 124–25
Moffett, Samuel Hugh, 109, 115, 164n.34
Moltmann, Jürgen, 37–38, 42
monasticism, 11, 113
Monophysitism, 111, 164n.29
Montanism, 139
Morse, Christopher, 80, 81, 151n.12
Mudimbe, V. Y., 77
Muller, Richard A., 154n.5, 154n.12

Nam-dong, Suh, 74
narrative: choosing the object of, 55–56; critique of the grand, of church history, 86–99; genealogies as uncovering ruptures in the grand, 116–22; and hermeneutics of the divine, 82–86; and history as God-bearing, 79–82; as the most effective means of organizing a tradition, 49; open-endedness of all, 49, 54–55; Ricoeur on, 18
Nestorianism, 164n.29
Niebuhr, H. Richard, 17, 18, 22, 23, 151n.6
Nietzsche, Friedrich, 11–12, 70, 71, 72, 102–3
Niles, D. Preman, 74, 158n.80
North Africa, 110–11, 113–14, 115
Not Every Spirit: A Dogmatics of Christian Disbelief (Morse), 80

Oduyoye, Mercy Amba, 159n.88
Ogbonnaya, Okechukwu, 169n.21
Orthodox churches, 60–61, 156n.29, 170n.35
orthodoxy, 39–43

Panikkar, Raimundo, 121
Pannenberg, Wolfhart, 65–66, 136, 170n.30, 170n.31
Patelos, Constantin G., 61
Patristics, 87
Pelikan, Jaroslav, 32, 139, 149n.49, 150n.70
Pentecost, 107, 108
Persian church, the, 108–10, 134, 164n.32, 164n.34, 165n.36
Peukert, Helmut, 43, 44
philosophy of history, 66–67
Pieris, Aloysius, 10–11
Pius XII, Pope, xi, 93–94
Placher, William C., 160n.11
Plaskow, Judith, 45, 49–50
Plato, 130
pluralism, 70, 138–43. *See also* diversity
poor, the, 10–11, 74–75
postcolonialism, 123, 167n.5
postmodernism: attempts to find meaning in history by, 22–23; black culture and, 167n.5; as emphasizing the particular and many, 123; Hodgson's critique of, 70–71, 158n.64; its overconcern with

INDEX

fragmentation, 45–46
Potter, Philip, 141
power, 102–3
praxis, 43, 70
preservationism, 160–61n.18
primitivism, 126, 145n.5
Protestantism, 4–5, 30–32, 88

Raboteau, Albert J., 20, 126
Rahner, Karl, 59–60, 65, 93, 145n.3, 155n.24, 161–62n.30
Rayan, Samuel, 75
Reformation, the, 31–32, 90
relativism, 24, 70
Religion des Alten Testamentes (Vatke), 67
Rendtorff, Trutz, 65–66, 157n.57
repentance, 10, 127
restorationism, 126, 145n.5
retraditioning, 50–52
revelation, 17–18, 57–72, 130–32
Revelation as History (Pannenberg), 65
rhizomes, 47, 48
Ricoeur, Paul, 18, 70, 154n.4
Rosenstock-Huessy, Eugen, 149n.52
Russell, Letty M., 31, 33

Said, Edward W., 105, 168n.14, 171n.41
salvation, 57, 60–64
salvation history, 60–62, 63–65, 67, 68, 155n.18
Sampson, Edward E., 46
Sartre, Jean-Paul, 168n.11
Schaff, Philip, 4–5, 6, 12, 145n.5
Schreiter, Robert J., 135
Segundo, Juan Luis, 10, 11, 43
Singh, Sadhu Sundar, 6–7
social scientific methods, 56
solidarity with the dead, 43–46
Solomon, Robert, 25
Song, Choan-Seng, 73–74
Souls of Black Folk, The (Du Bois), 84
Spivak, Gayatri Chakravorty, 142, 168n.15
Standing Again at Sinai: Judaism from a Feminist Perspective (Plaskow), 49–50
Stewart, I. D., 5
Stoics, the, 130

Sunquist, Scott, 164n.27
Systematic Theology (Tillich), 62, 63

Taylor, Mark C., 71, 72, 158n.64
technology, 29
Theodore of Mopsuestia, 109, 110
theology of history: divine revelation and, 57–72; and solidarity with the dead, 43; tradition as the meaning of, 53–57; and the whole *oikoumene,* 72–78
"Theses on the Philosophy of History" (Benjamin), 42
"Thesis on History" (Benjamin), 44
Thomas, M. M., 41
Thomas, St., 164n.27
Thomas Aquinas, St., 87
Tidy, M., 77
Tillich, Paul, 28, 42, 62–65
Towards a History of the Church in the Third World, 96
tradition: benefits of focusing on the plurality of, 138–43; churches' various views of, 35–39; connotations of the term, 30; critical practices and the meaning of, 7–14; and defining heresy and orthodoxy, 39–40; distinguished from traditionalism, 149n.49; the Enlightenment's denigration of, 29–30; genealogical ruptures in European, 116–22; historicity and, 54; meaning of term in the Bible, 40–41; Orthodox churches' conception of, 60–61; Protestant views of, 30–32; the rhizomatic structure of, 46–50; as the theological meaning of history, 53–57; treason and, 41–43; Trent on the diversity of, 168n.9; various definitions of, 28–29; ways of uncovering the subjugated, 101–2
"Tradition and Individual Talent" (Eliot), 28
traditioning, 27–33, 41, 124. *See also* retraditioning
translation, 135–36
treason, 41–43
Trent, Council of, 168n.9
Trimiew, Darryl M., 151n.6

INDEX

Trinity, the, 48, 136–37
Troeltsch, Ernst, 4, 24, 25–26, 32, 43, 69, 149n.47, 167n.72

urbanization, 29

Vatican II, 60, 61, 93, 100, 162n.30
Vatke, J. K. Wilhelm, 67
Vischer, Lukas, 170n.34
von Hofmann, Johann C. K., 67
von Rad, Gerhard, 68

Waldensians, 139
Walker, Williston, 89–91, 92, 161n.24
Walls, Andrew, 81
Ware, Kallistos, 155n.27
Warfield, Benjamin B., 32, 150n.68
Weber, Max, 157n.46
Wessels, Anton, 151n.13
West, Cornel, 167n.5
"What Is Enlightenment?" (Kant), 24
White, Hayden, 49
Wolfson, Harry Austryn, 168n.16
womanist theology, 43
World Christian Encyclopedia, 98
World Council of Churches, 141
Wright, G. Ernest, 67

Yong-bock, Kim, 74–75